CONSERVATION
UNDER
F.D.R.

CONSERVATION UNDER F.D.R.

A. L. Riesch Owen

PRAEGER

PRAEGER SPECIAL STUDIES • PRAEGER SCIENTIFIC

Library of Congress Cataloging in Publication Data

Owen, A. L. Riesch (Anne Lou Riesch), 1919-
    Conservation under F.D.R.

    Bibliography: p.
    Includes index.
    1. Conservation of natural resources — Government
policy — United States — History — 20th century. 2. Conservation of natural resources — United States — History
— 20th century. 3. Roosevelt, Franklin D. (Franklin
Delano), 1882-1945. I. Title.
S930.093 1983   333.7′2′0973   83-3966
ISBN 0-03-063166-1

333.72 097c

Owen, A. L. Riesch 191

Conservation under F.I

Published in 1983 by Praeger Publishers
CBS Educational and Professional Publishing
a Division of CBS Inc.
521 Fifth Avenue, New York, New York 10175 U.S.A.

©1983 by Praeger Publishers

3456789 052 987654321

Printed in the United States of America
on acid-free paper

*To my friend and colleague
Genevieve Winchester*

Foreword

Conservation in America, beginning in the late nineteenth century, and burgeoning during the Progressive Era, came to maturity during the New Deal. The depression decade of the 1930s, far from bringing serious cutbacks, led to Federal undertakings on a far larger scale than had previously been possible in an infinitely greater number of areas.

In considerable part the triumph of conservation during the New Deal came because of President Franklin D. Roosevelt's keen interest and considerable knowledge. It was an area in which Roosevelt had been involved since his youth, profoundly influenced by his wife's uncle, Theodore Roosevelt, and by T.R.'s chief conservationist, Gifford Pinchot. As a boy, Roosevelt had been something of an ornithologist and naturalist; he never lost his interest in birds. By 1911, he was in the State Senate, assuming the lead in state measures ranging from wildlife and fisheries management to the nurture of forest preserves. He began planting trees at Hyde Park in cooperation with the state forestry experts and, from this time to his death, used his land for demonstration purposes. He once described himself as a tree farmer. As Governor of New York, he actively fostered both conservation and public power development and became interested in technical areas like rural planning and zoning. He was acquainted with some of the most innovative experts and their ideas.

As President, Roosevelt was not as spectacular a conservationist as Theodore Roosevelt who had reserved large areas of the national domain for public use. He had, as was to be expected of someone of the next generation, a much broader technical knowledge and could draw upon a host of well trained specialists. Strong conservation organizations existed to back him—or force him to modify his plans. All the innovations to that point put him in a position to launch large-scale, significant Federal programs.

From the outset of the New Deal, Roosevelt acted decisively to foster conservation. The exigencies of the depression forced the Federal government to spend unprecedented sums on public works and work relief. These sums not only could keep millions of Americans from starving; their flow into the economy could stimulate recovery. Roosevelt was determined that as little of the money as possible should be wasted; he channeled large amounts of it toward both conservation and resource development. Thus in the first few weeks of his presidency he obtained legislation creating the Civilian Conservation Corps, enlisting otherwise wasted manpower at a trivial cost to plant trees, build firebreaks and recreational areas, and in many ways to improve the national domain. He enthusiastically backed George Norris's proposal to create a Tennessee Valley Authority, to foster flood control and power development, to check soil erosion, and improve the living standards of an entire region. He sought not only regional planning but also national planning through what became the National Resources Planning Board. If he had had his way, he would have transformed the Interior Department, over which the zealous Harold L. Ickes presided, into a Department of Conservation.

In outline, the involvement of Roosevelt and the New Deal with conservation has long been recognized. Edgar B. Nixon in 1957 brought out two volumes of documents on *Franklin D. Roosevelt and Conservation, 1911–1945*. Much has been written on the involvement of New Dealers in various aspects of conservation, and there have been excellent studies of a number of programs. Until now, however, there has been no comprehensive synthesis and analysis of both President Roosevelt's leadership and involvement and of the many programs, ranging from the breeding of waterfowl and planting of shelter belts to the contour plowing of eroding fields. Professor Anne Owen makes a fine contribution through her organization and synthesis of this multiplicity of issues and activities, of achievements (and some setbacks). Her analysis is shrewd, and her conclusions persuasive. She proves how large and permanent the New Deal contribution was to Federal conservation policies.

Frank Freidel
Bullitt Professor of American History
University of Washington

Preface

How did a man of wealth and social position take to heart the welfare of the American people—all the people? Why was he labeled a radical, a socialist, a conservative? Franklin Delano Roosevelt was a controversial figure in his time and remains so today. Why? The Great Depression called for immediate action. F.D.R. appealed to the masses when he said, "You have nothing to fear but fear itself." Conditions were ripe for a dictator, a leader, a reformer. Americans elected a saviour who promised them hope and gave them faith. Were they mistaken?

The unique conditions of the times combined with a resolute, innovative, experimental, and confident president gave the American people a legacy of a national government with new dimensions. Relief, recovery, and reform were the three Rs of the New Deal and in carrying out these goals F.D.R. brought together all sectors of our society. In doing so he carried out experimentation combined with his pragmatism. He embarked on greatly increased budget expenditures to help the unemployed, the farmer, businesses, victims of floods and the dust storms. His persuasiveness, his charm, and the marvelous fireside radio chats made the people believe they belonged to this country and could conquer the impossible. His first 100 days in office saw a multitude of legislation, programs, and projects. Again and again his hand of leadership was seen. It was his pencil during his first day as president that drafted the Civilian Conservation Corps. His call that brought the administrators together to bring the C.C.C. into being. It was but one of many projects to bring relief and recovery to his citizens. More and more reform loomed on the scene. The T.V.A., A.A.A., Social Security, Public Securities Exchange Commission, and so on, were initiated until the New Deal alphabet days arrived and with it the welfare state. President Roosevelt convinced the citizens that wealth must be distributed so those in need would be cared for, and that the national government had responsibilities that transcended state and local lines.

How did all of this come to pass? What set F.D.R. apart from other presidents? Hopefully, this book will assist the reader in answering these questions. I believed there was so much that was controversial about Franklin Roosevelt that selecting a specific area approach, enabling a detailed examination of him, would prove to be enlightening. Hence, the task of writing a microscopic book on Franklin D. Roosevelt was undertaken for a dual purpose: primarily, to present a detailed pragmatic analysis of F.D.R. and, secondly, an account of the conservation activity and policy developed during the Roosevelt years. F.D.R.'s page of history as a conservationist tells us much about him. He had a personal commitment to conservation and experimentation when a country squire at Hyde Park. His continuing commitment and innovations while governor of the state of New York were but mere rumblings of what was to become the nation's New Deal. At this early date he clearly showed that conservation to him meant more than natural resources. He included human resources. Once he became president he implemented on a grand scale what he had done in New York. His boundless energy, willingness to use a trial-and-error approach, assessment of the value of propaganda and the press, use of diplomacy, flair for the dramatic, and his constant humor was repeatedly demonstrated in his leadership in Congress, relationships with fellow office-holders, and in dealing with the American public. Nowhere was it better seen than in his conservation work.

Perhaps of even greater significance were his innovations, cooperation, commitment, determination, and prodding when necessary. All well illustrated in his ongoing battles for a shelterbelt, to be vindicated only on his birthday celebration in 1982. Greater in magnitude was his clarion call for a T.V.A. No private utility company's opposition would daunt him. F.D.R., with his collaborators and supporters, gave us the "yardstick" principle still in use today. With daring he argued continuously for a permanent planning board even in the face of charges of socialism. Indeed, the development of the concept of planning, far from impinging on the freedom of the individual, should provide greater individual opportunity and participation. At no time did F.D.R. desert the democratic framework and institutions of his country. The concept of "grassroots" administration appears throughout the conservation work of the 1930s. F.D.R. gave us a meaningful planning legacy worthy of careful attention at the present time. On a lighter side and as an illustration of his ever-present humor, is his dealing with his Chief of the Bureau of Biological Survey. He tied conservation to world cooperation and international peace. Nor did World War II cause him to neglect this pledge. Nothing was to endanger the permanent conservation policy he so ardently supported and led. His was close to a missionary cause. Never before had so much work in forestry, water, soil, minerals, wildlife, and recreational resources been accomplished at the national, regional, state, and local levels.

At the forefront of this accelerated conservation activity and national policy was F.D.R. He was a leader who changed the role and responsi-

citizens in themselves and their institutions. How did he do it? May this book enlighten the reader and add to our knowledge of Franklin Delano Roosevelt.

A. L. Riesch Owen

Acknowledgments

It is difficult for any author to include all of those who contributed to a book and certainly to do so by name is an impossible task. My sincere gratitude is extended to all who made this work possible whether herein named or not. Certainly, appreciation is due and given to my many colleagues,students, friends, and immediate family.

Specifically, I wish to express my gratitude to the staff of the Franklin D. Roosevelt Library, Hyde Park, New York. As one of the first scholars to complete research there I was met not only with excellent assistance but courtesy and enthusiasm. The first planned published work of the Franklin D. Roosevelt Library was to be on conservation. As a result, by this priority of effort and labor concentrated on conservation, I was greatly aided by the classification of materials and guidelines already completed on that subject. In addition to access to the Franklin D. Roosevelt Papers I had fine conversations and interviews with members of the library staff and personnel at Hyde Park. Director Herman Kahn was of great assistance; as well as editors Edgar Nixon and Carl Spicer, archivists George Roach, Margaret Suckley, Marion Towles, and Gloria Kidd, museum curator Raymond Corry; superintendent George Palmer; and historian George Wilkins. Speaking with William H. Plog, superintendent of grounds, Hyde Park, and Frank Draiss, assistant gardener, was invaluable.

To those people who graciously granted me invaluable interviews over the years, I would like to express my gratitude: Frank Draiss, Harold Ickes, Herman Kahn, William Plog, Eleanor Roosevelt, and Margaret Suckley.

The National Archives staff, Washington, D.C., was most helpful and cooperative in their assistance in using many varied materials. Faculty and staff at the Universities of Wisconsin and Colorado are too numerous to express my specific indebtedness to everyone who contributed in one way or another to this book. Numerous were the individuals and I express my appreciation. In particular, thanks are given to the staff of the Government Documents Division at the University of Wisconsin-Madison for its never-failing assistance and cooperation in my exhaustive examination of government documents and publications.

I am deeply indebted to Merle Curti and Edwin Witte for their stimulating and scholarly challenges. Their influence on me goes far beyond the realms of this book. As a personal student and assistant of Merle Curti and Edwin Witte, I should like to express my appreciation of their work and influence on me, and my indebtedness to them for high standards and support; specifically for their reading of parts of the manuscript and valuable detailed suggestions and stimulating general criticism that proved most helpful.

The critical reading of the entire manuscript and detailed suggestions by Genevieve Winchester are deeply appreciated. I am indebted to colleagues Dorothea and Ragaei El Mallakh for their academic and personal support over the years. Gratitude is extended to the assistance and support of Virginia Laney, Leo Ibler, and my brother, Louis Riesch. Students in my classes have contributed during the years by their stimulating questions and friendship, which are sincerely appreciated. Above all, I am deeply grateful to my children Deann, Todd, and John for their interest and cooperation.

No book is complete without those long hours of labor of typing, checking and rechecking, and numerous detailed tasks. It is not possible to express my gratitude to all by name who have contributed to those hours of labor. I am especially indebted to the comments and interest of my typists Eloise Pearson and Rosalie Hage.

Contents

CONSERVATION
UNDER
F.D.R.

ᴄᴏ 1 ᴄᴏ
Franklin Delano Roosevelt, the Conservationist

Franklin Delano Roosevelt took the oath of office as president of the United States on March 4, 1933. This was a time of crisis and uncertainty in the nation's history. The very survival of the time-treasured principles that composed the American Way of Life was at stake. In the years that followed Roosevelt's inauguration, this crisis was overcome. But this was not all. These also proved to be formative years for new developments in our social, economic, and political life. Several new and important elements were to take a permanent place in the U.S. scene. One such element was a concerted governmental policy for the conservation of our natural resources.[1]

Conservation development under Roosevelt was in part an emergency program, but most important was the permanent imprint that the policy of his administration left on the life and ideas of the American people. Government responsibility in conservation was tested and found to be a necessary component in the working of the United States democracy. Such a phenomenon raises several questions.

It is common knowledge that conservation was connected with Roosevelt's New Deal, but just how important was it in this total program and why was it important? Was conservation merely a product of vision and leadership on the part of F.D.R. himself? What part did his colleagues play? To what extent was conservation a natural product of emergency or just a normal sequence to an obscure but rich heritage of conservation history? Was it a result of a combination of these influences? If F.D.R. was an important factor in this development, what were his objectives? Who were his outstanding supporters and opponents with

1

respect to conservation? To what extent were the conservation objectives of the Roosevelt administration achieved and how sound were they, both in part and in whole? Why did the public accept this increased conservation zeal in the 1930s and how can its lasting effects be explained? Finally, what is the probable future of conservation in the United States political economy?

These are questions that this book is designed to illuminate. The proper historical perspective for the book is the whole American experience. Specifically, however, it is a book on the development of conservation in the United States economy over the period dating from the inauguration of President F. D. Roosevelt until the outbreak of the second world war in the early 1940s. Across this stage a leading character was the dynamic personality of F.D.R. with his many ardent followers and equally ardent opponents. A concrete approach, such as a book on conservation in this period, should also contribute to the needed evidence for a sound evaluation of the role and effectiveness of Roosevelt as a leader in a democracy.

CONDITIONS IN THE 1930s

President Roosevelt's vigorous conservation policy had behind it a long story. Conservation, properly defined as the conscious protection, judicious use, and perpetuation of our natural resources, had its beginnings in our early history. However, it was Franklin D. Roosevelt, who took office as president of the United States in the momentous spring of 1933 when the nation in despair faced the depths of the worst depression ever experienced by the American people, who implemented a never before seen all-encompassing conservation program.

Americans had witnessed the stock market crash in October 1929. Unemployment rolls increased annually from 6 or 7 million workers at the end of 1930 to double that number two years later. President Herbert Hoover's promise of two chickens in every pot proved to be mere words, and he eventually accepted the necessity of federal government action by his approval of the Reconstruction Finance Corporation. The Great Depression, first met with "have faith," now turned to necessity of action and the newly elected president Franklin D. Roosevelt. The economy was in disarray—the United States was in a crisis, a state of financial collapse. Scenes illustrating the economic sickness of the nation were duplicated and reduplicated throughout the country. Problems such as the banking crisis and lack of purchasing power remained to be solved by the newly inaugurated Democratic president who also faced a growing cry of restlessness and a demand that something be done.[2] Mother Nature also contributed her share of ill fortune. The occurrence of dust storms and floods in the 1930s further intensified the economic depression. As if in punishment for the human abuse of natural resources, the great drought of 1934 occurred. The resulting dust storms and the second serious drought of 1937 warned that soil erosion produced disaster. The skies were filled with ominous black clouds of dust, which carried the soil fertility of Kansas, Oklahoma, Colorado, North Dakota, South Dakota, New Mexico, and Texas eastward. It was the beginning of the long trek of the migrant, who left behind a fallen shed half buried in sand, an idle plow on a desert that once had been fertile wheat lands, a sun-blistered home, vacant with its steps covered with dust. It is paradoxical that out of the dust came the floods. In 1935 and 1936, the mighty bodies of water overflowing the land dramatized the crucial problem of flood control. Attention was focused anew upon the old fact that humans could not occupy and use the floors of the great valleys without suffering the consequences of the habits of uncontrolled rivers. Tragic illustrations were given to the American people that the laws of nature could not be ignored. The raging Ohio and Mississippi rivers in 1937 swung back and forth, biting off sections of rich land and swallowing them with hungry ferocity. The land laid ravished and wasted and 892 human beings who had busily walked and worked upon it lay dead. The overflow of the rivers covered the good land with sterile silt and left a burden of $300 million. The physical plus economic suffering caused demands for aid to resound from coast to coast.[3]

President Franklin D. Roosevelt as the leader of the federal government attempted to meet the cries of his constituents by the adoption of measures that were termed the "New Deal." Supporters hailed the New Deal as an answer to the multiple problems of the country. Critics challenged it as being un-American. Conservation was a vital and important part of this so-called New Deal program. To President Roosevelt, conservation was "one of the primary responsibilities of the federal government at all times." He had long favored measures of conservation. Now the sickening jolt to the nation's economy and the ruinous inroads into the natural wealth in forest and soil confronted him with a unique opportunity. Now he could institute conservation projects on a national scale.[4]

F.D.R.'s COMMITMENT
TO CONSERVATION

The application of such measures both explicitly as part of the New Deal and generally throughout his presidential administration was no sudden thing, improvised in the hour of disaster from the drought on the farms, in the banks, and in the withered hopes of the common citizen. This came out of his own childhood, his personal and political life. Conservation had enormous worth; of this he was morally and practically convinced: practically, because his experiences in conservation as a farmer and state office holder were successful. Now it was economically and socially feasible for him to develop conservation, also providing an opportunity for promotion of his personal philosophy. What had been the experiences and training that convinced him of the value of conservation? Wherein did he acquire the stature and drive that made him an outstanding exponent and leader of conservation? How did he attain his leadership? What were his motivations and goals in achieving a conservation policy? To answer these questions, it is necessary to examine Franklin Roosevelt's entire life as it related to conservation. His early childhood and environment reflect a sensitivity to beauty and practical awareness of conservation found in the adult man Roosevelt.

Roosevelt's Childhood
and Love of Nature

As a child, Franklin Roosevelt spent many hours in the outdoors. He early showed his love for nature. When but a young boy he collected birds and carefully guarded his mounted treasures. Pride in his knowledge of the types of birds and his own collection led him to make it a commendable project. His interest in collections did not end with birds. Young Franklin undertook one nature study after another, including the collection of insects. Interest in nature, however, did not revolve merely around gathering things of the forest. Franklin Roosevelt spent hours taking woodland walks, horseback riding, and sailing. The beauties of nature were not lost to him. He was instilled with an appreciation for trees at an early age by his father and his father's friend, Colonel Rogers. Both men were tree lovers who taught young Franklin the sentimental value of trees. In later years Roosevelt would demonstrate his love for his trees at Hyde Park by pointing out his favorites. There was an old tree along one of the woodland drives that frequently caused him to pause and make some comment. His favorite trees, however, were the English Oaks that stood in the field adjoining the entrance way of Hyde Park and still stand along the driveway to the Franklin Roosevelt Library. President Roosevelt constantly watched these English Oaks and checked on their health. He did love trees. He insisted that a large, damaged oak in front of the Roosevelt Library be left standing because the tree was old and he had played under it as a lad. After the completion of the library, the question arose as to whether the decayed oak whose trunk was barely able to support the branches should be cut down. Doubtless, sentimental memories of the tree and his love for its beauty and landmark value determined the president's action to save the tree. It was braced and repaired with the stipulation it was not to be cut.[5]

A Practical Conservationist

Roosevelt's love of trees, however appealing, was sentimental. He showed his practical attitude toward trees by practicing scientific forestry on his Hyde Park estate, located between Poughkeepsie and Hyde Park, New York. This estate, the Roosevelt Farm, consisted of 1,250 acres, of which 450 acres was in forest. Here, Roosevelt pioneered in farm forestry and showed his Hudson Valley neighbors how their land could be used wisely and profitably. He carried out good forestry practices by preventing fires, planting up the cut-over and poorer farmlands, and cutting out the defective, mature, and undesirable trees. His woodland tracts steadily produced cordwood, piling, and crossties, which were sold locally.[6]

His practical attitude was illustrated in yet another way. Franklin Roosevelt began planting trees at Hyde Park in the early 1900s. He recorded in his journal the planting of a white pine lot in 1911. Records were also made of plantings in 1912, 1913, and succeeding years, which enabled pruning of pine plantation by 1930.[7] The president started a number of plantation plots in the second decade of the twentieth century: a white pine and red pine plantation 1914—pruned in 1930; a white pine and Scotch pine plantation 1916—pruned in 1930; a white pine plantation 1915—pruned in 1930; a Norway Spruce plantation 1916; and a tulip poplar plantation 1917 after the stock had been held in the nursery for two years. This plot was pruned in 1929 under Roosevelt's direct supervision. The tulip poplar was one of his favorite trees and he started another poplar plantation in 1928.[8]

A person may love a tree because it is a thing of beauty, and may, as a loyal American, respect the beauty that ruthless, insensitive people so readily and rapidly destroy. But conservation has its hard-boiled angle, too. Franklin Roosevelt knew this by direct participation. He cooperated with the New York State Forester and the State Conservation Commission in obtaining trees and information.[9] When ordering trees from the State Conservation Commission, he wrote to William Overfield of Hyde Park on December 2, 1923, that others might want to place orders to save time and shipping charges. Even then he demonstrated a shrewd business ability and promoter's flair by declaring, "I am firmly convinced that it pays to plant these trees, and almost every farm has some section of rocky or otherwise unsuitable land for crops which could be planted to trees which in time would have real commercial value."[10]

Experimentation

All of the forestry work on the Roosevelt Farm was not along strict conventional lines. Franklin Roosevelt entered into experimentation with zest. Some of his projects were of his own choosing, whereas others were in cooperation with the N.Y. State College of Forestry. The first experiment conducted was the planting of all kinds of species during 1924–26. Another project was the plantings in the Tamrack Swamp, which was Roosevelt's idea and proved to be quite successful. It was necessary to keep replanting the trees in the humus, which made it very unprofitable. On the other hand, Roosevelt's Christmas tree experiment proved to be more satisfactory. Christmas trees were planted in 1926 and harvesting began in 1935. In 1936 the net proceeds of a cutting of 132 Christmas trees amounted to $134.55. The next year a cutting of 1,000 Christmas trees netted $480.00. Franklin Roosevelt was as pleased with this venture as a child with a highly prized toy. He had seen the trees planted, mature, and cut. It was the completion of a successful experiment. He witnessed a cycle of forestry. Other projects consisted of demonstration plantations and experimental plantations done in conjunction with the N.Y. State College of Forestry. This work brought him into a close relationship with the State College faculty, particularly Nelson Brown, who became a very influential friend.[11]

Friendship and Assistance
of Nelson Brown

Most of the tree planting done on the Roosevelt Farm took place between 1925 and 1940. During this period the friendship of Nelson Brown and Franklin Roosevelt was apparent in the forestry work accomplished at Hyde Park. Each man influenced the other. Brown encouraged Roosevelt's forestry endeavors and gave him information, and Roosevelt, in turn, opened to Brown the fulfillment of a lifetime goal of building the nation's forest resources. The two men worked together. A steady stream of correspondence between the two showed minute details of planning, cooperation, and promotion in carrying out forestry practices on Roosevelt's land. Nelson Brown aided Franklin Roosevelt in carrying out demonstration plantings at Hyde Park and in interesting neighbors in doing likewise. Roosevelt was delighted with Brown's success in interesting Vincent Astor in forestry. He complimented his friend on the great help it would be in stimulating additional reforestation.[12] Roosevelt was always ready to seize opportunities to promote forestry conservation. He cooperated in forestry programs, tours, and meetings. In September 1931, he participated in a Society of American Foresters' program by having the group tour his farm and accompanying them personally. He had his farm included in tours conducted by the N.Y. State College of Agriculture, the U.S. Department of Agriculture, and the Duchess County Farm Bureau in October 1934. Indeed, the Hyde Park estate was a show place of conservation forestry practices, a fine example of what could be done by fellow New Yorkers and people elsewhere.[13]

In working with Nelson Brown, the owner of Hyde Park kept a close check on all forestry projects and experiments. In 1933 he requested Brown to tabulate carefully the forestry operations in progress on the farm. Roosevelt not only checked the work by correspondence and reports, but also frequently invited Brown to Hyde Park to examine work in progress in those woods and to discuss improvement and reforestation. These were less business meetings than friendly exchange and cooperation. In a telegram dated November 3, 1939, for example, Roosevelt suggested that Brown lunch with him at Hyde Park on election day, if there were no exciting election in Syracuse. Any such excitement, replied Brown, would not compare with the opportunity of seeing the president on election day.[14]

Thus, Brown constantly advised President Roosevelt as to the Hyde Park estate and faithfully reported the tree plantings. By the 1930s these had become extensive: 26,000 trees were planted in 1937 and 29,500 in 1938. In planting trees, Roosevelt took full advantage of lessening direct costs, as when, in 1934, the N.Y. State College of Forestry furnished 42,000 trees free of charge to continue demonstration and experimental plantings in Hyde Park. This continued the custom of past years. Other needed trees Brown ordered and billed to Roosevelt, also advising methods of planting and suggesting various experiments. One of these which Roosevelt approved was to plant Asiatic chestnuts to replace a native eastern variety that was nearly extinct. Following another practical suggestion, Roosevelt contracted Hyde Park lumber in 1942. By this time the conservation measures here had contributed substantially to United States defense. Lumber cut from selected trees went to shipbuilding; Nelson Brown and the superintendent of grounds, William Plog, cropped the stand scientifically. The trees cut totaled 1,335, yielding 287,123 board feet of lumber.[15]

Publicity

The president was justifiably proud of his personal accomplishments in forestry. He gladly told the press about his tree plantings, his experiments, and what he had done on the recommendation of the N.Y. State College of Forestry. On February 23, 1937, in showing reporters his bill for 26,000 trees for Hyde Park planting, he said, "I am practicing what

I preach . . . that is, stopping erosion." That year he took newspaper correspondents on a tour of his farm to show them the result of the forestry practices he had been talking about.[16]

Assistance of William Plog

He could have accomplished none of this work, however, without the loyal support and hours of labor by men like William Plog. Mr. Plog knew the land thoroughly, having worked on the estate since 1891. He entered into the tree plantings wholeheartedly and supported Franklin Roosevelt's forestry projects. A constant correspondence was maintained between the president and his superintendent of grounds, which kept Franklin Roosevelt currently posted on the work done on the Roosevelt farm. It was a job the two men were doing together, and both took pride in their joint achievements.[17]

The good will that existed between Franklin Roosevelt and his staff at Hyde Park was best illustrated by the woodland roads. After being stricken with infantile paralysis and handicapped by a crippled body, the master of Hyde Park was no longer able to travel through the woodlands on foot and by horseback. The solution was the building of 20 miles of woodland roads that enabled Franklin Roosevelt to drive a specially constructed car on his estate. These roads were built under the direction of William Plog and Frank Draiss who contributed their energies in aiding the president to overcome his affliction. Roosevelt delighted in speeding along a woodland trail and setting up a screen of dust, enabling him to lose his secret guard, much to the latter's alarm and to Roosevelt's laughter. These woodland roads gave the president much pleasure and sorely needed hours of relaxation. They also enabled him to have the personal satisfaction of seeing his conservation projects and work on his own farm.[18]

Conservation Contributions as a New York State Senator

As a "country squire" Franklin Roosevelt had a keen interest in the problems of forestry and conservation. He did not merely direct this interest to his personal dealings and practices, but carried it with him to public office. As a N.Y. state senator from 1911–1913, he built up the reputation of a conservation-minded legislator. He served as chairman of the New York Commission on Forests, Fish, and Game, and cooperated closely with T. M. Osborne, state commissioner of forests. The two men worked together to pass a "top lopping" law, which saved trees from fire. They also decided to set up a State Department of

Conservation. To persuade favorable feeling toward this idea, Franklin Roosevelt invited Gifford Pinchot to an evening meeting in 1912 to show slides of a Chinese valley in 1510 and slides of the same valley in 1910, which illustrated a sharp contrast and the necessity of conservation. Senator Roosevelt by no means overlooked opportunities to use propaganda. He took advantage of chances given to him to teach and spread the "gospel" of conservation.[19]

Discussing the usefulness of competition up to a certain point and then the need for cooperation, Franklin Roosevelt introduced the subject of conservation when speaking before the Peoples' Forum in New York in 1912. He asserted that conservation to the American people was still a theory, whereas in Germany it had been practiced 150 years ago through restrictions on the unwise cutting of trees. In his address he emphasized that the Germans had passed beyond the liberty of individuals to do as they pleased with new property to the stage of checking liberty for the benefit and freedom of the whole people. He declared that the same situation was true in New York. That is, if the health and happiness of the New York citizens were to be protected, the lumber companies could not do as they pleased with the wooded growths of the Catskills and Adirondacks. Roosevelt had supported a bill for the preservation of the Adirondacks. In his fight he encountered opposition from lumber interests that opposed state regulatory powers for cutting on private lands. Roosevelt, however, never weakened under strong resistance to his conservation measures and continued his crusade.[20]

The citizens of New York considered Senator Roosevelt one of their outstanding spokesmen in initiating and passing conservation legislation. They wrote to him requesting his support of wildfire and forestry legislation and commended him on his conservation work.[21] Indeed, it was with regret that the people of New York saw him leave the state legislature and accept the position of assistant secretary of the navy.[22]

Assistant Secretary of the Navy

In this new governmental post, held from 1913 to 1920, Franklin Roosevelt continued to direct his energies toward the conservation of natural resources. He found time while assistant secretary of the navy to accept an appointment in November 1913, as a New York delegate to the Conservation Congress, Washington, D. C., and to accept his election in June 1914, as vice-president of the N.Y. State Forestry Association.[23] His new naval secretarial duties did not prevent him from carrying on correspondence on conservation matters and actively supporting federal conservation legislation. Also while serving as assistant secretary of the navy, Roosevelt was able to help protect and preserve naval oil resources.[24]

Governor of New York: Conservation Leadership

Franklin Roosevelt's promising youthful political career was seemingly blighted in 1920 when he went down to defeat as the Democratic nominee for vice-president and shortly afterwards was stricken with infantile paralysis. The door to an active public life seemed closed to the rising Democratic party man. Heavy as the blows were, Roosevelt did not stay down. He set himself to master his crippled body. His success was demonstrated when his friend Al Smith persuaded him to return to politics in 1928. He was elected governor of the state of New York and reelected in a landslide vote in 1930. Little did the people of the United States realize that this Governor Roosevelt was carrying out policies that would one day be used in the entire nation. His policies of state reforestation, land utilization, water power protection and development, pollution control, and use of unemployed on conservation projects were but a miniature of what was later to be adopted on a national scale when he became president of the United States.[25]

In taking office as governor of New York State, Franklin Roosevelt presented his views on conservation in his inaugural address:

> In the brief time that I have been speaking to you, there has run to waste on these paths towards the sea, enough power from our rivers to have turned the wheels of a thousand factories, to have lit a million farmers' homes—power which nature has supplied us through the gift of God. It is intolerable that the *utilization of this stupendous heritage should be longer delayed by petty squabbles and partisan dispute.* Time will not solve the problem, it will be more difficult as time goes on to reach a fair conclusion. It must be solved now.[26]

Action followed his hoisting of the conservation banner and he immediately set about working out a definite, far-reaching reforestation plan for New York State. Reforestation legislation was initiated and passed in 1930–31. Then Governor Roosevelt went on to champion state forest preserves against exploitation for private profit. He gave his support to a proposed amendment to the state constitution providing for acquisition and reforestation of land, management of forests, and establishment of forest tree nurseries.[27]

Roosevelt clearly showed his interest in land utilization and planning by discussing the "land policy for the state of New York" at a New York

Agriculture Society dinner in 1931. He told the guests that the policy was founded upon scientific approach based upon study and evaluation of land resources of the state. Its adoption would mean retirement of some land, reforestation, better roads, electrification of more farms, and the building of more recreational areas.[28] This land policy became reality when inferior agricultural land was retired by the state government and planted for future state forest plantations. A soil and crop survey was carried on by the state of New York to encourage a balance in production. Indeed, the premonitory rumblings of an Agricultural Adjustment Administration (A.A.A.), Tennessee Valley Authority (T.V.A.), Federal Erosion Service, and Civilian Conservation Corps (C.C.C.) were apparent in the New York land policy.[29]

Democratic Party Endorses F.D.R. as Presidential Candidate: A Foretelling of His Conservation Plans

Governor Roosevelt's commitment to conservation was further seen by his putting 10,000 of the state's unemployed to work on conservation projects. Roosevelt saw the possibilities of utilizing public works and conservation projects in solving the unemployment problem. The state government could make relief constructive, thereby converting a curse into a blessing.[30] Franklin Roosevelt's governorship of New York was heralded with success, and he became the preconvention presidential favorite of the Democratic party in the 1930s. His party formally endorsed him as the Democratic presidential candidate in 1932, and Roosevelt broke all precedents when he flew to Chicago to receive the nomination in person. It was a foretaste of the man's active nature and his use of the dramatic, and an example of his limitless personal interest and energy. In accepting the Democratic nomination on July 2, 1932, Roosevelt again showed the public his interest in conservation by revealing a plan, then taking shape in his mind, to help relieve distress among the unemployed through a great public works project of forest and land restoration.[31] He told the party members they should use common and business sense in solving the problem of unemployment, and he offered as a hopeful and immediate means of relief for the unemployed and agriculture a plan to convert millions of acres of marginal and unused land into timberland through reforestation and other conservation practices. This undertaking, said Roosevelt ". . . can give work to one million men." Pointing to his current success in the utilization of his conservation scheme for the relief of the unemployed in New York, he concluded, "I know the Democratic Party can do it successfully in the nation."[32]

Conservation Commitments
during the Presidential Campaign

Roosevelt lost no time in incorporating his conservation beliefs in offering such a solution to the problem of unemployment. Here was the
resolute leader for whom the desperate people were longing. The man
meant what he said; he was a man of deeds. In a letter to James W.
Sewall, a consulting forester of Old Town, Maine, he declared,

> When I spoke in my acceptance address of the use of a million men
> in reforestation work I had in mind, as you have inferred, more
> than mere planting of young trees. I thought of the general oppor-
> tunities in the care of our forests and the increasing of our forest
> assets which I think may properly be embraced under the title "Re-
> forestation."[33]

In another personal letter in 1932, Roosevelt stated explicitly that he
was keenly interested in forestry and reforestation not only as a temporary means of promoting employment, but also as a permanent national policy, and that he regarded it as one of the important matters to
be taken up in the campaign. Here was undoubted vision far beyond
the immediate economic problems[34]

Throughout his campaign Roosevelt stressed the positive energy,
the native resourcefulness of Americans, awakening them from the
nightmare of failure to a dream of resolute endeavor. As he developed
the campaign, he made these general assurances explicit. He spoke of
recovery and reform and discussed reciprocal tariff agreements, protection of the investor, sound money, federal power projects on the
Tennessee and Columbia rivers, the easing of farm mortgage burdens,
social security, and relief. The Democratic candidate promised the American people a New Deal.[35]

ELECTED PRESIDENT

Franklin D. Roosevelt's campaign promises were telling promises. The
people demonstrated the verve of their acceptance and faith by the vote
of nearly 23 million to less than 16 million, which elected Franklin Roosevelt to the presidency of the United States. Only four states in the
Union failed to carry for him; and with him the people swept the Democratic party to power in both houses of Congress. With immense relief
and a faith almost childlike, the American people loaded their collective
problems upon the new regime.[36]

On March 4, 1933, the Capitol was the national cynosure. Spectators by the thousands packed the 40 acres of lawn and pavement before the east front of the building to witness the president-elect take the oath of office. Others by millions, distributed over the land, bent eagerly to their radios. Into this universal hush of strained attention came the smooth and confident voice of the new president. There reverberated in it a note of solemnity appropriate for such an occasion: "This is a day of national consecration." But it was the bold decisiveness that followed that released within the listeners some of the long tension of the anxious years: ". . . this nation asks for action and for action now." There was no moment for the rhetorical cloaking of problems that faced them all and ground so many thousands into acute misery. "We must restore the soundness of the currency. We must secure the banks. We must save homes. We must save the farmers from bankruptcy. We must find jobs for the American people." Franklin Roosevelt felt his greatest task was to put people to work. He asserted that this could be accomplished in part by

> . . . direct recruiting by the Government itself, treating the task as we would treat the emergency of a war, but at the same time, through this employment, accomplishing greatly needed projects to stimulate and reorganize the use of our natural resources.

This was the sort of drastic action that he had promised in accepting the nomination.[37]

Drafting of the Civilian Conservation Corps

By the end of his first day in office, Roosevelt's busy pencil had blocked out an organization that would both give young people healthful work and directly conserve important national resources.[38] On the afternoon of March 9, 1933, the president invited to the White House the men immediately concerned with this project and put it before them: the secretaries of war, interior, and agriculture, the director of the budget, the solicitor of the Department of Interior, and the judge advocate general of the army. What was their opinion? Wholeheartedly, they agreed that it was practical and adapted to the country's needs. Could it be put into effect at once? It could.[39]

This was the support he needed. On the twenty-first of that month, only 17 days from the inauguration address, the president put the matter in a message to Congress:

> I propose to create a civilian conservation corps to be used in simple work, not interfering with normal employment, and confining itself

to forestry, the prevention of soil erosion, flood control and similar projects. I call your attention to the fact that this type of work is of definite, practical value, not only through the prevention of great present financial loss but also as a means of creating future national wealth. . . .

I estimate that 250,000 men can be given temporary employment by early summer if you give me authority to proceed within the next two weeks. . . .

This enterprise . . . will conserve our precious natural resources. It will pay dividends to the present and future generations. . . .

More important, however, than the material gains will be the moral and spiritual value of such work. . . . We can take a vast army of these unemployed out into healthful surroundings. We can eliminate to some extent at least the threat that enforced idleness brings to spiritual and moral stability. It is not a panacea for all unemployment but it is an essential step in this emergency. I ask its adoption.[40]

The message went on to request legislation to permit the federal government to enroll people in work not competing with private business. It proposed grants to states largely for direct relief to feed and clothe the unemployed. Then, with a program of public works, he concluded his first move in the strategy of immediate relief.

The public works program developed into the Public Works Administration, nationally familiar as the P.W.A. Direct aid to the needy flowered as Federal Emergency Relief. Also, Roosevelt's proposal to use the youth on federal projects met with effective congressional action in a bill passed under the official title "An act for the relief of unemployment through the performance of useful public works and for other purposes." It became effective with the president's signature on March 31, 1933, and under its authority was created the C.C.C. Dear to the president's heart, it developed into one of the most popular New Deal measures.[41]

Tennessee Valley Authority

The implementation of the public works program and the C.C.C. was only the beginning of President Roosevelt's guiding hand in instigating and developing conservation projects or projects that would contribute to the cause of conserving natural resources. In a message to Congress on April 10, 1933, President Roosevelt suggested legislation to create the Tennessee Valley Authority (T.V.A.). For 12 years Senator George W. Norris and other conservationists had waged a battle to develop the resources of the Tennessee Valley. Their labors never materialized in the passage of legislation, until, supported by Roosevelt's conviction that a project should be undertaken in the Tennessee Valley for the service of the people, the T.V.A. was created on May 18, 1933. Roosevelt in proposing the legislation envisioned the T.V.A. as more than mere power development, transcending to the fields of flood control, soil erosion, and land planning. As created, the T.V.A. was a corporation with the power of government to promote flood control, navigation, electric power production, proper use of land and forest, and "the economic and social well being of the people." The new agency was to deal with all natural resources as a single problem. Interstate in character, it worked cooperatively with seven state governments and many local ones. It constituted a project that gave regional planning a go-ahead signal.[42]

Roosevelt later admitted that before he came to Washington, he had determined to initiate a land use experiment embracing many states in the Tennessee River watershed. He felt that the T.V.A. was the beginning of the fulfillment of the pledge of the Democratic platform of 1932 calling for the conservation, development, and use of the nation's water power in the public interest. The president believed that the T.V.A. could serve as example and incentive for similar developments. It was to be a laboratory for the nation to learn how to make the most of its vast resources for the lasting benefit of the ordinary man and woman.[43] On June 8, 1933, President Roosevelt issued Executive Order 6161, directing the T.V.A. to initiate surveys, plans, experiments, and demonstrations needed or desirable to aid in the proper use and development of the natural resources of the Tennessee River drainage basin and adjoining territory.[44] The people of the states were at least going to be given a chance to face the future with the confidence that something of a long-range nature was being attempted.

Shelterbelt Proposal

By no means did the president, having initiated two major pieces of conservation legislation, tarry with self-satisfaction. He was continually at work seeking new ideas, new solutions, and information on possible projects, and studying the feasibility of planning and the value of scientific inquiry. As early as August 1933, Roosevelt was seeking cost estimates for tree desert planting and the cost of a series of 100-foot shelterbelts. During the first months of his administration, the germ of the shelterbelt idea sprouted.[45] He believed that the planting of trees in a line would serve as a windbreak and prevent the blowing away of top soil. The president was personally interested in a shelterbelt project, and by executive order on July 11, 1934, allocated $15 million for shelterbelt tree planting.[46] However, Congress refused to appropriate funds to continue the shelterbelt, and the entire project was ready to collapse without trial. The Secretary of Agriculture Henry Wallace suggested a legislative appropriation simply for tree planting on a broad, cooperative plan. "Yes," was his chief's comment, "if you can put it through." Money was obtained, but the shelterbelt project limped on precariously. Its value, cost, and practicability were challenged by ardent critics and supporters alike.[47] However, Roosevelt was not convinced by their attacks. In May 1939, he urged Secretary Wallace to undertake a special drive to bring the shelterbelt more prominently before Congress and the country. He conferred repeatedly with officials associated with the scheme. However the shelterbelt never achieved the popularity of the C.C.C.[48]

President Roosevelt did not limit his energies merely to proposing legislation to Congress and issuing executive orders during his first months in office, nor did he confine himself to a limited period in which he was active. Throughout his presidential administration he devoted a goodly share of his energy toward the protection of the nation's natural resources against unwise utilization. Conservation was not just a tool to implement a relief program, but a policy that was to be permanent. This objective of permanency caused the president to give attention to routine matters as well as the more spectacular acts. He was interested in the conservation of all natural resources, but was particularly devoted to that of forests, wildlife, soil, and water. A detailed discussion of these resources follows.

FORESTRY

What he had achieved on a personal and state basis in forestry, Roosevelt believed he could achieve on a national scale. The scope of reforestation in the nation meant work to be done on private lands as well as national lands. In 1933 Roosevelt made clear his opinion that the federal government could not properly undertake to reforest privately owned lands without some provision for getting its money back. Immediately, plans and studies were begun for the adoption of lumber codes, governmental cooperation with private owners in reforestation, and federal and state governmental cooperation in forestry.[49]

F.D.R.'s Appreciation
of Public Opinion and Support

The president also displayed an astuteness in appreciation of public opinion and support in carrying out forestry measures. In a memorandum to Henry Wallace, June 24, 1933, Roosevelt advised that purchase of lands for national forests from the $20 million allotment should be widely distributed to create public interest and promote education in organized forestry.[50] He did not miss an opportunity to urge scientific forestry. In January 1935, he sent letters to all of the state governors requesting state cooperation in forest conservation.[51] Likewise he addressed the governors in asking their cooperation in the National Industrial Recovery Act (N.R.A.) Lumber Code.[52] The president saw the need for tact and wisdom in developing a national forestry policy that would include the cooperation of governments and citizens at all levels. When writing to Senator Duncan U. Fletcher of Florida on March 30, 1935, about forest conservation, the president said

> . . . as to Federal legislation, I have only been awaiting the most favorable opportunity to present a program for the consideration of Congress. What I have in mind is a rounding out of existing legislation supplemented by new provisions and altogether something which will supply an organic basis, so far as we can now foresee it, for the next ten or fifteen years.[53]

F.D.R.'s Leadership

Roosevelt had an eye for gauging the most opportune time to push legislation and when to dip into the treasury for funds. The president had suggested that a plan be worked out for federal aid to stimulate the acquisition and development of state forests.[54] Such a plan was incorporated in the Fulmer Bill in 1935. When writing to Wallace on July 13, 1935, President Roosevelt said that the Fulmer Bill was an excellent law but, at that time, appropriation was impossible. He hoped the legislation could be postponed until purchases of land could be financed.[55] In this same manner the president conferred time and time again with his fellow office holders.[56] As well as giving advice and using his influence to gain his goals, the president asked for advice. As circumstances would warrant, he could be humble in asking for consideration or sarcastic with a razor edge in disciplining a political bedfellow or discouraging a proposal. These tactics were apparent in his forestry maneuvers. On August 2, 1935, he wrote to Secretary of State Cordell Hull and Secretary of Agriculture Wallace, asking their consideration of a plan to reduce cutting of trees for pulp.[57] The same month in corresponding with Governor C. H. Martin of Oregon, he stated plainly that passage to private ownership of so much of the accessible and productive forest land in Oregon had aggravated rather than diminished the problems of permanent forest management. The president pointedly said it would be necessary to restore to public ownership a great deal of forest land that unwisely was let pass into private control.[58] Just as Roosevelt could be pertinent in his remarks, he could temper his refusals with tact that took the sting out of rejections. He told Senator Fletcher in September 1935, that he approved of the purposes in proposed legislation to aid in the conservation of forests through a Forest Credit Bank, but that the proposal was not in accord with his financial program.[59]

F.D.R.'s Reliance on Information and Facts

In dealing with those whose help he sought, Roosevelt came loaded with facts. His fellow government officials constantly supplied him with detailed information, which he usually had at his fingertips when conferring with officials in forestry problems,[60] or before presenting messages to Congress. For instance, he requested on January 27, 1938, that Secretary of Agriculture Wallace prepare for him a short message to Congress on the general forestry situation.[61] Addressing Congress on March 14, 1938, Roosevelt set forth the nature of this great problem and recommended a study by Congress. And the following year he urged them to pass legislation on it.[62] Such legislation, however, was never considered to be the final goal. Results had to be shown—and good results. Investigate, experiment, devise—any expedient to improve forestry in the United States. In 1941 he suggested that Secretary of Agriculture Claude Wickard and Secretary of Interior Harold Ickes appoint a representative outside the professional forestry field to prepare a report on the forestry problem.[63] Nor was he content to pass along only broad recommendations, for the records show a lively attention to detail. Inspired perhaps by a warning from Harold Ickes in August 1941, Roosevelt early the next month wrote to Secretary of Agriculture Wickard about a proposed release of timber-cutting rights on the Morse Creek watershed of the Mount Olympic Park. He requested Wickard to send him a map of the area and to hold up any such proposed action until he had cleared it. Fortunately, Wickard could assure him that no sale of timber was contemplated on the Morse Creek watershed, but the incident illustrates Roosevelt's alertness.[64]

Impact of World War II

The effect of the war upon forestry called upon all of Roosevelt's flexibility of means in attaining firm objectives, of which he had by then shown himself a master. In 1942 he outlined a governmental forestry policy for the war's duration: let Congress impose no federal regulation of forestry practices on private lands; let farmers' woodlots lying within forest areas not be put under regulation but under a county agent system; let appropriations for insect and disease control not increase in time of war. This did not desert an earlier policy but readjusted emphasis to meet the vast emergency of war.[65] Scientific forestry would not cease, nor would the nation ruthlessly cut its timber for war needs, but energy and expenditure would go toward the most efficient use of forest resources within the conservation framework. In this, the president set an example by selling his own scientifically cut timber on Hyde Park for shipbuilding. Also he requested Harold Ickes to find out if there was any usable timber in the national parks, and he repeatedly reminded the American people not to discard sound, long-range principles under stress of war.[66]

WILDLIFE

Dear also to Roosevelt was the wildlife of the country, though sentimentality did not describe his attitude toward its protection. His policy was efficiently practical. Writing to Secretary Wallace, October 18, 1933, he asserted that he had heard that the Biological Survey spent too much time on scientific experimentation: "We ought to have a more practical spirit—would you look into the whole subject?"[67] And in May 1934, ever-mindful of expense, he asked Wallace for definite suggestions for wildlife expenditure. He hoped to add 5 million to the 1 million dollars already received. As an afterthought, he concluded: "by the way, the congressmen say the million dollars which I allocated has got lost somewhere. Will you conduct a search party? F.D.R."[68] Though his subtlety of humor sometimes made it difficult to determine whether he was teasing or sarcastic, he always appeared basically sincere.

Humorous Correspondence
with Biological Survey Chief

A delightful exchange took place between Roosevelt and Jay N. Darling, chief of the Bureau of Biological Survey. Darling sketched a letterhead picturing a confident F.D.R. with mammoth pencil writing $4,000,000 while a diminutive Darling jumped and pulled his hair shrieking, "Hey look what you're doin!" (See drawing). Under this dramatic heading he wrote:

We can make better use of retired agricultural land than anybody. Others just grow grass, trees, marshes, lakes, ducks, geese, furbearers, impounded water and recreation. The six million we get from Congress and which you think is enough, is mostly going to buy Okefenokee, the ranches on the winter elk range in Jacksons Hole, the private lands that lie in the midst of the Hart Mountain antelope range, and for rehabilitation [dams and dikes] of the duck ranges we bought last year.

By the way, Secretary Ickes wants me to give him Okefenokee. Do you mind? I don't, only that it cuts into our nesting area funds.

I need $4,000,000 for duck lands this year and the same bill which gave us the $6,000,000 specifically stated that at your discretion you could allocate from the $4,800,000,000 money for migratory waterfowl restoration.

We did a good job last year. Why cut us off now?[69]

Darling closed the letter with sketches of patch-attired ducks and ducklings saying "Redistribution of wealth eh? Where do we come in?" "Yeah, how about subsistence homesteads for us?" (*See drawing*). The president promptly picked up the quip, replying:

As I was saying to the Acting Director of the Budget the other day—
"this fellow Darling is the only man in history who got an appropriation through Congress, passed the Budget and signed by the President without anybody realizing that the Treasury had been raided."

You hold an all-time record. In addition to the six million dollars
($6,000,000) you got, the Federal Courts say that the United States
Government has a perfect constitutional right to condemn millions
of acres for the welfare, health and happiness of ducks, geese, sand-
pipers, owls, and wrens, but has no constitutional right to condemn
a few old tenements in the slums for the health and happiness of
the little boys and girls who will be our citizens of the next generation.

Nevertheless, the more power to your arm! Go ahead with the
six million dollars ($6,000,000) and talk with me about a month hence
in regard to additional lands, if I have any more left.[70]

Darling came back by return mail with another hand-drawn letterhead.
He pictured a small, confident Darling with a "Time's Up" exclamation
to a startled president and his secretary. (*See drawing*). Darling's letter
carried the message:

About recognizing wildlife as a valued agency of public service . . . it
hasn't been so far you know . . . the only money specifically allocated
to wildlife out of the emergency funds so far was your one million
last year. All the rest we have had to suck through borrowed straws
out of some one else's barrel!! . . . and it's been tough going.

And about that six million which I believe you mentioned. You
suggested that I try to get a special act of Congress for Okefenokee
and the Jackson Hole elk. Remember? When I found where the
money was and how to get it, that Mr. Ickes was sitting on it and
didn't have anything in particular he was going to do with it. I added

just a little change for the antelope range in Hart Mountain so we won't have to pass the tin cup every winter to buy hay.

We could do a swell job with four million and a fair one with three. It's o.k. with Congress.[71]

The president cooperated actively with his chief of the Bureau of Biological Survey, offering his help if Darling ran into any coordination difficulty in carrying out his wildlife measures. When a dispute between Darling and the Reclamation Service reached an impasse, Roosevelt offered his services for a conference.[72]

Roosevelt's Attention to Detail

Roosevelt kept track of the work of the men engaged in wildlife conservation and of legislation and projects adopted. Never did the relative smallness of a matter leave him indifferent. When David Wagstaff criticized the unnecessary slaughter of bears in Alaska, President Roosevelt immediately sent a memorandum to Harold Ickes stating,

This horrifies me as much as it does my friend David Wagstaff. If these bears come under your jurisdiction will you please have the matter checked up? It seems to me that that kind of slaughter ought to be stopped.[73]

SOIL

Similarly, Roosevelt did not limit himself to certain phases of the conservation policy being developed in the nation. He also guided and influenced in all fields, devoting as much attention to saving the soil as to saving the forests and wildlife. According to what was appropriate or effective, his action was by administration, science, or publicity. In administration, for instance, Roosevelt announced his decision on March 22, 1935, to transfer the Division of Erosion Control from the Department of the Interior to the Department of Agriculture on the grounds that soil erosion was more congruous with the latter.[74] The same year he gave the A.A.A. publicity by discussing its objectives.[75] He was often quick to further a project by such a public comment in its favor. Thus, in a press conference on January 10, 1936, he discussed the dangers of plowing up buffalo grass on the Great Plains and pointed to the current dust storms as ominous warning against a renewed plowing-up of land that should be in pasture or woods.[76] Ever eager to push the soil conservation program, he wrote to J. B. Huston, acting administrator of the A.A.A., July 1936, "I am told there is a growing interest in the soil conservation program in upstate New York and this would be a good time to push it. Will you do everything possible?"[77] To ward off critical attacks, he pointed to the experimental work in soil conservation done by Louis XIV in the Loire Valley in France in the eighteenth century.[78]

State and Local Cooperation;
Great Plains Drought Committee;
Dust Bowl Trips

The president was keenly aware that a national program required state and local cooperation. The black blizzard that blew off soil to the measure of millions of tons in 1934 laid bare that haggard truth: people where they are must care for their soil, else the soil of the nation is gone. Not merely land was lost from the Dust Bowl, but the souls of homeless embittered men. A vast and swelling army, the new American migrants, scattered in dismay, in despair, from the parched and dying earth became the angry theme of John Steinbeck's *The Grapes of Wrath,* and sent through the country a chill of realization that the Sahara could happen here. Roosevelt appointed a Great Plains Drought Area Committee on

July 22, 1936. Its difficult task was to discover the most efficient ways to utilize the resources of the Great Plains area, and especially to explore practicable measures for remedying the truly dreadful losses and distress of the people there.[79] At the same time, he continued his extensive Dust Bowl Trips. From July 15 to September 15, 1936, his travel from state to state brought the conditions of soil and drought directly under his eye, and sharpened his insight into the problems they produced. In a series of Governors' Conferences, he discussed with state officials the extent of hardships and possible remedies. En route he received numerous invitations from organizations, individuals, political office holders, and educators to attend dinners, to address groups, and to visit. The president also received suggestions of places to see. No state or local area wanted him to overlook its need for aid in trying circumstances.[80]

Reports of the Great Plains Drought Area Committee

The president and the Great Plains Drought Area Committee appreciated the seriousness of the situation. On August 29, 1936, the Great Plains Committee reported that stopping the waste of soil by erosion and increasing efficient use of the regional water resources were basic to any rational long-range program for the Great Plains Drought area.[81] This report plus another on the Great Plains of the Future in December 1936, caused President Roosevelt to attempt to put the whole thing before Congress.[82] He requested M. L. Cooke, Rural Electrification administrator, to prepare a short message that he could use in transmitting the report. Cooke, with an eye as quick as his commander-in-chief's for a chance for publicity, advised him to hold back the report until the current flood of January 1937, had passed its crest. Cooke believed that within three or four days the newspaper reporters, anxious for a fresh lead, would be receptive to the relation between drought and flood, the fundamental unity of the problems they produce.[83] The president and his fellow office holders were ever-mindful of favorable publicity and public support, and the administration was successful in teaching that no one conservation problem stood alone, but was related to others.[84]

Cooperation with State Governors in Soil Erosion Control

In tackling the national soil erosion control problem, President Roosevelt urged state cooperation. On February 26, 1937, he wrote to the state governors, requesting their cooperation in promoting an effective soil erosion program by adopting a uniform soil conservation law. He pointed out that soil erosion control was a part of flood control and protective land use practices, that "dust storms of the last few years have underscored the importance of programs to control soil erosion . . . the nation that destroys its soil destroys itself. . . ."[85] He told Governor Olin D. Johnston of South Carolina that "only by cooperation of the various states with the efforts of the Federal Government can we make soil conservation a national achievement."[86]

WATER

The president's interest and leadership in the development and conservation of the nation's water resources were manifold. The ink had barely dried on his signature approving the T.V.A. when he indicated his desire to get something started on the lower Columbia River.[87] The development of water resources was to be a part of the public works program. By executive order on August 19, 1933, he designated the Federal Power Commission as an agency to aid the Federal Emergency Administration of Public Works, in preparation of that part of the program of public works pertaining to the development of water power and the transmission of electrical energy. The Federal Power Commission also had the responsibility of making a survey of the water resources of the United States as they related to the conservation, development, control, and utilization of water power. The president approached the conservation of water resources from every possible aspect and, as the new national leader, immediately made known his interest in them.[88]

Early in his administration Roosevelt submitted reports to Congress on a comprehensive plan for the control and development of water resources. He did not intend to drop the matter there. He informed Congress that water resources were going to receive his direct attention.[89] This promise he fulfilled by helping to direct and shape flood legislation. In May 1936, he opposed the Copeland Flood Control Bill under debate on the basis that it was unsound.[90] Flood control legislation as finally passed June 15 and 22, 1936, received the president's sponsorship by the encouragement of surveys and studies that would enable the federal government intelligently to sponsor worthwhile projects.[91] However, before he endorsed any major flood control measures, he conferred with Cabinet members and the National Resources Board.[92] President Roosevelt was very much in support of flood control, but he desired that the work be done scientifically, cooperatively, and with a long-range view.[93]

F.D.R.'s PERSONAL ATTENTION
TO VARIED CONSERVATION ENDEAVORS

With almost uncanny ability, F.D.R. seemed able to keep track of and in touch with all conservation endeavors and projects. Whether the conservation work was of major or minor importance, Roosevelt's presence and influence were felt. He showed interest in the control of grazing of livestock on the public domain, and once the Taylor Grazing Act was passed, he supported it by promoting cooperation and offering advice.[94] The president used his influence in pushing legislation through Congress providing for the Mount Olympic National Park project. He favored enlarging Olympic National Park and concentrated his efforts in that direction.[95] Another project that caught his attention was the Colorado Big Thompson Project.[96] Ever varied were his conservation efforts. In 1936 he supported a constituent's request to unlock Glacier National Monument for gold exploration. In no way did the president think that mining on a glacier would impair conservation. He saw no threatened harm to scenic beauty and believed that harm to wildlife could be avoided by requiring miners not to carry firearms. This particular incident of relative unimportance compared with the major conservation problem facing the nation illustrates the president's great flexibility and energy in carrying out his executive duties and his practical conservation attitude.[97]

CRITICISM OF PRESIDENT ROOSEVELT

President Roosevelt was subject to critical charges of being impractical in his leadership and sponsorship of planning. He was charged with being a supporter of planning and thus endangering the true function of democratic processes of government. His actions favored national planning in all phases of conservation of natural resources. He could not deny that he believed in and supported planning. Money was granted for surveys, studies, conferences, mapping, committee studies, and the work of a National Resources Board. The president wholeheartedly endorsed planned projects. He made great personal use of scientific and research reports in determining his own conclusive opinions and directive influence.[98]

F.D.R.'s DIPLOMACY AND TACT

President Roosevelt constantly used diplomacy and tact in showing the American public his interest in conservation and in encouraging fellow conservationists to continue their worthwhile efforts. Whether in press conferences, personal letters, dinner addresses, or public speeches, the president made use of every opportunity to direct attention to the nation's natural resources.[99] A chronological sampling of his diplomatic technique illustrates how varied were the areas in which he dealt. When writing to Marshal N. Dana, president of the National Reclamation Association, on November 23, 1933, Roosevelt said, "Reclamation as a federal policy has proved its worth and has a very definite place in our economic existence."[100] Roosevelt sent a telegram to Commissioner L. Osborne of the Conservation Department, New York, on May 15, 1935, to be read at a celebration of the 50th anniversary of conservation in New York, giving his best wishes for their celebration and promising his "unqualified support" of conservation.[101] The same year he sent a statement to the Washington State Sportsmen's Council complimenting them on their cooperation with the Washington State Planning Council in carrying out effective use of land and water resources.[102] Writing to R. U. Johnson, director of the Hall of Fame of New York University, August 7, 1935, Roosevelt addressed him as "My Dear Mr. Ambassador" and went on to give him information on the Appalachians and concluded with "At least the nation is becoming conservation minded."[103]

The president displayed his humor when writing to Secretary Ickes on June 17, 1935, concerning an appropriation that he was taking in stride,

> I suppose there is nothing to do but approve the allotment of $350,000 to cover item one for a third double fish lock at Bonneville. All I can hope is that the salmon will approve the spillways and find them really useful even though they cost almost as much as the dam and the electric power development.[104]

But when speaking to the press about the Norris Dam on March 4, 1936, he said "The Norris Dam is a practical symbol of better life and greater opportunity for millions of citizens of our country."[105]

On January 25, 1937, Roosevelt sent a message to Ickes to be read by him at a banquet of the New York Rod and Gun Editor's Association. Part of this message he made a plea for dedication of all self-protection and the cause of true conservation.[106] The chief executive showed shrewd diplomacy in his advice to Director Fechner of the C.C.C. in 1937. He cautioned Fechner against too many projects on privately owned land that would naturally incur criticism.[107] In other messages in 1937, he appealed to the pride of the people. A telegram sent on the occasion of the dedication of the Wheeler Dam read:

As all sound conservation projects should do, Wheeler Dam makes an incidental contribution to the public welfare by adding another important unit to the nation's parks and providing sanctuary for the conservation of wildlife.[108]

Writing to Joseph H. Black, national president of Future Farmers of America, Roosevelt pointed to the shame of America of heedless exploitation of natural resources in the past and the determination that future policy of the government would be wise conservation.[109] He complimented C. L. Miller, vice-president of the Cincinnati Beautiful Association, on the planting of elms by school children on Arbor Day.[110] A letter to W. Davis, president and publisher of *The Southern Planter,* Richmond, Virginia, on October 2, 1939, expressed Roosevelt's faith in current conservation measures' stopping destruction and waste of land resources.[111] On February 21, 1941, the president commended Richard Neuberger, Hall of Representatives, Salem, Oregon, on his work in Oregon's advancement in conservation.[112] It was but another example of a "politic gesture." Indeed, the president was a master of tact and diplomacy.

PRAISE FOR PRESIDENT ROOSEVELT

There was no lack of praise for the leadership and work of President Roosevelt in the field of conservation. Honors of recognition were bestowed upon him. As early as April 29, 1933, he was honored by being unanimously elected honorary national president of the Izaak Walton League of America in appreciation of his good work and interest in conservation.[113] John Hermsted, president of the Forestry Club and editor of the annual *Empire Forester,* dedicated the year's publication, 1933, to Roosevelt as the outstanding exponent of conservation in the country.[114] In 1934 Roosevelt was elected honorary member of the Society of American Forester and was the first recipient of the Schlich Memorial Medal.[115] On December 24, 1936, Fred Fletcher of the New York Rod and Gun Editor's Association sent information to the White House that the association planned to present President Roosevelt with a boat award for being the outstanding conservationist in the United States.[116]

In addition to awards, President Roosevelt received messages of congratulations and praise. In 1933 he was complimented in Congress on the success of his reforestation program, on the Tennessee River Valley project, and on his protection of wildlife.[117] Appreciation of the president's conservation effort was oft repeated throughout his administration, not only by private citizens but by fellow political office holders as well.[118] Harold Ickes, secretary of the interior, praised his executive for past and future vision of conservation.[119] Congressman Robertson of Virginia claimed that Roosevelt was making real contributions to the happiness of the average citizen,[120] and Morris L. Cooke, Rural Electrification administrator, credited Roosevelt for being largely responsible for current interest in soil conservation.[121] Even a long-standing ardent Republican saw fit to compliment the president. Molly Dewson wrote to Roosevelt on January 4, 1935,

> You will like to hear this. A friend of mine motoring West this summer stopped in New Mexico one night with a Navajo Indian trader who said "though he was a Republican that in the twenty five years of his connection with the Indians this administration was the only one which had done anything constructive for the Indians." The Navajos were building innumerable dams for soil conservation.[122]

F.D.R.'s PERSONAL COMMITMENT

Without a doubt Franklin Roosevelt was a great leader in reawakening the American people to the need for conservation of their country's natural resources and provoking and developing a national conservation policy. His personal interest and political office as chief executive of the United States enabled him to accomplish what no preceding president had ever dreamed possible. Nor did the threat of war deter his conservation efforts. Conservation as envisioned by President Roosevelt was not a temporary policy that would terminate with an emergency or the ending of his presidential administration. To him his work was but the beginning of a necessary remolding and expansion of conservation policy in the United States.[123] In so doing he was carrying on a historical conservation legacy; however, there had never been such an encompassing and expansive conservation policy and program as under the incumbent president.

NOTES

[1]Documentary evidence of this is found in the following chapters. The following specific citations indicate merely the type of information available. Robert H. Randall, "Conservation of Natural Resources," *Annals of the American Academy*, 206:142–46 (November 1939); "Democracy: Its Essentials and Its Problems," *Scholastic*, 35:18S–20S (December 11, 1939); W. Wilcox, "Economic Aspects of Soil Conservation," *Journal of Political Economy*, 46:702–13 (October 1938); *New York Times*, March 12, 16, June 25, 1933; Stuart Chase,

Rich Land Poor Land (New York, 1936), 3–333; Richard Lieber, *America's Natural Wealth* (Harper's, 1942), 1–241.

²*New York Times,* March 12, 16, June 25, 1933; "Democracy: Its Essentials and Its Problems," *Scholastic,* 35:18S–20S (December 11, 1939); Wilcox, "Economic Aspects of Soil Conservation," *Journal of Political Economy,* 46:702–13 (October 1938); *United States Statutes at Large,* 43:22; National Archives, Washington, Box 572, "Western Water Problems," Folder *Drought Conditions,* General correspondence of secretary of agriculture.

³"Roosevelt and Conservation," *Nature Magazine,* 21:269 (June 1933); Chase, *Rich Land Poor Land* (New York, 1936), 3–353; Lieber, *America's Natural Wealth* (Harper's, 1942), 1–241; *Congressional Record,* 75 Congress, 1 session (1937), Appendix 473–75, speech made by Harold Ickes, secretary of the interior before N.Y. Rod and Gun Editor's Association in Commodore Hotel, N.Y.C., February 23, 1937, broadcast over N.B.C.; 74 Congress, 2 session (1936), 4643–44, address by Senator Guffey of Pennsylvania; 73 Congress, 2 session (1934), 6709–11; 75 Congress, 1 session (1937), 1336–40, address of Will M. Whittington of Mississippi before the American Forestry Association, May 31, 1937; *New York Times,* January 28, February 27, 1934, March 14, 1937; "The Ohio Mississippi Valley Flood Disaster of 1937," *Report of American Red Cross* (Washington, 1938), 1–252; Bennett Swenson, "Monthly Weather Review," *U.S. Weather Bureau,* 65:71–86 (February 1937).

⁴*New York Times,* April 30, 1933, March 31, April 9, 1935; Theodore M. Knappen, "Operating on a Continent," *Reader's Digest,* 28:59–60 (March 1936); "Dust Bowl into Grazing Land," *Literary Digest,* 121:9 (March 7, 1936); "Save Our Soil," *Colliers,* 97:86 (March 14, 1936); W. I. Drummond, "Dust Bowl," *Review of Reviews,* 93:37–40 (June 1936); Coyle David Cushman, "Balance What Budget?" *Harper's Magazine,* 175:449–59 (October 1937); H. H. Bennett, "Emergency and Permanent Control of Wind Erosion in the Great Plains," *Scientific Monthly,* 47:381–99 (November 1938); Morris L. Cooke, "Twenty Years of Grace," *Survey Graphic,* 24:276–82 (June 1935); Charles W. Collier, "At Last—A Soil Erosion Program," *New Republic* 83:68–70 (May 29, 1935); A. W. Malone, "Desert Ahead," *New Outlook,* 164:14–17 (August 1934); "The Grassland," *Fortune,* 12:58–67 (November 1935); *Congressional Record,* 74 Congress, 2 session (1936), 4643–85.

⁵Interview with Mr. William Plog, superintendent of grounds of the Hyde Park estate (June 1950); Olin Dows, *Franklin Roosevelt at Hyde Park* (New York, 1949), 1–156.

⁶Leaflet folder "Forestry Practice on the Roosevelt Farm" (N.Y. State College of Forestry, August 1931); Plog interview.

⁷F.D.R. Papers, Franklin D. Roosevelt Journal 1911–17, material on farm activities at Hyde Park, (notes are written in longhand). This journal is included in the Franklin Roosevelt papers at the Franklin D. Roosevelt Library, Hyde Park, New York; Group 14, Papers of Franklin D. Roosevelt relating to family business, and other personal affairs, 1882–1945, Subject Files, Hyde Park matters: General 1909, 1933, Box 5.

⁸Plog Interview; Leaflet, "President Roosevelt Practices Selective Logging," *Southern Lumberman,* (December 15, 1942); F.D.R. Papers, Group 14, Subject Files, Hyde Park: Farming on the Roosevelt estate, 1911–33, Box 6, Group 9, papers of Franklin D. Roosevelt as assistant secretary of the navy 1913–20, personal papers (letters on tulip poplars).

⁹F.D.R. Papers, Group 9, Papers of Franklin D. Roosevelt as assistant secretary of the navy 1913–20, personal papers, February 19, 1916, F.D.R. to B. H. Paul, N.Y. State Foresters; Group 14, Subject File, Hyde Park: Forestry 1912–33, Box 7, Adrianic Platt Company to F.D.R..

¹⁰Ibid., Group 14, Subject Files, Hyde Park: Forestry 1912–33, Box 7, December 2, 1933, F.D.R. to W. Overfield, Hyde Park, New York.

¹¹Plog interview; F.D.R. Papers, Group 14, Subject File, Hyde Park: Forestry 1912–33, Box 7, letters for N.Y. State College in Forestry on demonstration plantings put out by college in Hyde Park; Group 14, "The President's Forests," *American Forests,* (January

1934), Nelson Brown, "President's Christmas Trees," *American Forests*, (December 1941); President's Secretary's File, PSF, Folder, Hyde Park, Box 1933–35, letter on demonstration plantings, June 14, 1932, Hugh P. Bokes to F.D.R., N.Y. State College Forestry; letter, June 12, 1934, Samuel H. Spring, dean, N.Y. State College, to F.D.R.; letter, April 19, October 8, 1935, W. Plog to F.D.R., on planting of acorns.

[12]F.D.R. Papers, President's Personal File 38, PPF, 1933–44, correspondence between F.D.R. and Nelson Brown; Group 12, papers of Franklin D. Roosevelt as governor of New York, 1929–32, February 12, 1930, Brown to F.D.R.; Group 12, March–1930, January 1932, Brown to F.D.R., correspondence with F.D.R. concerning conservation matters and other subjects.

[13]Leaflet, "Forestry Practice" (N.Y. State College, August 1931); F.D.R. Papers, mimeographed—*Announcement Cooperative Extension Work*, Poughkeepsie, New York, October 15, 1934; mimeographed—*Demonstrations at Roosevelt's Farm*, Hyde Park, New York; program—*Joint Meeting New York and New England Sections*, Society of American Foresters, Poughkeepsie, New York, September 3–4, 1931.

[14]F.D.R. Papers, Group 12, Box 21, May 22, 1930, F.D.R. to Brown; Box 240, June 29, 1931, F.D.R. to Brown; Group 13 PPF 38, March 8, 1933, Brown to F.D.R.; September 23, 1933, Brown to F.D.R.; October 20, 1933, Brown to F.D.R.; March 22, 1934, Brown to F.D.R.; October 1, 1938, F.D.R. to Brown; October 17, 1939, Brown to F.D.R.; October 19, 1939, F.D.R. to Brown; November 3, 1939, Watson, secretary to president to Brown; November 3, 1939, Brown to F.D.R.

[15]Ibid., Group 13, PPF 38, March 14, 1934, Samuel N. Spring, dean, State College of Forestry, to F.D.R.; June 26, 1937, Brown to F.D.R.; June 29, 1937, F.D.R. to Brown; April 16, 1936, Brown to F.D.R.; February 1, 1937, F.D.R. to Brown; October 1, 1942, Brown to F.D.R.; February 23, 1942, Brown to F.D.R.; January 19, 1942, F.D.R. to Brown; April 3, 1942, F.D.R. to Brown.

[16]Ibid., PPF 1-P, President's press conference, Number 186, 10–12, February 27, 1935; press conference, Number 347, 1, February 23, 1937; press conference, Number 378, 1–12, July 4, 1937.

[17]Plog interview; F.D.R. Papers, President's Secretary's File, PSF, folder, Hyde Park, Box 1, 1933–35, April 15, 1935, Plog to F.D.R.; April 24, 1935, F.D.R. to Plog; October 8, 1935, Plog to F.D.R.

[18]Plog interview. One of the most humorous woodland road stories is the disagreement F.D.R. and Frank Draiss, assistant gardner, had while building the road. They argued about a certain turn that the president desired. Frank Draiss insisted that the turn could not be constructed because the angle would be too sharp. When the president insisted it could be done, Draiss replied that it was impossible and refused to do it. One of the president's guards mumbled, "Just who in the —— does that guy think he is to tell the president what to do?" Interview with Frank Draiss, June 1950.

[19]F.D.R. Papers, Group 13, White House Official File, OF, OF-1, Agriculture, May 20, 1935, Tugwell to F.D.R.; PPF 2265, July 15, 1939, M. A. LeHand to I. Van Meter (statement, letter not for publication nor to be quoted from); OF-1, Agriculture, May 15, 1935, "Conservation Redefined," address by R. G. Tugwell, under-secretary of agriculture, before 50th anniversary of founding of N.Y. State Forest Preserve.

[20]*Poughkeepsie News Press*, March 5, 1912, F.D.R.'s address before the Peoples' Forum, Troy, New York, on March 3, 1912; F.D.R. Papers, Group 8, Papers of Franklin D. Roosevelt as New York senator, 1911–13, File 26, Box 13, February 22, 1912, F.D.R. to D. Stockton, Poughkeepsie, New York.

[21]F.D.R. Papers, Group 8, N.Y. State Senatorial File, extensive correspondence to F.D.R. asking him to support certain legislation, work against legislation because it was harmful to wildlife, and conservation pleas; correspondence on wildlife and fish conser-

vation; letters commending F.D.R. on conservation work; File 26, March 14, 1911, F.D.R. to W. W. Grant, 140 Nassau St., N.Y.C.; Box 13, March 16, 1911, F.D.R. to Charles D. Haines, N.Y.C.; File 259, Box 32, March 16, 1911, F.D.R. to Samuel H. Ordwary, attorney, N.Y.C.; Box 34, February 20, 1912, H. S. Rivenburgh, Commission of Public Works, Hudson, New York, to F.D.R.; Box 13, February 27, 1912, F.D.R. to George C. Boldt, N.Y.C.; File 82, Box 23, March 10, 1912, F.D.R. to Charles L. Bullymore, Buffalo; Box 31, March 19, 1912, F.D.R. to John F. Murtaught, N.Y. state senator, Albany; Group 8, File 175, Box 28, March 25, 1912, A. S. Houghton, vice-president of the Camp Fire Club of America, N.Y.C., to F.D.R.; File 177, Box 28, March 26, 1912, F.D.R. to Houghton; Speeches, March 31, 1912, F.D.R. to the press, Albany, New York; Group 8, File 105, Box 24, April 5, 1912, F.D.R. to T. F. Conway, Lt. Gov., New York.

[22]Ibid., Group 9, assistant secretary of the navy, Box 75, March 11, 1913, A. S. Houghton, chairman, Camp Fire Clubs of America, N.Y.C., to F.D.R.; Box 73, March 18, 1913, M. H. Hoover, Conservation Commission, Albany, New York, to F.D.R.; Box 75, April 3, 1913, F.D.R. to Houghton.

[23]Ibid., Box 82, November 1, 1913, Governor Martin H. Glynn, New York, to F.D.R.; March 20, 1913, F.D.R. to Governor Martin; Box 89, June 28, 1914, F.D.R. to Hugh P. Baker, reelected to vice-presidency of N.Y. State Forestry Association, 1915 and 1916— letters; Box 96, February 2, 1915, F.D.R. to Frank F. Moon; Box 107, January 26, 1916, Moon to F.D.R.

[24]Ibid., Box 80, September 8, 1913, Thomas M. Upp to F.D.R.; Box 84, January 26, 1914, F.D.R. to J. F. Coleman, New Orleans, Louisiana; Box 154, November 1, 1918, F.D.R. to Dwight W. Huntington; Group 14, Forestry and Conservation, 1921–25, January 2, 1924, F.D.R. to Charles C. Adams, director of N.Y. State College of Forestry, Syracuse; Group 14, relating to family, business and other personal affairs. In the 1920s people wrote to F.D.R. for advice on conservation, his sponsorship of certain projects, and articles; Group Records of Office of Governor of New York State—Albany Papers, October 31, 1928, F.D.R. to Association for the Protection of the Adirondacks, Adirondack Civic Association, Saranac Lake Cambiv of Commein, Adirondack Property Owners Association (Jaboc Gould Shurman, Jr.). The Governor papers in deposit at Hyde Park were borrowed from the Albany records *Congressional Record*, 75 Congress, 1 session (1937), Appendix 473—75.

[25]F.D.R. Papers, Group 12, Roosevelt as governor of New York, Box 256, February 21, 1929, M. H. Hoover, editor, *New York State Conservationist*, to Cross; Group Records of Office of Governor, State of New York, March 31, 1931, radio address by F.D.R., "Conservation Week and Conservation"; Group Records of Governor of New York, 1929– 32, May 9, 1930, Irving Snow, 737 Delaware Avenue, Buffalo, New York to N.Y. State Committee of Unemployment; May 31, 1930, F.D.R. to Daniel Mitchell, president of the Enfield Community Men's Brotherhood, Ithaca, New York; April 1, 1931, Roosevelt radio address; June 30, 1931, F.D.R. to Charles E. Roesch, mayor, Buffalo, New York; December 5, 1931, F.D.R. to Arthur S. Hopkins, chairman, Society of American Foresters, Conservation Commission Albany, New York; Group 12, Roosevelt as governor, Box 223, September 9, 1931, F.D.R. to Wilbur L. Cross, governor of Connecticut.

[26]Ibid., Group 13, PPF 1820, November 6, 1936, D. E. Lilienthal to F.D.R., speech material.

[27]Ibid., Group 12, Roosevelt as governor, Box 91, February 4, 1929, F.D.R. to Robert Underwood Johnson, New York University; Box 147, February 16, 1929, Nicholas Roosevelt, *New York Times*, to F.D.R.; Group Records of Governor of New York, February 27, 1929, F.D.R.'s address to N. Y. State Forestry Association, 17th annual meeting, Albany, New York; Group 12, Box 91, March 12, 1929, F.D.R. to R. U. Johnson, New York University; Box 31, January 10, 1931, Nelson Brown to F.D.R.; Group Records of Gov-

ernor of New York, October 28, 1931, F.D.R. statement; November 12, 1931, James C. Langley to F.D.R.; Group 12, November 1931, William G. Pond, Elmira, New York, to F.D.R.; Box 140, November 2, 1931, F.D.R. to Robert Anderson Pope, Harvard Club, N.Y.C.; November 5, 1931, Nelson Brown to F.D.R.; November 18, 1931, Francis A. Bartlett, Stamford, Connecticut, to F.D.R.; November 21, 1931, F.D.R. to Barrett, St. Augustine, Florida; Group Records of Governor of New York, March 2, 1932, E. E. Elliott, 122 South Kensington Avenue, Kansas City, Missouri, to F.D.R.

[28]Ibid., Group Records of Governor of New York, January 21, 1931, address of Governor Roosevelt at annual dinner, N.Y. State Agricultural Society of Conservation, Aurania Club.

[29]Ibid., Group 12, Roosevelt as governor, Box 242, April 23, 1931, Tom Catheart, editor of *Country Home*, to F.D.R.; Group Records of Governor of New York, March 9, 1932, F.D.R. to G. W. Avery, Cimarron, Kansas; April 8, 1932, F.D.R. to George H. Sankey, 511 1st National Bank Building, Great Falls, Montana; Group 12, Box 60, May 19, 1932, Roosevelt's statement prepared for the *Forestry Geological Review*.

[30]Ibid., Group Records of Governor of New York, May 9, 1930, Irving M. Snow, 737 Delaware Avenue, Buffalo, New York, to N.Y. State Committee on Unemployment; October 9, 1930, I. M. Snow to F.D.R.; October 14, 1930, F.D.R. to Snow; *Congressional Record*, 74 Congress, 2 session (1936), 3098; Albert Atwood, "Is this Conservation." *Saturday Evening Post*, 209:23 (September 26, 1936); *Time*, 33:10 (February 6, 1939); "Roosevelt and Conservation," *Nature Magazine*, 21:269 (June 1933); National Archives, Washington, (1936), folder, letter from Paul H. Appleby, general correspondence of secretary of agriculture.

[31]*The Civilian Conservation Corps* (Washington, 1941), not paged. A bulletin reprinted from *American Conservation* (Washington, 1941); "Roosevelt and Conservation," *Nature Magazine*, 21:269 (June 1933); F.D.R. Papers, Group 12, Roosevelt as governor, November 5, 1931, N. Brown to F.D.R.; November 18, 1931, Francis A. Bartlett, Stamford, Connecticut, to F.D.R.; Group Records of Governor of New York, March 2, 1932, E. E. Elliott, 122 South Kensington Avenue, Kansas City, Missouri, to F.D.R.; Group 12, Box 242, April 23, 1931, Tom Catheart, editor of *Country Home*, to F.D.R.

[32]Franklin D. Roosevelt, "Issues Defined in the Speech of Acceptance," in *Campaign Book of Democratic Party: Candidates and Issues* (New York, 1932), 26, address by F.D.R. before the Democratic National Convention at the Stadium, Chicago, Illinois, July 2, 1932, accepting the presidential nomination.

[33]F.D.R. Papers, Group Records of Governor of New York, July 25, 1932, F.D.R. to James W. Sewall, consulting forester, Old Town, Maine.

[34]Ibid., July 29, 1932, F.D.R. to Stephen J. Adams, 130 West 42nd Street, N.Y.C.; July 29, 1932, F.D.R. to C. A. Cobb, editor, *The Progressive Farmer and Southern Ruralist*, Atlanta, Georgia; August 15, 1932, F.D.R. to Ovid Butler, The American Forestry Association, Washington.

[35]*The Public Papers and Addresses of Franklin D. Roosevelt: (1933) The Year of Crisis* (New York, 1938), 622; Roosevelt, "Issues Defined in Speech of Acceptance," *Campaign Book of Democratic Party* (New York, 1932); Dixon Wecter, *The Age of the Great Depression* (New York, 1948), 41–61.

[36]U.S. Department of Commerce, Bureau of the Census, *Vote Cast in Presidential and Congressional Elections, 1928–1944* (Washington, 1946), 171 pp.; Wecter, *Age of Great Depression*, 1–61; Edgar Eugene Robinson, *The Presidential Vote 1896–1932* (Stanford, Calif.: Stanford University Press, c. 1934), 27–30.

[37]*Congressional Record*, 73 Congress, special session (March 1933), 5; Wecter, *Age of Great Depression*, 1–61; Roosevelt, "Issues Defined in Speech of Acceptance," *Campaign Book of Democratic Party* (New York, 1932).

[38]F.D.R. Papers, Group 13, PPF 2265, July 15, 1939, M. A. LeHand to I. Van Meter

(*Time* Magazine); James F. Kieley, *C.C.C.* (United States Department of the Interior, processed, Washington, 1938), 3. A great amount of the basic material in the booklet was supplied by the office of the director of the C.C.C. and the various departments cooperating in the work of the Corps.

³⁹Alfred C. Oliver, Jr., and Harold M. Dudley, eds., *This New America: The Spirit of the Civilian Conservation Corps* (New York, 1937), 20. Much of the material for this book was taken from *Happy Days*, the C.C.C. weekly newspaper, and assembled data in government files made available to the editors; F.D.R. Papers, Group 13, OF 268, Box 1, March 14, 1933, F.D.R. to secretaries of war, interior, agriculture, and labor.

⁴⁰*Congressional Record*, 73 Congress, 1 session (1933), 650.

⁴¹Ibid., *United States Statutes at Large*, 48:22; Oliver and Dudley, *This New America*, 21; F.D.R. Papers, Group 13, PPF 2265, March 4, 1935, F.D.R. to Henry S. Graves, president, American Forestry Association; April 29, 1936, F.D.R. to Fechner; See Chapter 6 on the C.C.C.

⁴²*The Public Papers and Addresses of Franklin D. Roosevelt: (1933) The Year of Crisis* (New York, 1938), 122–29, Item 36, "A Suggestion for Legislation to Create the T.V.A." Roosevelt's Fireside Chats, messages to Congress, executive orders, and public addresses; *United States Statutes at Large*, 48:58–72; F.D.R. Papers, Group 13, PPF 5850, May 17, 1933, F.D.R. to editor of *Knoxville Journal* (Tennessee).

⁴³*The Public Papers and Addresses of Franklin D. Roosevelt: (1933) The Year of Crisis* (New York, 1938), 125–29, Item 36; F.D.R. Papers, Group 13, OF 42, Box 1, October 17, 1933, David E. Lilienthal, director and counsel of T.V.A., address before Rotary Club of Memphis.

⁴⁴Executive Order 6161.

⁴⁵F.D.R. Papers, Group 13, OF 1-C Agriculture, August 8, 1933, R. Y. Stuart, forester, to F.D.R.; August 19, 1933, F.D.R. to Stuart; September 13, 1933, F.D.R. to Wallace.

⁴⁶Ibid., June 26, 1934, F. A. Silcox, chief forester, to secretary of agriculture; executive order, July 17, 1934; July 31, 1934, Tugwell memo; September 7, 1934, Under-Secretary of Agriculture Tugwell to F.D.R.; September 18, 1934, memo, F.D.R. to director of budget; PPF 1-P, Box 204, September 21, 1934, press conference, Number 144, 4–5.

⁴⁷Ibid., May 27, 1936, Wallace to F.D.R.

⁴⁸Ibid., May 15, 1939, F.D.R. to Wallace; OF 79, May 3, 1940, Harold D. Smith, director of budget, to F.D.R. OF 1-C, May 6, 1940, F.D.R. to Wallace; OF 149, November 4, 1940, Secretary of Agriculture Wickard to F.D.R.; November 6, 1941, Harold Smith to F.D.R.; February 15, 1945, Cooke to F.D.R.; February 26, 1945, F.D.R. to Cooke; April 6, 1945, Cooke to F.D.R.; April 9, 1945, F.D.R. to Cooke.

⁴⁹Ibid., OF 149, May 11, 1933, F.D.R. to Byrnes; PPF 1-P, Box 203, February 23, 1934, press conference, number 100, 3–5.

⁵⁰Ibid., OF 149, June 24, 1933, F.D.R. to Wallace.

⁵¹*Public Papers and Addresses of Franklin D. Roosevelt; 1935* (New York, 1938), 25–26.

⁵²F.D.R. Papers, Group 13, OF 149, January 2, 1935.

⁵³Ibid., March 30, 1935, F.D.R. to D. U. Fletcher, Florida.

⁵⁴Ibid., July 11, 1935, Wallace to F.D.R.

⁵⁵Ibid., July 13, 1935, F.D.R. to Wallace; July 26, 1935, F.D.R. to Wallace.

⁵⁶Ibid., March–July, 1935, 16 items consisting of correspondence and draft of bill relating to proposed legislation to provide for extending credit to aid the conservation and operation of forest lands.

⁵⁷Ibid., OF-1 Agriculture, August 2, 1935 F.D.R. to Hull and Wallace.

⁵⁸Ibid., OF 149, August 12, 1935, F.D.R. to Martin.

⁵⁹Ibid., September 21, 1935, F.D.R. to D. U. Fletcher; September 21, 1935, F.D.R. to

Acting Director of Budget Bell; December 3, 1935, F.D.R. to Russell T. Edwards, editor, *Forest News Digest*, Washington.

[60]Ibid., OF 1-C, Box 20, December 20, 1937, F.D.R. to Wallace; PPF 1-P, Box 207, August 1, 1936, press conference, Number 311, 3.

[61]Ibid., OF 1-C, Box 20, January 27, 1938, F.D.R. to Wallace.

[62]Ibid., OF 149, March 14, 1938, President's message to Congress.

[63]Ibid., OF-1 Agriculture, June 18, 1941, Wickard to F.D.R.

[64]Ibid., OF 1-C, September 3, 1941, F.D.R. to secretary of agriculture; September 6, 1941, Grover B. Hill, acting secretary of agriculture, to F.D.R. Ickes wrote to F.D.R. on this matter August 27, 1941.

[65]Ibid., OF 149, May 19, 1942, F.D.R. to director and assistant director of budgets.

[66]Plog interview; F.D.R. Papers, OF 446, October 1942, F.D.R. to Ickes; October 9, 1942, Newton B. Drury, director of National Park Service, to Ickes.

[67]F.D.R. Papers, OF-1 Agriculture, October 18, 1933, F.D.R. to Wallace, memorandum.

[68]Ibid., OF 378, May 24, 1934, F.D.R. to Wallace.

[69]Ibid., President's Secretary's File, 1933–35, Box 7, July 26, 1935, Darling to F.D.R.

[70]Ibid., July 29, 1935, F.D.R. to Darling.

[71]Ibid., August 26, 1935, Darling to F.D.R.

[72]Ibid., Group 13, OF-1 Agriculture, February 8, 1935, F.D.R. to secretary of agriculture and chief of Bureau of Biological Survey; OF 1-F, May 13, 1935, F.D.R. to Darling; May 23, 1935, Darling to F.D.R.; June 13, 1935, Early to McIntyre.

[73]Ibid., OF 1-F February 18, 1936, F.D.R. to Wallace and Ickes; February 21, 1936, Ickes to F.D.R.; OF 6-CC, February 21, 1941, F.D.R. to Ickes; PPF 1-P, Box 206, December 20, 1939, press conference, Number 258, 1–2; OF 6, Box 46, February 21, 1941, Ira Gabrielson, director, Fish and Wildlife Service, to Ickes; OF 378, June 6, 1934, F.D.R. to Ickes; June 6, 1934, F.D.R. to David Wagstaff; June 19, 1934, Ickes to F.D.R.

[74]Ibid., OF 6, Box 45, March 22, 1935, F.D.R. to Ickes. See Chapter 5 for discussion of Soil Erosion Service.

[75]Ibid., PPF 1-P, Box 206, October 25, 1935, press conference, Number 243, 2–3.

[76]Ibid., Box 207, January 10, 1936, press conference, Number 265, 3–5.

[77]Ibid., OF 1-K, July 11, 1936, F.D.R. to Huston.

[78]Ibid., Group 13, PPF 1-P, Box 207, August 7, 1936, press conference, Number 313, 9–11.

[79]*Public Papers and Addresses of Franklin D. Roosevelt: (1936), The People Approve* (New York, 1938), 264–69, 301–15, Item 90 "White House Statement on the Appointment of the Great Plains Drought Area Committee," July 22, 1936; Item 104, "Summary of the Great Plains Drought Area Committee's Preliminary Report and Conclusions Submitted During Drought Inspection Trip," August 27, 1936.

[80]F.D.R. Papers, 200-EE 1936, four boxes of material on the drought trips of F.D.R.; Box 31, Folders 1 and 2, Dust Bowl Trip, July 15–August 26, August 26–September 15, 1936; Box 32, Governor's Conferences; Box 33, folders by states (invitations from organizations, individuals, political office holders, educators, etc.); Box 34, folders by states (invitations and suggestions of places to see); July 23, 1936, Cooke to McIntyre; August 12, 1936, L. T. Alverson, acting executive director to F.D.R.; September 3, 1936, Presidential Drought Conference for the States of Missouri, Kansas, Iowa, Oklahoma, and Nebraska; general correspondence to F.D.R. in the drought.

[81]Ibid., OFF 2285, Report of the Great Plains Drought Area Committee, August 1936.

[82]Ibid., Great Plains of the Future, Report of the Great Plains Committee, December 1936.

[83]Ibid., OFF 285, January 7, 1937, F.D.R. to Cooke; OFF 2285, January 25, 1937, Cooke to F.D.R.

[84]Ibid., OF 402, August 26, 1937, F.D.R. to Ickes; Group 13, PPF 1-P, January 21, 1938, press conference, number 427, 9.

[85]Ibid., Group 13, OF 732, February 17, 1937, F.D.R. to state governors; February 23, 1937, F.D.R. to governors; March 17, 1937, F.D.R. to secretary of agriculture; *The Public Papers and Addresses of Franklin D. Roosevelt: The Constitution Prevails, (1937)* (New York, 1941), 102–4, Item 25, "The President Urges the Adoption by All the States of a Uniform Soil Conservation Law," February 26, 1937.

[86]F.D.R. Papers, Group 13, OF 1-R, April 26, 1937, F.D.R. to Johnston.

[87]Ibid., OF 402, August 7, 1933, F.D.R. to Ickes.

[88]*The Public Papers and Addresses of Franklin D. Roosevelt: (1933) The Year of Crisis* (New York, 1938), 325–28, Item 116, "The Federal Power Commission Designated as an Agency of the Public Works Administration," Executive Order, Number 6251, August 19, 1933.

[89]*National Resources Committee,* "Planning Our Resources" (March 1938), 1–27; *National Planning Board,* "Federal Emergency Administration of Public Works," 1–119, final report; U.S. Congress, *Miscellaneous Senate and House Hearings 1935–1936,* Committee on Public Lands, "Establishment of a National Resources Board," *Hearing before the Committee on Public Lands,* House of Representatives, 74 Congress, 2 session, on H. 10303, "Bill to Provide on the Establishment of National Resources Board and the Organization and Function Thereof," February 20, 24, March 3, 1936 (Washington), 1–95.

[90]F.D.R. Papers, Group 13, OF 132, May 1, 1936, F.D.R. to Robinson, senator, Mississippi.

[91]Ibid., PPF, 1-P, Box 207, June 30, 1936, press conference, Number 305, 23.

[92]Ibid., OF-1 Agriculture, May 7, 1937, F.D.R. to Wallace; OF 132, May 17, 1937, F.D.R. to McIntyre.

[93]Ibid., PPF 1-P, Box 210, April 8, 1938, press conference, Number 449, April 3–4; President's Secretary's File 1940, Interior Department, Box 58, December 21, 1939, F.D.R. to Ickes; OF 79, June 15, 1940, F.D.R. to Milton H. West, Texas, member of Congress.

[94]Ibid., OF 633, April 27, 1933, Ickes to F.D.R.; June, 1934, Ovid Butler, American Forestry Association to F.D.R.; OF 378, January 28, 1935, F.D.R. to Ickes and Wallace; OF 633, January 3, 1936, F.D.R. to Ickes; President's Secretary's File 1940, Agriculture, Box 58, March 3, 1940, Wallace to F.D.R.

[95]Ibid., OF 6-P, March 21, 1938, F.D.R. to Cammerer and Silcox; December 11, 1939, Irving Brant to F.D.R.; December 11, 1939, E. K. Burlow, acting secretary of interior, to F.D.R.; OF 6, Box 36, December 21, 1939, F.D.R. to Clarence D. Martin governor, Washington; PPF 1-P, January 2, 1940, press conference, Number 161, 1–3; September 22, 1937, Irving Brant (*St. Louis Star Times,* editor of editorial page) to F.D.R., part of material on the Olympic Peninsula kept in F.D.R.'s desk for years.

[96]Ibid., OF 402, July 1, 1937, W. P. Wharton, president of the National Parks Association, to F.D.R.; July 8, 1937, A. Z. Gray to F.D.R.; July 9, 1937, J. C. Gregory, director of Izaak Walton League of America, to F.D.R.; August 4, 1937, F.D.R. to A. Z. Gray; December 20, 1937, Ickes to F.D.R.

[97]Ibid., OF 928, Box 1, December 23, 1935, Rex Beach to F.D.R.; January 9, 1936, F.D.R. to Beach; January 15, 1936, F.D.R. to Ickes; May 4, 1936, F.D.R. to Ickes.

[98]*Public Papers and Addresses of Franklin D. Roosevelt: (1938) The Continuing Struggle for Liberalism* (New York, 1941), 144, Item 34, "The President Suggests a Comprehensive Congressional Study of the Forest Land Problem of the United States," March 14, 1938; *House Miscellaneous Documents,* Number 539, 75 Congress, 2 and 3 session (1938), 10264, 1–4; F.D.R. Papers, Group 13, OF 132, November 21, 1933, F.D.R. to Ickes; OF 378, January 23, 1934, "A Plan for National Conservation"; January 31, 1934, press conference,

Number 93, 3; OF 1092, April 20, 1936, F.D.R. to Joe Robinson, Speaker of Senate; February 14, 1934, press conference, Number 97, 3–5; OF 1-F, February 12, 1935, Wallace and Darling to F.D.R.; OF 114, July 2, 1935, F.D.R. to Ickes; OF 114-A, July 19, 1936, F.D.R. to secretary of commerce; OF 1092, July 31, 1936, Ickes to F.D.R.; OF 1092, September 9, 1936, F.D.R. to F. D. Delano; OF 1092, February 3, 1937, F.D.R. to Congress, OF 132, August 12, 1937, F.D.R. to secretaries of war, interior, agriculture, and treasury and acting director of budget; OF 1092, December 3, 1938, F.D.R. to W. I. Meyers.

⁹⁹F.D.R. Papers, Group 13, PPF 191, February 14, 1933, editorial, "Jobs on Trees," clipping from *Kankakee*, (Illinois) *Republican News;* PPF 1-P, March 15, 1933, press conference, Number 3, 5–7; August 11, 1933, press conference, number 43, 5–6; November 7, 1934, press conference, Number 156, 8; November 28, 1934, press conference, Number 161, 17; December 26, 1934, press conference, Number 168, 4; May 6, 1938, press conference, Number 448, Appendix 5–6; PPF 993, October 8, 1941, F.D.R. to O. S. Warden, president of the National Reclamation Association; OF 3-E, February 23, 1937, F.D.R. to C. B. Miller.

¹⁰⁰Ibid., PPF 993, November 23, 1933, F.D.R. to Dana.

¹⁰¹Ibid., PPF 771, May 15, 1935.

¹⁰²Ibid., PPF 2570, May 9, 1935, F.D.R. to E. French Chase, Washington, Sp. Consul.

¹⁰³Ibid., PPF 1742, August 7, 1933, F.D.R. to Johnson.

¹⁰⁴Ibid., OF 108, Box 1, June 17, 1935, F.D.R. to Ickes.

¹⁰⁵Ibid., OF 42, Box 6, March 4, 1936, F.D.R. to press.

¹⁰⁶Ibid., PPF 4301, January 25, 1937, F.D.R. to N.Y. Rod and Gun Editor's Association.

¹⁰⁷Ibid., OF 149, July 28, 1937, F.D.R. to Fechner.

¹⁰⁸Ibid., OF 42, September 9, 1937, F.D.R. to Arthur E. Morgan.

¹⁰⁹Ibid., PPF 1922, October 6, 1937, F.D.R. to Black.

¹¹⁰Ibid., PPF 128, June 29, 1937, F.D.R. to Miller.

¹¹¹Ibid., PPF 6250, October 2, 1939, F.D.R. to Davis.

¹¹²Ibid., PPF 7398, February 21, 1941, F.D.R. to Neuberger.

¹¹³Ibid., PPF 383, April 29, 1933, A. C. Willford, senator, Iowa, to F.D.R.

¹¹⁴Ibid., PPF 38, November 28, 1933, Nelson Brown to F.D.R.

¹¹⁵Ibid., PPF 1112, December 12, 1934, H. H. Chapman, president, Society of American Foresters, to F.D.R.

¹¹⁶Ibid., PPF 4301, December 24, 1936, Fletcher to Marvin McIntyre.

¹¹⁷Ibid., Group 14, Subject Files, Hyde Park: Forestry 1921–23, March 1, 1933, N. Brown to F.D.R.; Group 13, OF 359, April 24, 1933, George L. Berry, Tennessee, to F.D.R.; OF 378, August 29, 1933, F.D.R. to Wallace.

¹¹⁸Ibid., Group 13, OF 378, October 28, 1936, N. Biddle, president, Board of Game Commissioners, Pennsylvania, to F.D.R.; PPF 4301, February 26, 1937, George Greenfield, editor, *Wood, Field and Stream,* to F.D.R.; PPF 1-G, Box 40, Brown to S. Early; OF 177, September 1, 1939, B. Schurr to F.D.R.

¹¹⁹Ibid., OF 6, Box 1, January 22, 1935, Ickes radio address.

¹²⁰Ibid., PPF 1935, June 29, 1935, A. W. Robertson to F.D.R.

¹²¹Ibid., PPF 940, April 7, 1941, M. L. Cooke to F.D.R.

¹²²Ibid., OF 296, January 4, 1935, M. Dewson to F.D.R.

¹²³Ibid., PPF 943, September 5, 1946, F.D.R. to O. S. Warden, president, National Reclamation Association; PPF 940, April 9, F.D.R. to Cooke; PPF 940, July 8, 1941, F.D.R. to Ickes; December 1, 1941, F.D.R. to Stimson, secretary of war; PF 268, December 19, 1941, F.D.R. to Ickes; OF 6, January 20, 1942, F.D.R. to Ickes; OF 79, October 28, 1942, Smith, Budget, to F.D.R.; PPF 943, October 21, 1943, F.D.R. to Warden; *Public Papers and Addresses of Franklin D. Roosevelt: 1940* (New York, 1941), 237–38, Item 52; *Congressional Record,* 76 Congress, 3 session (1940), 269.

ᔕ 2 ᔕ
Background and Setting for Conservation under Franklin Delano Roosevelt

Before Franklin D. Roosevelt's accelerated conservation activity, Americans had already engaged in some conservation work. The conservation of our natural resources had its beginnings in colonial times. The ideas of the American colonists were a legacy of their mother countries expressed in their early legislation. In 1626 Plymouth Colony passed an ordinance prohibiting the cutting of timber on colony lands without official consent. Timber was the first resource for which legislation was enacted in all the colonies. The people were interested in its accessibility to settlement and its lucrative source of income in British trade. By 1650 a number of the New England colonies had enacted ordinances regulating fires to ensure the protection of timber. During the same time, other regulatory devices appeared. Massachusetts, New Hampshire, and Connecticut prohibited timber cutting on public land, unless it had been sanctioned by local government, and penalities were incurred for trespassing on private land. In 1681 William Penn's ordinance for Pennsylvania required that in clearing land, 1 acre be left in trees for every 5 acres cleared. Indeed, resemblances to modern forestry practice were already present. Furthermore, by the eighteenth century the social implications of conservation were apparent. The first community forest in America was established in 1710 at Newington, New Hampshire, where a 110-acre forest owned by the town has continued to yield benefits to the community. Another of America's earliest community forests was established in 1760 at Danville, New Hampshire. A committee was appointed to manage the town's 75-acre woodland "to keep the parson warm." Over the years the forest has yielded some $10,000 worth of products.[1]

EARLY ROLE OF
THE FEDERAL GOVERNMENT

Early in its history, the federal government appeared as an interested party in the disposal of the nation's timber resources. For example, the Federal Timber Purchases Act in 1799 appropriated $200,000 to buy timber for naval purposes. After the War of 1812 and the expansion of the navy, the interest of the federal government in the continued supply of suitable timber for naval construction was reemphasized in the passage of a law in March 1817. This authorized the secretary of the navy to employ a surveyor and agents to select tracts that included timber suitable for naval purposes and gave the president power to establish reservations out of tracts selected.[2]

During the early days of the federal government, however, few people in public life clearly recognized a need for governmental care of the nation's resources. True, some timber legislation had been passed, agricultural societies devoted attention to improved soil practices, and agricultural experiments were conducted; but there was a failure to translate findings and recommendations for private lands into policies of conservation for the public domain. Only now and then was insight displayed. For example, Noah Webster foresaw the need for conservation of land and timber resources and called attention to the fact "that the improvidence of the people of this country for timber would some day be regretted," but he did not recommend governmental action.[3]

PUBLIC POLICY OF
JOHN QUINCY ADAMS

It remained for John Quincy Adams to be the only statesman of the first half of the nineteenth century whose outlook toward natural resources included a definable public policy of conservation. He wanted to conserve the public domain and begin a management of resources that would finance other undertakings for the general good. He recognized the relationship of natural resources to the internal improvement of the nation.[4] The enlightened views of John Quincy Adams enabled him, during his presidential administration, to carry out the first public experiment in tree culture. Through his influence, a resolution was sponsored in Congress providing for an inquiry into the preservation of timber on public lands and the "expediency of forming plantations for rearing of live oak for the future supply of that timber."[5] This resolution, incorporated into law in March 1827, enabled President Adams to withdraw 30,000 acres of live oak land on a peninsula jutting into the Bay of Pensacola, Florida, which became known as the Santa Rosa reservation. Here, by the planting of live oak seedlings and acorns, the first forest experiment station was established. President Adams, with his realization of the importance of live oak timber in the construction of battleships for the United States Navy, also had surveys made of the live oak supply near the coasts of Georgia, North Carolina, and Florida.[6]

Santa Rosa Reservation

During Adams' presidency, work on the Santa Rosa reservation progressed satisfactorily and Adams referred favorably to the experiment in his last annual message to Congress. Unfortunately, his Santa Rosa project became a "political football" and work was dropped after two years. With the election of Andrew Jackson and the appointment of John Branch as secretary of the navy, political opposition to the project began to develop. There were charges of financial abuse by Branch, which were investigated by Congress and not substantiated. After its investigation Congress concluded that the acorn venture was unsound; however, it did not recommend its discontinuance. It ceased to function with the retirement of the director and the gradual neglect of the preserve by the Navy Department. Thus ended one of the first federal government experiments with an active conservation venture.[7]

Impact of Adams' Conservation Contributions

The efforts of Adams, however, were not lost between his administration and the Civil War. It is true, no action or legislation clearly pointed to a national policy in this field. There was no approach—even less an organized one. But, by 1850, many people were aware of the depletion of resources on a local level. They saw the decline of the fur industry, the exhaustion of soil in old farming communities, and a diminishing fund of usable timber. The exploitation of United States resources before 1860 was not wholly unconscious and blind, as labeled by some conservation enthusiasts. It must be remembered that the social and economic outlook of the people for their time dictated natural resources practices. It is true that during the period of formation of the new government, the American people abandoned the restrictive conservation features of the colonial period. But, with the technological age of the nineteenth century, new attitudes developed as a result of intellectual discernment and social protest. The intellectual discernment came about as scientists, professionals, and public officials acquired new insights into the use of natural resources. Social protest reflected the agitation for changes on the part of groups adversely affected by prevailing policies for the control of resources. This provided a foundation for the development of a national policy.[8]

PRESIDENT JACKSON: TIMBER TRESPASS ACT AND LATER CONSERVATION DEVELOPMENTS

A very definite step in the development of a national policy was the enactment of the Timber Trespass Act during President Jackson's first term of office. This prohibited the destruction without proper authorization of live oak and other trees on the public domain. Actually it became the basis for the present-day law for the prevention of timber trespass on government land. There were also several other important developments pointing in the same general direction. Evidence of interest in the preservation of wildlife is seen in the establishment of the New York Association for the Protection of Game in 1844.[9] A conservation landmark came into being with the establishment of the Department of the Interior in 1849.[10] Indeed, as early as 1858, the state of Georgia turned to the federal government for guidance by asking Congress to appoint a federal commission to inquire into the extent and duration of the southern pine belt.[11] Specific events here and there illustrated that conservation was within the knowledge of office holders and the American people. They might not have had a clearly formulated policy, but the framework existed for one.

STATE CONSERVATION MEASURES

During the 1860s states undertook to protect fish and to control stream pollution. In 1867, the Michigan and Wisconsin legislatures provided for inquiries into forest conditions and needs and set up tree-growing bounties and tax exemptions. A Forestry Committee was appointed under the State Board of Agriculture in Maine in 1869 to develop a state forest policy. The states showed a determination to protect their resources. During the 1870s they took steps to protect game, and during the 1880s to preserve forests. In the next decade, states directed attention to the preservation of oil, gas, and water.[12]

FEDERAL CONSERVATION ACTIVITY IN THE 1870s

The interest of the federal government in conservation was maintained. From a growing concern over the decline of fisheries came the creation of the office of U.S. Commissioner of Fish and Fisheries in 1872.[13] In the same year a federal act provided $5,000 for "protection of timberlands," primarily naval timber reservations. It was the first appropriation made directly to protect publicly owned timber in the United States from spoliation.[14] A major conservation act went into effect in 1872 when Congress created Yellowstone National Park, which comprised 3,500 square miles in Wyoming. In 1873 Congress passed the first timber culture act, which granted homesteaders a patent to 160 acres of land in the Great Plains if they agreed to plant one-fourth of it to trees. That year also saw the American Association for the Advancement of Science at its annual meeting in Portland, Maine, appoint a committee "to memorialize Congress and the several state legislatures upon the importance of promoting the cultivation of timber and the preservation of forests and to recommend proper legislation for securing these objects."[15] This started the movement that led ultimately to the establishment of the Forest Service.[16]

ORGANIZATION OF THE AMERICAN FORESTRY ASSOCIATION

On September 10, 1875, the American Forestry Association was organized for public promotion of forestry and timber culture. This movement was one of the first well-organized attempts to influence public sentiment in the United States. Congress responded to the work of the American Forestry Association by granting an appropriation of $6,000 for the purpose of obtaining information preparatory to establishing a Division of Forestry. Carl Schurz, German immigrant, statesman, and student, who became secretary of the interior in 1877, was among the first to propose and urge the establishment of federal forest reservations and the scientific handling of forests. In Germany he had witnessed forest management by regular selection and replacement of trees. He believed the same could be done in the United States.[17]

DIVISION OF FORESTRY

The idea of scientific forestry gained enough support by 1881 to raise the forest agency in the Department of Agriculture to a full-blown Division of Forestry. Actually, the department had no forests or forest lands under its control, but it did serve as a fact-finding agency. A growing interest in forestry is apparent from such events as the organization of an American Forestry Congress in 1882, the transformation of the Senate Standing Committee on Agriculture into the Committee on Agriculture and Forestry in 1884, and the presentation of the first course of technical forest lectures for a body of students in the United States by Dr. Bernhard Fernow at Massachusetts Agricultural College in 1887.[18]

NATIONAL FOREST SYSTEM

Steps toward a national conservation policy reached a climax in the institution of the National Forest System in 1891. By act of Congress, approved March 3, the president was given power to establish forest reserves from the public domain. On March 30, President Harrison created the first—the Yellowstone Timberland Reserve, made up of 1,239,040 acres in Wyoming. Harrison added to such lands by withdrawing 1,198,080 acres in Colorado on October 30. Before ending his presidential term, he had set aside forest reservations totaling 13 million acres. President Cleveland, next in office, withdrew an additional 25 million acres from the national domain and placed them in the forest reserve system, to which President McKinley added 7 million acres.[19] Thus, the development and administration of the national reserves were slowly worked out. In 1898, Gifford Pinchot, who had been active in urging forest conservation, was appointed head of the Division of Forestry in the Department of Agriculture. The national reserves, however, were in the Department of the Interior, which meant that the government foresters had no authority in the national reservations. Nevertheless, Pinchot, with great energy and leadership, enlarged and extended the scope of the Division of Forestry beyond the confines of the office to make it a vital and useful service.[20]

OTHER CONSERVATION MILESTONES

While this forest conservation development was taking place, other conservation developments marked the beginning and extension of federal responsibility. These were: the establishment of the Geological Survey in 1879, the function of which was to study water supplies, soil erosion, and land use; the creation of the Division of Economic Ornithology and Mammology in 1886, which later became the Bureau of Biological Survey; the beginning of the soil survey in 1899; the establishment of the Bureau of Reclamation in 1902; the passage of an act to protect Alaskan fisheries in 1906; establishment of the Inland Waterways Commission in 1907; and the creation of a mining branch in the United States Geological Survey in 1907. To a large degree the purposes of the agencies set up in this period were informative and investigative.[21]

POPULARIZATION OF CONSERVATION BY PRESIDENT THEODORE ROOSEVELT

Conservation groundwork was laid, but it remained for the strenuous energy of Theodore Roosevelt to popularize the movement and achieve noteworthy results. Like many crusaders, he found inspiration in others. His zeal for enlarging the national forests was ignited partly during the many hours he spent with John Muir, naturalist, conservationist, and gifted writer. Among those who were influential, none outranked Gifford Pinchot, a pioneer in forest conservation in the United States. The conservation trail had also been blazed for Theodore Roosevelt years before by such individuals as Major J. W. Powell, Professor N. S. Shaler, and Arthur J. Mason. But Theodore Roosevelt, by his leadership, official acts, writing, and cooperation with conservation-minded citizens, was able to captain an exceptional period of conservation activity.[22]

National Forests and Reclamation

Under the law of 1891, President Roosevelt set aside almost 1.5 million acres of government timberland as national forests. Following Senator La Follette's advice, he withdrew from public entry some 85 million acres more in Alaska and the Northwest, pending a study of their mineral and water power resources by the United States Geological Survey. He was able to transfer the national forests to the Department of Agriculture, thereby bringing them under the scientific administration of Clifford Pinchot. Roosevelt lent his support to the enactment of the Reclamation Act in 1902, which provided that irrigation be financed from the proceeds of public land sales under the supervision of the federal government. Under this act a new reclamation service was established, which was under the administration of Frederick H. Newell. In addition, Roosevelt created 5 national parks, 4 national game preserves, and 51 wild bird refuges.[23]

Need of Public Support:
National Conservation Conference of Governors

President Roosevelt realized that the newly created governmental agencies needed public support to carry out conservation work successfully. He encouraged forestry conservationists to join hands with those individuals interested in developing inland waterways by appointing an Inland Waterways Commission in 1907 to study the whole question of the relation of rivers, soil, and the forests. Out of the recommendations of the commission and by its persuasion, the president called a national conservation conference of governors to consider the conservation of natural resources. He also invited the vice president of the United States, Cabinet members, justices of the Supreme Court, members of Congress and the Inland Waterways Commission, representatives of national societies, and individuals of politics, education, and science.[24] The conference was held May 13, 1908, and President Roosevelt opened the convention by saying:

> So vital is this question that for the first time in our history the chief executive officers of the States separately, and of the States together forming the Nation, have met to consider it. It is the chief problem that confronts us, second only—and second always—to the great fundamental question of morality. . . .
>
> This conference on the conservation of natural resources is, in effect, a meeting of the United States called to consider the weightiest problem now before the Nation.[25]

He emphasized the value of wise management of natural resources and pointed out that their various uses were so closely connected that they should be coordinated in one coherent plan. Others who spoke reiterated those ideas and called attention specifically to the problems of minerals, soil, water, and forests. The conference issued a declaration of principles stressing conservation of natural resources and recommending that the government retain all lands containing minerals and power sites. The conference spread the idea that the purpose of conservation of natural resources was the greatest good for the greatest number for a long time. It sought to teach the people of the United States the meaning of the word "conservation." Without a doubt the conference helped popularize conservation.[26]

As a result of the recommendations issued from the conference, a number of states established conservation commissions, and in 1909, a National Conservation Association, with President Eliot of Harvard as its president, was organized as a center for education and propaganda. Another outgrowth of the 1908 conference was the appointment of a

National Conservation Commission by President Roosevelt. This commission was assigned the task of taking an inventory of existing natural resources, which was submitted to the president of the United States in January 1909.[27]

That President Theodore Roosevelt's conservation interests were not limited to the national level was evident when, by calling a North American Conference in February 1909, he extended the movement internationally. At this meeting the broad principles of conservation were discussed and met with general approval.[28]

T. Roosevelt's Conservation Record

Theodore Roosevelt's record as a conservationist was outstanding. He encouraged legislation, withdrew lands, stimulated meetings, popularized conservation, and grasped the problem of conservation in its totality as it related to the national welfare. Yet, although so much conservation work was accomplished under his administration, there remained much to do, and even before the close of his term, a reaction in Congress set in that severely curtailed conservation activity.[29]

PRESIDENT TAFT'S ADMINISTRATION

President Taft was sympathetic to conservation objectives, but lacking Roosevelt's enthusiasm, he encouraged greater congressional opposition. Also, his administration witnessed the dramatic quarrel between Pinchot, who had been placed in charge of national forests since their transfer from the Interior to the Agriculture Department in 1905, and Secretary of the Interior Ballinger. Pinchot accused the Department of the Interior of corruption in connection with the Alaskan coal land. Upon investigation President Taft decided that the charges were unwarranted and removed Pinchot from office. Ballinger later resigned from his office.[30] This quarrel directed the public mind anew to the reaction of Congress against conservation and the decreased tempo and intensity of conservation work since Theodore Roosevelt's administration. Nevertheless, Taft did carry out some conservation measures, and under his administration the objectives of conservation of natural resources became, in principle, an accepted function of the United States government. During his presidency, the Bureau of Mines was established in 1910 to promote safety in mines and conduct research in the efficient use of minerals. An important piece of legislation, the Weeks Act (1911) established a new national policy involving the purchase by the federal government of forest lands protecting the flow of navigable streams. Most of the

National Forest east of the Great Plains, where there was little land left in the public domain, was acquired by purchase under this act and acts amending it.[31]

Societies Promoting Conservation and Conservation Education

Congressional opposition encountered during President Taft's administration did cause some public-spirited citizens to organize societies for the promotion of conservation. This movement was strengthened by the Izaak Walton League and by the interest of the Audubon Societies in the cause of conservation in the 1900s. Interest was also maintained by education in conservation. Outstanding in this service was Charles R. Van Hise, a geologist by training, president of the University of Wisconsin at the time of the White House Conference of Governors, and active in bringing to the students of the university the findings of the conference and of the National Conservation Commission. His teachings were spread orally and through the publication of his lectures, entitled *The Conservation of Natural Resources in the United States*, in 1910. A pattern for conservation education was set. Theodore Roosevelt had left his imprint alongside those of earlier conservation pioneers, and the American public had been awakened. Conservation might encounter opposition and exist through periods of relative inactivity, but seeds had been too well sown not to struggle for life and full growth. President Taft's contributions were added to by succeeding presidents.[32]

PRESIDENT WILSON'S ADMINISTRATION

During President Wilson's administration, Congress in 1916 passed the act creating the National Park Service in the Department of the Interior. The service was to protect and preserve wilderness areas for the benefit of all the people. This legislation was followed by the organization of the National Parks Association, which was to promote the welfare of the National Park System and safeguard high standards in the development of national parks. President Wilson, like Roosevelt, saw a worldwide conservation problem. He attempted to obtain world cooperation in natural resources but was unsuccessful.[33] On the domestic level, however, conservation continued. Additional pieces of legislation such as the Federal Water Power Act of 1920 kept alive not only the idea of conservation but also the role of the federal government in it.

PRESIDENT HARDING'S ADMINISTRATION

President Warren Harding's administration, frequently associated with the famous story of the Teapot Dome scandal, was not without its conservation aspects. The scandal involving fraud and misuse of naval oil reserves is not to be underestimated. It is possible, however, to discern within the corruptness of the Harding administration some attention to conservation and a sufficient continuance of past endeavors to carry conservation forward in its historical development. In 1921 President Harding proclaimed the first nationwide Forest Protection Week, and during his administration Congress appropriated money for the improvement of public campgrounds in the national forests. Furthermore, Harding considered conservation important enough to direct full attention to it in a message to the Mountain West. Herein he stated that reclamation meant more to him than merely constructing dams, ditches, and reservoirs. He envisioned a wealthy mountain empire where streams were harnessed to great electrical units. He declared the West had all the resources to make it great—that it needed merely to be developed, but that care should be taken to prevent "monopolization of resources and opportunities." His conception of conservation did not consist of locking up the resources as treasures but rather a judicious use of them.[34]

FORESTRY LEGISLATION, 1920s;
SENATOR NORRIS AND
PRESIDENT HOOVER'S ATTITUDE

Forests continued to receive attention in the 1920s. The Clarke McNary law, passed in 1924, extended the federal land purchase policy under the Weeks Law of 1911, and in 1927 a cooperative board called the Forest Protection Board was established, which was to prevent and suppress forest fires. The federal government also sponsored extended forest research by the passage of the McSweeney-McNary Act in 1928, which authorized a ten-year program of forest research. Forest conservation had evidently proved to be acceptable as a government responsibility. On the other hand, Senator Norris of Nebraska met serious opposition in 1928 when he fought to have Congress provide for government operation of the dams at Muscle Shoals. He was not a man easily defeated. Governmental interest in dam construction was kept alive by Norris' introduction of a bill in Congress in 1931 calling for the construction of a second dam on the Tennessee River and for government manufacture and sale of fertilizer and power. Congress passed the bill, but it was vetoed by President Herbert Hoover. It remained for the approval of the T.V.A. to bring Norris' fight to a victorious end. President Hoover's veto on the Tennessee River proposal, however, by no means indicated an anticonservation attitude. It was under his auspices that Boulder Dam was initiated.[35] Also, he supported waterway and flood control development by recommending increased appropriations for such projects as the floodway from the Arkansas River to the Gulf of Mexico. His veto on the Tennessee River proposal indicated that he did not favor government operation of power business. The action, however, did not change his attitude that "conservation of national resources is a fixed policy of the Government." He recognized that there were some urgent problems that needed to be solved.[36]

The evidence shows that after Theodore Roosevelt's dynamic conservation record, the governmental care of resources quietly continued. Regularly assigned conservation work of departments was carried out, and there was steady, if rather slow, progress in conservation development. Nothing took place to compare with the scope, enthusiasm, and attention given to conservation during Theodore Roosevelt's administration. It remained for the administration of Franklin D. Roosevelt to reawaken attention and by the impetus of this leadership to bring new and immense projects and secure the funds to help make them actual. In doing so, he continually encouraged cooperation and support of conservation work.

NOTES

[1] Ernest A. Engelbert, "American Policy for Natural Resources: A Historical Survey to 1862" (doctoral dissertation, Harvard University, April 1, 1950), 1–31; J. R. Whitaker and E. A. Ackerman, *American Resources* (New York, 1951), 210; "Highlights in the History of Forest Conservation," pamphlet prepared by Forest Service, U.S. Department of Agriculture (Washington, January 1948).

[2] "Highlights in the History of Forest Conservation" (Washington, 1948), 2; Engelbert, "American Policy for Natural Resources," 182–83.

[3] Engelbert, "American Policy for Natural Resources," 137.

[4] Loomis Havemeyer, ed., *Conservation of Our Natural Resources* (New York, 1930), 3–17; Charles Richard Van Hise, *The Conservation of Natural Resources: In the United States* (New York, 1910), 1915; Engelbert, "American Policy for Natural Resources," 138.

[5] Engelbert, "American Policy for Natural Resources," 184.

[6] "Highlights in the History of Forest Conservation" (Washington, 1948), 2; A. E. Parkins and J. R. Whitaker, *Our Natural Resources and Their Conservation* (New York, 1939), 1–21; Havemeyer, *Conservation of Our National Resources*, 3–17.

[7] "Highlights in the History of Forest Conservation" (Washington, 1948), 2; Engelbert, "American Policy for Natural Resources," 185–196.

[8] Engelbert, "American Policy for Natural Resources," 222–23, 235, 251, 396–99.

[9] "Highlights in the History of Forest Conservation," (Washington, 1948), 2.

[10]"Conservation: The Resources We Guard," pamphlet issued by the U.S. Department of the Interior (Washington, 1940), 27.

[11]"Highlights in the History of Forest Conservation" (Washington, 1948), 2.

[12]Robert H. Randall, "Conservation of Natural Resources," *Annals of the American Academy,* 206:142–46 (November 1939); C. J. Hynning, *State Conservation of Resources* (Washington, 1939), published by the National Resources Committee; Merle Fainsod and Lincoln Gordon, *Government and the American Economy* (New York, 1948), 737–38; "Conservation Program of the United States Government," Record of National Resources Planning Board, N.E.C. (May 1939), National Archives, Natural Resources Record Division, Washington, Box 631–636.2, Folder 635.1; "Highlights in the History of Forest Conservation" (Washington, 1948), 2.

[13]U.S. Department of Agriculture, *The Yearbook of Agriculture, 1940: Farmers in a Changing World* (Washington, 1940), 33, 531.

[14]"Highlights in the History of Forest Conservation" (Washington, 1948), 3.

[15]Ibid.

[16]U.S. Department of Agriculture, *Farmers in a Changing World,* 421.

[17]"Conservation Program of the United States Government" (May 1939), Box 631–636.2, Folder 635.1; Fainsod and Gordon, *Government and the American Economy,* 738; Parkins and Whitaker, *Our Natural Resources and Their Conservation,* 3–5; "Conservation of Natural Resources," *Annals of the American Academy,* 206:142–46 (November 1939).

[18]"Highlights in the History of Forest Conservation" (Washington, 1948), 4.

[19]"Conservation Program of the United States Government" (May 1939), Box 631–636.2, Folder 635.1; Whitaker and Ackerman, *American Resources,* 271–72; "Highlights in the History of Forest Conservation" (Washington, 1948), 6.

[20]Gifford Pinchot, *Breaking New Ground* (New York, 1947), 105–87; "Highlights in the History of Forest Conservation" (Washington, 1948), 6; "Geologist's Conservation Warning," *Literary Digest,* 120:19 (July 13, 1936).

[21]U.S. Department of Agriculture, *Farmers in a Changing World,* 421–22; "Conservation: The Resources We Guard" (Washington, 1940), 27; "Facts and Background about the Reclamation Program" (Washington, 1949), mimeographed article issued by the Department of Interior in connection with the 100th anniversary of the Department of the Interior; Randall, "Conservation of Natural Resources," *Annals of the American Academy,* 206:142–46 (November 1936).

[22]Whitaker and Ackerman, *American Resources,* 33–34; Pinchot, *Breaking New Ground,* 197–361; "Democracy: Its Essentials and Its Problems," *Scholastic* 35:18S–20S (December 11, 1939); "Geologist's Conservation Warning," *Literary Digest,* 120:19 (July 13, 1935); Henry A. Wallace, "The War at Our Feet," *Survey Graphic,* 29:109–14 (February 1940); Randall, "Conservation of Natural Resources," *Annals of American Academy,* 206:142–46 (November 1939); B. W. Allen, "Is Planning Compatible with Democracy?" *American Journal of Sociology,* 42:510–20 (January 1937).

[23]Morris Llewellyn Cooke, "New Steps to Save the Land," *Survey Graphic,* 29:246 (April 7, 1940); *Congressional Record,* 76 Congress, 3 session (1940), Appendix 1444–45, address of Major General Julian L. Schley, chief of engineers, before the Mississippi Valley Flood Control Association, May 13, 1940; "Facts and Background about the Reclamation Program" (Washington, 1949); Pinchot, *Breaking New Ground,* 319–44; Harold L. Ickes, "Balancing Our Resources Budget," *The Reclamation Era,* 27:258 (November 1937).

[24]*Congressional Record,* 76 Congress, 3 session (1940), Appendix 1444–45; Pinchot, *Breaking New Ground,* 344–60; Parkins and Whitaker, *Our National Resources and Their Conservation,* 6.

[25]*Congressional Record,* 76 Congress, 3 session (1940), Appendix 4002, address by Gif-

ford Pinchot, "Conservation as a Foundation of Permanent Peace," at the 8th American Scientific Congress.

[26]Ibid.; Pinchot, *Breaking New Ground*, 344–60; Whitaker and Ackerman, *American Resources*, 33; Parkins and Whitaker, *Our Resources and Their Conservation*, 6–9.

[27]Pinchot, *Breaking New Ground*, 344–60; Whitaker and Ackerman, *American Resources*, 33; "Conservation: The Resources We Guard" (Washington, 1940), 27; *Congressional Record*, 76 Congress, 3 session (1940), Appendix 4002.

[28]Pinchot, *Breaking New Ground*, 361–72.

[29]Owen P. White, "Land of the Pilgrim's Pride," *Colliers*, 96:12–13 (July 27, 1935); "Roosevelt and Conservation," *Nature Magazine*, 21:269 (June 1933); Randall, "Conservation of Natural Resources," *Annals of American Academy*, 206:142–46 (November 1939); Allen, "Is Planning Compatible with Democracy?" *American Journal of Sociology*, 42:510–20 (January 1937); Whitney R. Cross, "Ideas in Politics: The Conservation Policies of the Two Roosevelts," *The Journal of the History of Ideas*, 14:421–38 (June 1953); "Democracy: Its Essentials and Its Problems," *Scholastic*, 35:18S–20S (December 11, 1939); "Geologist's Conservation Warning," *Literary Digest*, 120:19 (July 13, 1935); Wallace, "The War at Our Feet," *Survey Graphic*, 29:109–14 (February 1940); Cooke, "New Steps to Save the Land," *Survey Graphic*, 29:246 (April 7, 1940); *Congressional Record*, 76 Congress, 3 session (1940), Appendix 1444–45; Appendix 4002; Parkins and Whitaker, *Our Natural Resources and Their Conservation*, 6–9; Pinchot, *Breaking New Ground*, 317–72; Whitaker and Ackerman, *American Resources*, 33.

[30]Harold L. Ickes, "Not Guilty" (Washington, 1940), 1–47, pamphlet from an official inquiry into the charges made by Glavis and Pinchot against Richard A. Ballinger, secretary of the interior, 1909–11; Fainsod and Gordon, *Government and the American Economy*, 740; James Lawrence Fly, "National Approach to Water Conservation," *Congressional Digest*, 17:19–21 (January 1938), address by Fly, general counsel of T.V.A., before the American Bar Association, September 28, 1937; Albert W. Atwood, "Is This Conservation?" *Saturday Evening Post*, 209:23 (September 26, 1936); Pinchot, *Breaking New Ground*, 403–510; Alpheus Thomas Mason, *Bureaucracy Convicts Itself: The Ballinger-Pinchot Controversy of 1910* (New York: Viking Press, 1941), 1–224.

[31]"Highlights in the History of Forest Conservation" (Washington, 1948), 9; Pinchot, *Breaking New Ground*, 391–403.

[32]Whitaker and Ackerman, *American Resources*, 34; *Congressional Record*, 76 Congress, 3 session (1940), Appendix 4002–03; Fly, "National Approach to Water Conservation," *Congressional Digest*, 17:19–21 (January 1938); Atwood, "Is This Conservation?" *Saturday Evening Post*, 209:23 (September 26, 1936).

[33]"Highlights in the History of Forest Conservation" (Washington, 1948), 10; "Conservation: The Resources We Guard" (Washington, 1940), 28; *Congressional Record*, 76 Congress, 3 session (1940), Appendix 4002–03.

[34]M. E. Ravage, *The Story of Teapot Dome* (New York, Republic Publishing Co., 1924), 198 pp.; F. L. Allen, *Only Yesterday* (New York, Harper, 1931), 136–42; Warren G. Harding, *Our Common Country* (Indianapolis, 1921), 173–94, edited by Frederick E. Schortemeier.

[35]"Conservation Program of the United States Government" (May 1939), Box 631–636.2, Folder 635.1; "Highlights in the History of Forest Conservation" (Washington, 1948), 10–12; George W. Norris, *Fighting Liberal* (New York, 1945), 156–61, 245–87, 374; Donald C. Blaisdell, *Government in Agriculture: The Growth of Federal Farm Aid* (Washington, 1940), Blaisdell formerly assistant to the under-secretary of agriculture; "Conservation Program of the United States Government" (Washington, 1934), 1–22, mimeographed publication of the Information Service Division of the Office of Government Reports, No. 1405; L. C. Gray, *Land Planning* (University of Chicago, 1936), 1–27, pamphlet; *Congres-*

sional Record, 76 Congress, 3 session (1940), Appendix 1444–45; J. R. Mahoney, *Natural Resources Activity of the Federal Government* (U.S. Library of Congress; Legislation Ref. Service, Publ. Affairs Bulletin, No. 76, Washington, January 1950), 64.

[36]William Starr Meyers, *The State Papers and Other Public Writings of Herbert Hoover* (New York, 1934), 150–58, Vol. I; March 4, 1929, to October 1, 1931.

◆ 3 ◆
Collaborators in
the Conservation Movement

Even as unchallenged leader of the conservation movement in the 1930s, Franklin D. Roosevelt could not carry on a conservation campaign and realize conservation objectives without the cooperation and advice of others. Legislation had to be passed to set up administrative and physical machinery to provide appropriations for the establishment of conservation projects. The nation's legislators controlled the financial "fuel power" needed to carry out the chief executive's conservation goals. It was essential to the continued development of the conservation program in the United States that the Congress and the president work in harmony.

ROOSEVELT'S LEADERSHIP
IN CONGRESS

Immediately after his inauguration, President Roosevelt summoned the new Congress, which was Democratic by large majorities and ready for strong leadership, to meet in a special session on March 9, 1933.[1] The Congressmen quickly demonstrated their desire to cooperate with the chief executive by giving blanket approval to his proposed legislation. Congress was as eager for confident guidance as was the vast multitude of citizens throughout the country. He electrified them with a new and needed fighting spirit that could, and would, attack the weakness, the ills, and the evils that beset the country. Gladly, therefore, did the House and Senate in passing legislation include those acts that provided for the C.C.C., T.V.A., and conservation public works projects.[2]

Congress did not stop, however, with merely approving the president's legislative proposals during the trying early days of the new administration. It also sought the president's support of additional conservation legislation and federal conservation aid for constituents. Senator G. M. Gillette of Iowa (Democrat) and 11 other senators and representatives sent a message to President Roosevelt on May 3, 1933, urging a forestation and water conservation program in Iowa, Kansas, Minnesota, Missouri, Montana, Nebraska, North and South Dakota, Oklahoma, Ohio, and Texas.[3] Roosevelt responded by notifying his secretaries of interior and agriculture and the director of the C.C.C. that he thought it was important to put some C.C.C. camps in the prairie states, thereby providing for the carrying on of forestry and water projects.[4]

Congressional Requests to the President

Varied were the Congressional requests that reached the president. Senator Duncan asked Roosevelt to support a bill establishing Everglades National Park when it came up in the House. In the same year, 1933, a Tennessee delegation in Congress called the president's attention to the erosion problem in their state. The congressmen pointed out that the state was reforesting as rapidly as funds permitted, but that this was not enough. They hoped to receive more federal aid.[5] Patrick McCarran of Nevada (Democrat) and nine other senators from western states sent a message to Roosevelt on July 25, 1933, requesting an appropriation for the improvement and construction of reclamation projects.[6] More and more congressional pleas and requests for presidential attention were received at the White House as the months passed. Representative Jed Johnson of Oklahoma (Democrat) in January 1934, expressed his concern for the menace of soil erosion and asked the president for an interview to discuss the problem. Roosevelt's reply expressed his interest in soil erosion and assured the congressman that corrective measures would be taken.[7] In the spring of 1934, Senator William G. McAdoo of California (Democrat) entreated President Roosevelt to support the Central Valley Water Project. McAdoo was convinced that the gradual subsidence of the water level in the San Joaquin Valley, owing to insufficient annual rainfall, had reached the point of seriously imperiling a great agricultural section of the state. He declared, "If a beginning could be made on the Central Valley Project it would hearten thousands of our best farmers and citizens and give promise of permanent relief from the danger now confronting them."[8] On June 15, 1934, Representative Muma F. Montet from Louisiana (Democrat) and 19 other congressmen and senators representing the Southwest wrote to President Roosevelt urging early action on four groups of projects for hydroelectric generation, navigation, flood control, erosion control, irrigation, and sanitation along the Red River.[9]

No congressman overlooked the opportunity to help his state. It is difficult to determine how many of them were genuinely interested in conservation, as opposed to those who merely sought the favor of their constituents by getting appropriations from the popular money train. No doubt, as is usual in human affairs, mixed motives led the individuals in their expression of interest in conservation. But whatever the cause, the important result was that Congress did help further the conservation movement. One thing is certain: In the formulation of congressional opinion, legislators never met with preoccupation and indifference on the part of Roosevelt as leader of the movement. The president gave attention to all requests by acknowledging letters and asking fellow office holders to investigate requests, suggest remedies, or take other steps necessary to meet the need. At times he indicated his appreciation of needs but reminded the legislators that funds had to be available as well as legislative authority.[10]

Congressional Conservation Support

While a broad base in Congress looked to the president for aid and leadership, it also went ahead in adopting additional legislative measures. For instance, during the second session of the 73rd Congress, January 3 to June 18, 1934, three wildlife conservation bills were passed.[11] This legislation was supported by Republicans and Democrats alike. In fact, both parties deemed the administration's conservation work to be praiseworthy. Congressman Roy P. Chase of Minnesota (Republican) asserted on March 8, 1934, "Conservation has made great forward steps in the past few months. Never before in the history of our country has there been such a pronounced interest on the part of the people in the preservation of our wildlife."[12] Harry Howes, former senator from Missouri, expressed the opinion that never before in American history had Congress and the federal administration given more attention, consideration, and assistance to wildlife conservation.[13] Speaker of the House Henry Rainey, in a radio broadcast April 8, 1934, discussed the need for soil erosion control after approving wildlife conservation. He also favored proposed legislation to control the use of the grazing lands of the United States. Rainey advocated a national conservation program.[14] Representative Einar Hoidale of Minnesota (Republican), speaking for the Middle West, directed attention to the problems of soil erosion and drought in that part of the country. Fellow congressmen reemphasized Hoidale's concern over drought problems and water conservation.[15] Congress did not limit itself to any particular phase of conservation.

The president himself submitted to Congress on June 4, 1934, a preliminary study of the control and development of water resources. The Congress was to regard this as a tentative outline; he urged them to allow him to complete the outline for the next Congress in the form of a comprehensive plan to be pursued over a long period of years.[16]

Midterm Election, 1934

In its first session (74th Congress, January 3 to August 26, 1935), the Democrats held 69 seats in the Senate and 322 seats in the House. Contrary to the usual experience of the party in power, the Democratic party made gains in both houses in the midterm election of 1934. In the Senate, the 69 Democrats constituted 72 percent of the membership (61 percent before election), and in the House the 322 Democrats constituted 75 percent of the membership (71 percent before election). No such combined majorities had been enjoyed by any party since the Republican majorities of the Civil War reconstruction period.[17] To this Congress President Roosevelt delivered his annual message on January 4, 1935. The keynote of his message was reform.

Obviously, the cooperative relationship between the president and Congress had continued beyond the famous First Hundred Days. The two branches of government attacked the relief and recovery problem with a program that included the wholehearted adoption of conservation projects. However, the hitherto almost ardently cooperative Congress lifted the head of revolt by March of 1935. This was touched off by the president's defeat at the hands of the Senate on the prevailing wage issue—the McCarran amendment—which threatened the legislative program of the 74th Congress. Legislation was delayed for nearly three weeks while the administration reformed its lines. Later the revolt spread to the House and was reflected in opposition to the bonus, inflation, and costs of Social Security. Nevertheless, Franklin D. Roosevelt went ahead with his New Deal program and continued to sponsor reform legislation.[18]

Continued Congressional Support

Disagreement in Congress, or threatened revolt, did not generally affect the conservation endeavors of the federal administration, except for a stiffening attitude toward appropriations for it and a tendency to voice divergent views on flood control. Congress agreed that the federal government must not dismiss the problem of soil erosion. President Roosevelt assured a large delegation of Western senators and representatives on April 11, 1935, that as much money as could be allocated in view of the general relief program would go to the prevention of soil erosion. Those who conferred with the president included members of Congress from states that were the most seriously effected by recent dust storms. During the same month, hearings before a subcommittee of the Committee on Agriculture and Forestry of the Senate investigated the need of protecting land resources against soil erosion. The investigation led to the proposal of bills on the control of soil erosion.[19]

Meanwhile, in congressional session, a dozen congressmen testified specifically to the need for such endeavor. In favoring legislation that would protect the land resources against erosion, they emphasized the importance of permanent measures. The need for a long-term program to combat the ruinous washing away of the soil was repeatedly stressed. In fact, there was no open opposition to a demand for this action.[20]

Members of Congress were also aware of the need of forestry conservation as well as flood control. In his messages in January 1935, the chief executive reminded them not only of the general value of conservation, but also of specific conditions in their own states, those natural depletions and the consequent sufferings of their fellow citizens that made conservation a compelling issue. Hearings before a subcommittee of the Committee on Agriculture of the House of Representatives on April 12, 1935, investigated the possibilities of a Program of Forest Land Management. In the same month, the House of Representatives held hearings before the Committee on Flood Control.[21] While studying forestry conservation practices, soil erosion control, and flood control, congressmen recognized the possibilities of power development in the nation and suggested the building of dams that would be of value to all citizens. Congress also took definite steps to attempt to control floods by the passage of legislation, which met with no success. The House did pass an omnibus flood control bill on August 22, 1935, designed to authorize those projects most urgently needed throughout the nation. This bill was revised, amended, and reported to the Senate. It then encountered a brilliant one-man filibuster by Tydings of Maryland (Democrat) that delayed its passage, and it was done to death by a motion to recommit. Amid shouts and criticisms of "pork barrel," the press of the country applauded its defeat. It remained for a future Congress, with further warnings from Nature, to achieve success in passing new flood control legislation.[22]

Congressional Attention to
Flood Control in 1936 and
F.D.R.'s Position

After punishing humanity with clouds of dust and a whirling array of millions of dollars worth of top soil, Nature seemed determined to teach with compelling vividness the evil results of a slack management of natural resources. Congressmen faced the problem of soil erosion, and the predominantly Democratic 74th Congress in its second session from January 3 to June 20, 1936, faced the tragic results of floods. The ravaging of the Susquehanna Valley and damages suffered in the Connecticut and Merrimack Valleys forced Congress to concentrate its conservation work on flood control legislation. The legislators generally agreed that they must adopt some form of flood control program. Any differences in opinion among them that did appear during discussion centered around how the program should be carried out and how far they should heed the president's advice. Encouraged by Majority Leader Robinson, the Senate Commerce Committee prepared a report on an omnibus measure authorizing a ten-year flood control program to cost approximately $1 billion. President Roosevelt intervened at this point by making known his desire that some form of flood control legislation be passed before Congress adjourned, but that such legislation be limited to authorizing emergency works made necessary by recent floods. The president wanted to use information prepared by the National Resources Committee in developing a long-range national water plan. This was due for submission by December 1.

The omnibus measure as reported by the Senate Commerce Committee and passed by the Senate was described by Royal S. Copeland of New York (Democrat) as the first porkless water bill in the history of Congress. In senatorial discussion, contests had to do with the sharing by the benefited areas of a part of the flood control expense and the granting of authority to the president to determine the order in which projects should be undertaken. An amendment to strike out provisions conferring power upon the chief executive to fix priority of projects was rejected by a vote of 40 to 31. An amendment to eliminate state and local contributions and place the entire cost of the program upon the federal government was rejected 55 to 15. The legislators did not lose sight of the national aspect of flood control.

Congressmen from Louisiana, Oklahoma, Mississippi, Washington, and New York favored a national flood control plan.[23] Faced with nationwide conservation problems, Congress had become increasingly aware of the advantages of national conservation planning. President O.S. Warden of the National Reclamation Association believed that within the government and country, a considerable movement had grown to establish a land policy that would be nationwide.[24] Whatever the future held was no longer purely a matter of speculation, because as early as June 22, 1936, Congress gave approval to flood control legislation "authorizing the construction of certain public works on rivers and harbors for flood control."[25] Congress thus recognized the nationwide magnitude of conservation by admitting that destructive floods caused a loss of life and property, including erosion of lands and the impairment of channels of commerce, all of which constituted a menace to the national welfare. Hence on this basis Congress felt that flood control was a proper activity of the federal government in cooperation with the states.[26]

Election of 1936

During the summer and fall of 1936, attention focused on the coming election. Who would win? The New Deal, with the future of conservation legislation and the whole activity of consolidation and development of the gains made so far, clearly hinged on the answer to this question. The chair of the executive and seats of congressmen were at stake. All attention was focused on the contending nominees, Landon and Roosevelt. Roosevelt won by a tidal vote of 27,751,000, nearly 60 percent of the popular ballots. The vote was spread through all sections, which enabled him to win 523 of the 531 electoral votes and to claim an unprecedented election victory. The congressional elections increased the Democratic majorities in both houses so that in the next session of Congress, three-fourths of the senators and almost four-fifths of the representatives would be of the chief executive's party. The only consolation for the Republicans was that such unwieldy Democratic majorities might be unmanageable.[27]

Continued Congressional Support
of Flood Control, 1937

This 75th Congress in its first session from January 5 to August 21, 1937, soon returned to the problem of flood control. It was quite evident that the Act of 1936 did not go far enough. This had provided for flood control projects, but hampered their development by lack of appropriations. Congressional discussion centered upon increasing expenditure for this purpose. Senator Royal S. Copeland of New York (Democrat) emphatically told the members of the U.S. Chamber of Commerce, on April 27, 1937, that money was absolutely necessary for flood control. Senator Bennett Champ Clark of Missouri (Democrat) in a radio address emphasized that expenditures on flood control should not be cut down.[28]

Nor was the public alone urged to support the expenditure for flood control. Within Congress proper the members used persuasion and repetition to remind fellow lawmakers that curbing the floods would take money. Representative William Whittington of Mississippi (Democrat) urged the Congress to grant more of it. In doing this, however, the legislators faced an administration that was attempting, in the interest of economy, to balance the budget. Also, the congressional agitation for a heavier outlay to control the floods became tainted with the odor of the "pork barrel." As early as February 1, Majority Leader Robinson warned that the flood control projects then advocated would wreck public credit. "I recognize the need for flood prevention and control," the president said in his budget economy message of April 20,

> but . . . such large immediate expenditures as are contemplated by the majority of the flood control bills now pending in Congress would impose an unjustifiable burden upon the federal treasury.[29]

The earmarking of relief funds for flood control was temporarily forestalled by a series of informal agreements with leaders of the House, and when a bill appropriating for nonmilitary work of the War Department passed the House, it allowed only the amount specified in the budget for flood control. The Senate doubled this amount; however, in conference, an agreement was reached whereby the Senate increase would come out of the $1.5 billion previously appropriated for relief. At the same time, authorization was given to separate river and harbor flood control bills of new projects totaling approximately $85 million. These projects included a new T.V.A. dam in Kentucky, an appropriation increase for the Blue Ridge Parkway, the Gila reclamation project in Arizona, and money to start work on Grand Lake Big Thompson transmountain diversion project in Colorado.[30] In the discussion of how to finance flood control, Congress recognized it as a national problem[31] to be dealt with, as their party leader had urged, along national lines. Roosevelt had made this clear when he explained the need for care of the national estate, both in curbing the continuing waste and in building up a higher productivity.[32]

F.D.R. Recommends Regional Planning to Underwrite National Planning

In line with recognition of flood control as a national problem, the president on June 3, 1937, recommended to Congress that it establish seven regional authorities to carry on national planning and the development of natural resources, a proposal viewed by the administration as the ultimate solution for a multitude of problems. Of these, the most important were drought and flood, waste of hydroelectric resources, and soil depletion.[33] The presidential proposal was presented to Congress by Representative Mansfield, chairman of the Committee on Rivers and Harbors, who introduced bill H.R. 7365. A companion bill S. 2555 was introduced by Senator Norris. Congress was largely hostile to the program so that it was never taken out of committee. The entire delegation in Congress from 13 western states opposed the measure. They objected to the Mansfield bill on seven grounds: it asserted the federal government's ownership of the country's waters, thereby preempting the property of the several states; it curtailed or duplicated many functions of existing federal agencies; it made likely the abridgment of state functions; it provided no assurance that relevant representations of state interests would be heard; it offered no assurance that water priorities in one state might not exist at the expense of another; and most alarmingly comprehensive of all, it plainly disclosed a movement to center control of the economic life of the country very largely in a succession of presidents.[34] Hearings in the House also disclosed opposition to the presidential proposal by public utility interests, the coal industry, and some state planning officials.[35]

Congress not only failed to cooperate with Roosevelt in passing legislation to establish seven regional authorities, but countered his suggestion with other proposals, which led to open disagreement between the president and Congress. A specific instance was Roosevelt's veto message on August 13, 1937, which accompanied his return without approval of the joint resolution (S.J.R. 57) entitled: "To authorize the submission to Congress of a comprehensive national plan for the prevention and control of floods of all the major rivers of the U.S., development of hydroelectric power resources, water and soil conservation, and for other purposes." President Roosevelt informed the Senate that he vetoed the bill because it was completely contrary to the philosophy and process proposed by him in his message of June 3, 1937. His major criticism was that in the proposed legislation, "the local and regional basis of planning would be ignored," and that prior to its presentation to Congress the whole program would have no review in reference to the national budget and national conservation policies.[36]

Cooperation Between Congress and the President on the Civilian Conservation Corps and Soil Conservation

On other conservation projects, however, the president and the 75th Congress in its first session did achieve action by compromise and cooperation. Roosevelt requested permanent status for the C.C.C.; in conference, compromise extended the life of the C.C.C. three years. Without substantial opposition, the House and Senate passed a bill authorizing the secretary of agriculture to continue soil conservation payments to individual growers util 1942. Under the Soil Act of 1936, direct payments to farmers were to end at the close of 1937. Grants were to be made instead to states, and a state soil conservation program was to be carried on. The president requested state governors to urge the enactment of state legislation to carry out the cooperative venture, and by 1937, 25 states had complied. But the bill to continue federal control of the program was pressed through Congress and signed by Roosevelt on June 28, 1937.[37]

On the whole, the 1937 session of Congress was considered to be a sharp defeat for the administration, even though two important new laws, the Farm Tenant Act and the Housing Act, were passed. Democratic congressmen had voted against the administrative program on various issues, particularly on the Judiciary Reorganization Bill. However, on the president's coast-to-coast tour after the close of the congressional session, the Democrats showed an eagerness to side with the president. Convinced during his travels that the majority of the people approved his policies, Roosevelt called a special session of Congress for November 16. During its five-week session, the administration did progress toward enactment of laws, but accomplished nothing final. The proposed seven regional authorities were still strongly opposed.[38]

Flood Control Act of 1938

However, whereas Congress disagreed with the president on the comprehensive regional scheme, it did not turn away from a national approach to the conservation of resources. The 75th Congress in its third session, January 3 to June 16, 1938, was too well indoctrinated by the president, by national sentiment, and by its own conviction of the national scope of conservation to ignore a national approach. Again, in their attention to conservation they were concerned mainly with flood control and its national aspects.[39] A series of floods and feeling of inadequacy of the 1936 Flood Control Act caused Congress to pass a comprehensive Flood Control Act in 1938. Even so, the bill encountered difficulty and opposition, although the House finally passed it with but four negative votes, and in spite of a threatened filibuster, the Senate passed it, too. Nevertheless, criticism of the act did not die with the closing of the 75th Congress, but was revived in the next session.[40]

At the same time that Congress urged expansion of flood control, it recognized the relationship of flood control and the development of power, a relationship discussed before 1938 in a radio address on February 11, 1937, by John E. Rankin of Mississippi (Democrat). Rankin accepted the doctrine that floods had to be controlled and emphasized that while controlling them hydroelectric power should be developed. In the same year, Whittington of Mississippi advocated the development of power in conjunction with flood control. Representatives John L. McCellan of Arkansas (Democrat) and Peter J. DeMuth of Pennsylvania (Democrat) in 1938 expressed the opinion that flood control was "tied up with power."[41]

Conservation Endeavors in 1938 and 1939

In the 1938 congressional election, the Republicans gained 7 seats in the Senate and 80 in the House, indicating that the 76th Congress in 1939 would be more conservative than its predecessors. This, however, did not seem to deter either the conservation efforts of the administration or the conservation activity of Congress. Congressmen asked for larger appropriations for flood control in 1939, and when doing so, cited the advantages of the flood control program.[42] Representative Clyde Taylor Ellis of Arkansas (Democrat) stated that additional appropriations for flood control were justifiable because it had value for conservation, water power, and recreation.[43] Another issue, intimately tied up with this, provoked scathing criticism and defiant challenge—the issue of states' rights. The Flood Control Act of 1938 caused lengthy discussion and debate as a violation of states' rights.

It should be noted that in its consideration of conservation during 1939, Congress did not devote its attention exclusively to flood control and closely related issues. It also considered wildlife, forestry, and soil erosion. Legislation was suggested for a nationwide forest survey, and favorable opinion was expressed concerning the continuance of investigations of wildlife conservation. Congress also granted money for projects to control soil erosion and for aid to farmers.[44]

Impact of War
on Conservation

During the third session of the 76th Congress from January 3, 1940, to January 3, 1941, a growing awareness of defense needs and the likelihood of a cut in conservation appropriations was apparent among members of Congress. Republicans and Democrats alike urged their colleagues to recognize the defense value of conservation projects and the grave dangers that slowing or halting endeavors would produce. Congressmen from Michigan, Washington, Oregon, Oklahoma, Idaho, Louisiana, and Arkansas called on their colleagues to support the appropriation measures for conservation. They particularly stressed the urgent need to continue the flood control program.[45] Nor was soil erosion work or reforestation neglected.[46] Both Republican Congressman H. Tibbott of Pennsylvania and Democratic Congressman C. Brooks of Louisiana stated well Congress' conviction of the value of conservation and its relationship to defense. Tibbott confessed that flood control was one of the principal aims of the people of his district, and that since coming to Congress he had done everything in his power to bring about an adequate program of flood control. However, he went on to explain that aside from "home politics," he was convinced that government investment in flood control was wise. For instance, factories of Pennsylvania in the flood area needed security for vital war production. He asked that a sufficient portion of national defense appropriations be set aside to complete flood control projects throughout the nation.[47] Brooks asserted, "This nation must build its flood control economy upon a rock. It must build well, provide adequate flood control regardless of the necessity of economy."[48]

The 77th Congress, January 3, 1941, to December 16, 1942, discussed the federal flood control program and also cited state needs in flood control. Interest in wildlife and soil conservation was again expressed. National defense, however, was beginning to capture the energy and attention of Congress. Men such as Representative Charles H. Leavy of Washington (Democrat) fought for appropriations to carry on the federal reclamation and water conservation rather than defense alone. He contended that, in truth, conservation was a part of the total defense program.[49] In spite of rumblings of war in their ears, with this connection made plain, congressmen did not desert the programs of national conservation.

PRESIDENT ROOSEVELT RELIES ON CABINET AND OTHER OFFICE HOLDERS

Congress recorded an extensive conservation legislative record and cooperated with President Roosevelt in bringing into reality his conservation goals. Nor were these efforts without the support of others. Roosevelt, while working with Congress, relied on his Cabinet and other federal office holders. He conferred and exchanged information with the director of the budget, the secretaries of agriculture and interior, and other administrative officials on legislation, the formulation of conservation measures, and conservation work in progress.

D. W. Bell,
Acting Director of the Budget,
and Director H. Smith

During the 1930s, D. W. Bell, acting director of the Bureau of the Budget, frequently corresponded with President Roosevelt, advising him on proposed legislation. Bell's advice was based on financial information or knowledge of interdepartmental promises or conflicts needing attention. For example, in the spring and summer of 1935, Bell advised Roosevelt that the forestry proposal (H.R. 6914) and flood proposal (H.R. 8455) were not in accord with the president's financial program.[50] In a like manner, Harold Smith, director of the budget, on April 10, 1941, advised President Roosevelt that the Fulmer forest-leasing bill was not in accord with Roosevelt's program because of budget limitations imposed by the defense program. Smith also volunteered reclamation information in working out a redefinition of the functions of the Departments of the Interior and Agriculture in the forestry field. The budget directors' comprehension of conservation went beyond the dollars-and-cents level, and they did not hesitate to offer their views and make recommendations to the chief executive.[51]

Secretary of Agriculture Henry Wallace

Secretary Henry Wallace of the Department of Agriculture worked constantly with his superior in carrying out measures of conservation. At the very beginning of President Roosevelt's administration, Secretary Wallace conferred with him on conservation needs and praised the administration for its wildlife program.[52] Wallace also exchanged information with the president on proposed forestry legislation. The secretary of agriculture did not devote his attention only to major issues. For example, on March 13, 1936, in reply to Roosevelt's memorandum of February 18 asking about certain stands of sugar pine still in private ownership near Yosemite National Park, Wallace reviewed the question of government purchase of this tract and recommended no special legislation on it.[53]

Wallace took the initiative, too, in making suggestions to President Roosevelt on both major and minor matters. Learning in the summer of 1936 that the president was going to Asheville in September, Wallace reminded him that the first step toward establishing national forests in the East was undertaken there. Likewise at a later date Wallace reminded F.D.R. of the recreational use of the national forests. Wallace told him in 1936 that the recent floods made it opportune to consider a program of flood prevention. The following year he urged that land purchase money be allowed for Biological Survey so the water fund conservation program could be carried on.[54] Indeed, he did not hesitate to voice to his superior his opinions on any subject. He urged an open conference on upstream engineering and the continuation of federal projects under the works relief program in 1939, and declared in 1937 that planting could be done on the Great Plains if there were continuity of financing.[55]

At the same time, Wallace acceded wholeheartedly to the president's requests for information whether as background for discussion with congressional leaders or as technical bureau reports. He was anxious to cooperate in carrying out conservation measures and projects. He sincerely wished to aid the farmer and directed his efforts toward halting erosion and educating farmers to use their land wisely.[56] His devotion to President Roosevelt was unquestionable. In his correspondence with him, he praised Roosevelt's tolerance and his love for peace, asserting that from these came his tremendous appeal to the American people. He added, "that is one of the reasons you have such a grip on me, one of the reasons I have felt free to talk and write to you as I have."[57]

Secretary of Agriculture Claude Wickard

The cooperation that existed between President Roosevelt and Secretary Wallace continued with the new Secretary of Agriculture Claude R. Wickard. Roosevelt sent memoranda to Wickard requesting his views on proposed legislation and technical information. The majority of correspondence between the two men dealt with forestry legislation and wartime lumber needs. Wickard worked closely with President Roosevelt in increasing lumber production under scientific conservation practices. Conservation was not to be sacrificed at any cost.[58]

Secretary of the Interior Harold Ickes

One of President Roosevelt's most ardent conservation supporters was his Secretary of the Interior, Harold Ickes. To Harold Ickes the conservation of natural resources was not merely his responsibility as the secretary of the interior but a responsibility of personal, moral conviction. He was committed by his personal convictions to a permanent policy of sound and inclusive national conservation. His sincerity rings through page after page of his annual departmental reports, and his ardor shone alike whether he spoke or wrote. Harold Ickes insisted on what he termed true conservation: "The principle underlying true conservation is the protection, upbuilding and prudent use of our natural resources for the greatest number of our people."[59] This thought ran throughout Secretary Ickes' work relating to conservation. Ickes believed that the nation's resources should be available to all citizens, future as well as present. He believed that no resource, including humans themselves, should be exploited for purely personal gain.

> I do not object to any man building up a great fortune providing he can do so without injury to others. But I do take serious objection to a man enriching himself at the expense of others. . . .
>
> No man has a right to become a multimillionaire through the waste or willful destruction of essential natural resources, especially if such destruction means loss of property and life to others.[60]

Honesty and Integrity of Harold Ickes

In Harold Ickes, President Roosevelt found a man who would fight political graft, and who did so where it appeared in conservation projects. When speaking at a dinner for contractors, Ickes stated emphatically there would be nothing like that. Work contracts were to be granted on open bidding, on assurance of good work with no cutback wages, skimping, or poor materials. His success in minimizing political theft was illustrated by the experience of the owner of the construction company who had a good many contracts. While working, this man bought much new machinery. One of Ickes' engineers, suspecting something wrong in the purchases, investigated, and got the satisfactory explanation that the contractor could buy new equipment because he did not have to waste any money on graft. Ickes thought that God was good in providing him an opportunity to cut out some of this deadly rottenness. Early in his career as secretary of the interior, he indicted two political office holders, a Republican and a Democrat, on charges of graft. Though neither man was convicted, the incident made clear the resolute stand of Ickes in his administration of public projects. His experience in Chicago enabled him to show public officials that he would permit only honest methods. Mayor Kelly sent a delegate to him requesting an appropriation for sewage work in the city. Ickes, knowing that the politics of the city were controlled by a corrupt machine, refused to discuss the matter. There was only one man he could trust, and he finally sent word to Mayor Kelly that he would approve an appropriation for the proposed work if the individual he had in mind were appointed. The machine went to work, and Kelly saw that the man was elected and made chairman of the board. Secretary Ickes, knowing there would be no mishandling of funds, then approved the grant of money.[61]

Ickes' Commitment to Permanency

Harold Ickes, as a lover of the out-of-doors, took a special personal interest in conservation. He did not view the project work of the Roosevelt administration merely as one of emergency and temporary relief. He looked for long-range objectives—for the permanent aspects of projects. On this question he often quarreled with Harry Hopkins who was more interested in emergency work.

Varied Support from Ickes

The secretary of the interior not only could aid the president in formulating conservation legislation and establishing projects, but he could and did serve as an endless source of technical advice and moral support. Ickes kept the president posted on the activities of the Department of the Interior and forwarded suggestions.[62] For example, on September 7, 1934, Ickes advised Roosevelt not to approve of a project controlling silt in the Yellowstone River and bringing new lands into cultivation through irrigation until he had a report from the National Resources Board.[63] On March 22, 1938, Ickes advised the president that proposed legislation to amend the Flood Control Act of 1936 might have bad effects in the states. This was because the amendment would reduce construction under Reclamation law that required repayment of federal investments.[64] The secretary of the interior did not lack a sense of humor when writing to his superior about the points of acute irritation between the Interior and Agriculture Departments. He asserted that the matter ought to have the attention of the chief surgeon. Ickes admitted he might be seeing ghosts, but said "my thought is that I ought to set up a Board of Erosion Control to prevent all of the good, rich soil of the Department from being washed into the hollows and crevices of Agriculture."[65] Indeed, the president had in Harold Ickes a capable, hard-working, cabinet member and a loyal supporter. Roosevelt's respect and need for this conservation supporter was expressed in his memorandum to Ickes when the secretary of the interior offered his resignation in February 1940. The president merely said, "You and I have been married 'for better or worse' for too long to get a divorce or for you to break up the home. I continue to need you. Affectionately, FDR."[66]

M. L. Cooke, Rural Electrification Administrator

Morris L. Cooke, President Roosevelt's Rural Electrification administrator, kept in touch with the chief executive on conservation matters. On February 2, 1937, he sent Roosevelt photographs of eroded lands and urged greater concentration on the problem of all eroded lands.[67] The next year he forwarded the exchange of letters between himself and David Coyle on what was needed to put over a conservation program.[68]

Cooperation and Support
from Varied Officials

Countless governmental officials such as Morris Cooke advised the president and cooperated with the administration in carrying out conservation projects.[69] Within the Departments of the Interior and Agriculture, government office holders and employees promoted conservation in various ways. Dr. H. H. Bennett, a soils specialist in the Department of Agriculture, had been aware of rapid deterioration of soil resources and for years had carried on a one-man crusade to arouse the country to the gravity of the situation. In the National Industrial Recovery Act passed on June 16, 1933, Congress authorized an erosion control program on an emergency basis. Dr. Bennett headed this emergency conservation service, which was established in the Department of the Interior.[70] Other professional and governmental office holders helped popularize and promote conservation. Major General Julian L. Schley, chief of engineers, speaking before the Mississippi Valley Flood Control Association on March 13, 1940, urged the continuation of conservation projects. He pointed out that conservation affected the operations of nearly every department of government and the general social attitude of the U.S. citizenry. He believed that conservation was a common-sense attitude indispensable to the best use of existing resources.[71] The associate chief of the Soil Conservation Service, D. Lowermilk, not only delivered addresses that kept conservation in the mind of the public, but in 1944 undertook a technical mission under the auspices of the State Department to advance conservation of soil in China.[72]

Senator W. Norris

One after another, these office holders could be specifically cited for their conservation efforts. From the lowly clerk in the office to the bureau chief, energy was directed toward the prudent husbandry of the natural wealth. Cooperation of all was necessary to carry out conservation projects. And alongside the "Joe Doakes" and the prominent office holders and conservation workers were the names of veterans in the conservation cause, such as Senator W. Norris of Nebraska. As father of the T.V.A., he had a long record behind him of legislative attempts to develop and operate Muscle Shoals.[73] His effort culminated in the legislative act of May 18, 1933, authorizing the creation of the T.V.A.[74] When speaking of the T.V.A. he stated,

> In 1933 a dream long in the back of my mind began to shape. It embraced a little TVA in Nebraska, including the Platte and its

tributaries; the Loop and its feeder streams; and the Republican Valley to which I had come as a young man. It was a long fight extending over years, with much confusion of honest origin and with the opposition, inevitably, of the private power interests contributing greatly to misinformation and conflict. It has in part been realized. On the upper Platte is Kingsley Dam, back of which is a great artificial lake . . . for the expansion and strengthening of irrigation on a semi-arid region where all that fertile soil needs in order to produce abundantly is water. . . .

I spent enormous energy upon these projects. I fought days and months against opposition. Now they are taking form.[75]

The interest of Norris in conservation was not restricted to the T.V.A.[76] He supported forestry legislation, remarking on one occasion, "I have always felt a tender interest in the labors of the Forest Service." He spent innumerable hours talking with the chief foresters about their enlightened efforts to reestablish the forests of the country. Senator Norris, devoted to bettering the lives of U.S. citizens, saw in the conservation of natural resources a way to do it.[77]

CONTRIBUTIONS OF
SCIENTIFIC ASSOCIATIONS AND WRITERS

The cause of conservation was advanced not only by the president, Congress, Cabinet members, administrative officials, and governmental employees, but also by members of scientific associations and writers. True, President Roosevelt's leadership was invaluable and stimulating, just as the cooperation and work of all governmental office holders and veterans in the cause were indispensable. Yet, even all this combined effort would have missed complete effectiveness without the understanding of conservation and belief in it by great numbers of the citizenry. To this end the members of scientific associations and writers made substantial contributions by studies and publications. Geologists wrote articles stating their approval of national conservation work and urging that additional conservation projects be undertaken.[78] Stuart Chase's *Rich Land Poor Land,* a pointed and readable book, made the best books list.[79] Others also lent an effective hand, including the Californian Pearl Chase, who was instrumental in making people in her home state aware of this vital issue. Although the idea of an annual Conservation Week originated in the East, Pearl Chase urged its adoption in California in 1933. Voluntary organizations and county conservation chairmen were sponsored by the state.[80]

POPULARIZATION OF
CONSERVATION AND EDUCATION

The popularization of conservation was further fortified by demands for federal aid. The state governors turned to the federal government for financial aid, guidance, approval of projects, and messages of hope for their people.[81] The citizens themselves advanced the movement by their demands for relief, for soil erosion control, and for aid to those striken by the dust storms and the floods.[82]

At the same time, a formal and informal educational campaign for the wise use of natural resources furthered the government's conservation work. Government officials recognized, as early as 1933, the value of educating the American people in conservation. Secretary Stephen Early suggested in April 1933, that a proclamation be issued for an American Forest Week, reminding the citizens of the value of the forests. He hoped to tie in this idea with the unemployment reforestation work started by President Roosevelt.[83] In the same year, Henry Wallace urged the president to pen a series of Farm and Home Hour Conservation Day broadcasts.[84] The Water Resources Section of the National Resources Board reflected the urgency of education on the conservation front in a message to Ickes on September 27, 1934. The board declared that a program of adult education was far more badly needed in the Big Horn River Basin than the proposed dam.[85] By the mid-1930s the North Carolina Conservation and Development Department could boast that for the first time, the dramatization of conservation appeared over radio as a regular feature.[86] The federal government was not far behind with its conservation propaganda material. Wallace reported to President Roosevelt on June 27, 1936, that the pamphlets "Soil—The Nation's Basic Heritage" were being distributed throughout the country. About 2,000 copies were to be sent to farm papers and country editors in the Midwest and the remainder to consumer papers.[87] Pamphlet after pamphlet on all phases of conservation issued by the federal government found their way into the hands of the U.S. citizen.[88]

SPEECHES

The printed word was reinforced by individual speeches. Representative Clare E. Hoffman of Michigan (Republican), in the course of a talk at a meeting of conservationists in December 1939, stated, "There is no more worthy cause than that of conservation. There is no more useful, unselfish, productive work in which man can engage than that of promoting the cause of true conservation."[89] Dr. Isaiah Bowman, president of Johns Hopkins University, declared that "conservation is not only a good idea; without it there will cease to be an America as we know it."[90] A radio address of Honorable G. Pinchot, former governor of Pennsylvania and a veteran in the cause, stressed the importance of cooperation between the farmer and the Forest Service in conservation work.[91] Federal and state governmental officials as well as educators saw the need for the understanding of conservation. The gospel of conservation had to be spread.

THE EDUCATION CONSERVATION SOCIETY AND EDUCATION LEGISLATION

An interesting society, headed by Harry Vavra and known as the Education Conservation Society, carried on an education campaign. The extent of its influence and true purposes are questionable. Its national president, Vavra, wrote letters on imposing stationery and seemed conscious of limelight. Whether his intentions were sincere or not, he did correspond with the president and Congress on conservation matters,[92] asserting that "conservation must be a matter of education as well as legislation." He proposed that conservation be introduced as a regular subject into every school.[93] The Education Conservation Society did submit a bill to Congress in 1934 providing for annual federal appropriation to states for the promotion of courses of study in public conservation in schools, colleges, and universities.[94] In 1937 bills on conservation education appeared in Congress. A bill was introduced in the House of Representatives providing for conservation education in schools, and another bill in the Senate providing for cooperation with states in promoting such instruction in their educational institutions. State legislation enabled individual states to carry on school conservation programs. Significant education was undertaken between 1930 and 1940 in Tennessee, Michigan, West Virginia, Ohio, Missouri, and Wisconsin, pioneer states in the addition of conservation to their public school programs. In other states, individual colleges and state or private agencies sponsored special programs.[95]

GROUP SUPPORT OF CONSERVATION

In March, 1940, a nonprofit society, Friends of the Land, met in Washington and decided to work with lay and professional people in conservation endeavors. The society resolved to publish a monthly magazine and to encourage research in land and water conservation. Part of their program was to give conservation awards and to encourage educational institutions to give such awards.[96] Attempts to educate the public and encourage interest in conservation were also promoted by other groups. *Nature Magazine* in 1935 adopted a new section in its publication that dealt exclusively with conservation.[97] The state of Iowa furthered the cause of conservation by designating Soil Conservation Week in 1941.[98] All these efforts aided in making the U.S. citizen aware of the necessity of conservation and made the term conservation a familiar one.

The record of conservation activity and accomplishment from 1933 to 1942 hence was not written by President Roosevelt alone. He was the popular and brilliant leader, a man of ideas and of faith, and undoubtedly, the mastermind in the shaping of conservation policy. But at the same time his collaborators—Congress, Cabinet members, governmental office holders, and veterans in the cause—were indispensable to the strides made in conservation achievement. Names like Ickes, Wallace, Bennett, Norris, Whittington, and the "Joe Doakes" are properly placed alongside their leader. Finally, the work of the governmental officials was supplemented and stimulated by the invaluable contributions of scientific associations, societies, writers, conservation educators, and the private citizen. It was such united effort that wrote one of the greatest pages in the history of American conservation.

NOTES

[1]First session of Congress (special session) May 9–June 26, 1933. Senate roll: 90 Democrats, 35 Republicans, 1 Farm Labor; House roll: 310 Democrats, 117 Republicans, 5 Farm Labors, 3 vacancies.

[2]The C.C.C. was established under the authority of "An Act for the relief of unemployment through the performance of useful public works," March 31, 1933; the T.V.A. was established under the authority of "Tennessee Valley Authority Act," May 18, 1933; and provision for conservation works on public works projects was authorized under the "National Industrial Recovery Act," June 16, 1933.

[3]F.D.R. Papers, Group 13, OF 268, May 3, 1933.

[4]Ibid., F.D.R. to Ickes, Wallace, Fechner.

[5]Ibid., OF 6, Box 34, May 30, 1933, Fletcher to F.D.R.; OF 149, April 22, 1933, Jere Cooper and others of Tennessee delegation in Congress to F.D.R.

[6]Ibid., OF 402, July 25, 1935, Pat McCarran, C. Hayden, J. B. Kendrick, F. Steimer, C. Menary, C. Dill, G. Pope, H. F. Ashurst, and J. G. Scrugham to F.D.R.

[7]Ibid., OF 732, January 4, 1934, Johnson to F.D.R.; January 15, 1934, F.D.R. to Johnson.

[8]Ibid., OF 402, May 9, 1934, William McAdoo to F.D.R.

[9]Ibid., OF 114, June 15, 1934, Montet and 19 other representatives and senators to F.D.R.

[10]Ibid., OF 732, January 15, 1934, F.D.R. to Congressman J. Johnson, Oklahoma; Group 13, OF 6, Box 45, April 9, 1935, Marvin Jones, congressman from Texas, to Marvin

McIntyre; OF 402, June 13, 1934, F.D.R. to Frank E. Merriam, governor of California; OF 114, June 30, 1934, Ickes to F.D.R.

[11]*Congressional Record,* 73 Congress, 2 session (1934), 4035–36, "The President"s Conservation Program."

[12]Ibid., 4035.

[13]Ibid., 6709–11. Memo of conservation progress in 1934 with brief digest of new laws prepared by Harry B. Hawes, former U. S. Senator from Missouri and former member and vice-chairman of Special Senate Committee on Conservation of Wildlife Resources.

[14]Ibid., 6777–78, "Conservation and Citizenship," address by Hon. Henry T. Rainey, Speaker of House of Representatives, over N.B.C., April 8, 1934; *New York Times,* April 9, 1934.

[15]*Congressional Record,* 73 Congress, 2 session (1934), 4748–52, "The Cost of Soil Erosion," Mr. Collins of Mississippi asked to extend remarks on cost of soil erosion by inserting a statement by Bennett; 6547, "Conservation of Natural Resources," remarks by Haverick; 6777–78, "Conservation and Citizenship," address by Hon. Henry T. Rainey, April 8, 1934; 10,311–12, "Drought Situation in Middlewest," remarks by Mr. Hoidale.

[16]Ibid., 10,399, "Message from the President of the United States to Congress on the Improvement and Development of Water Resources"; *Public Papers and Addresses of Franklin D. Roosevelt: (1934) The Advance and Recovery and Reform, 1934* (New York, 1938), 283–85, Item 99, "The President Plans for Control and Development of Water Resources," June 4, 1934.

[17]*Editorial Research Report,* (Washington, 1935), 1(10):184.

[18]Ibid., 1(10):184–85.

[19]*New York Times,* April 11, 1935; *Congressional Record,* 74 Congress, 1 session (1935), 13,505–07, 8905–06; U.S. Congress, Senate, Committee on Agriculture and Forestry, *Miscellaneous Senate Hearings 1935–1936,* "Protection of Land Resources Against Soil Erosion," *Hearings before a subcommittee of the Committee on Agriculture and Forestry,* 74 Congress, 1 session, on S. 2149, S. 2318, and H.R. 7054 bills to provide for the protection of land resources against soil erosion, April 2–3, 1935, 1–78.

[20]*Congressional Record,* 74 Congress, 1 session (1935), 4770–71, remarks by Mr. Whelchel; 4803–10, remarks by 10 different Congress members on soil erosion; 6012–14, remarks by three senators favoring soil erosion control; 1263–64, remarks by Mr. Sutphin; 3550–53, remarks by Mr. Ferguson; 4127–28, radio address by Mr. Nichols of Oklahoma, March 1935; 8905–06, remarks by Mr. Johnson of Oklahoma; 13,505–07, remarks by Mr. Hoeppel; 14,686–87.

[21]U.S. Congress, House of Representatives, Committee of Agriculture, *Miscellaneous House Hearings 1935–1936,* "Program of Forest Land Management," *Hearing before a subcommittee of the Committee of Agriculture,* 74 Congress, 1 session, on H.R. 16914 by M. Fulmer, April 12, 1935, 1–39; U.S. Congress, House of Representatives, Committee on Flood Control, *Miscellaneous House Hearings 1935–1936,* "Flood Control in the Mississippi Valley," *Hearings before the Committee on Flood Control,* 74 Congress, 1 session, on a plan to modify and extend the project for flood control and improvement of the Mississippi River authorized by the Flood Control Act of 1928, April 10–13, 1935, 1–832.

[22]*Congressional Record,* 74 Congress, 1 session (1935), 12,002, remarks by Mr. McNary; 14,686–87, "Conservation and Use of Natural Resources," remarks by Mr. Gray of Indiana; 2573–74, "Light and Power Rates Compared"; 75 Congress, 1 session (1937), 184–86, radio address by Hon. Bennett C. Clark of Missouri, February 8, 1937.

[23]F.D.R. Papers, Group 13, OF 132, May 1, 1936, F.D.R. to Joe Robinson; *Congressional Record,* 74 Congress, 2 session (1936), 4511–12, "The Flood in Connecticut," remarks by Mr. Kopplemann; 4643–44, address by Senator Guffey of Pennsylvania on "Averting the

Flood Peril"; 6245–49, address by Mr. Whittington delivered April 27, at 31st Annual Convention of National Rivers and Harbors Congress; 830–32, "Tributary Flood Control," remarks by Mr. Ferguson; 4197–98, article by Senator Robert F. Wagner in *New York Times*, March 22, with reference to flood control situation; 6315–16, radio address by Mr. Wallgen, member of Flood Control Committee; 6138, Mr. Wilson of Louisiana asked consent to include in *Record* an address he made before the Rivers and Harbors Congress, April 27; U.S. Congress, Senate, Committee on Agriculture and Forestry, *Miscellaneous Senate Hearings 1935–1936,* Control of Flood Waters in the Mississippi Valley, *Hearings before a subcommittee of the Committee on Agriculture and Forestry,* 74 Congress, 2 session, on S. 3524, "A Bill to Provide for the Control of Flood Waters on the Mississippi River and Its Tributaries, to Provide for the Irrigation of Arid and Semiarid Lands and for Other Purposes," March 24–April 15, 1936, 1–366; U.S. Congress, House of Representatives, Committee on Flood Control, *Miscellaneous House Hearings 1933–1936,* "To Provide for a Permanent System of Flood Control and for Other Purposes," hearing, 74 Congress, 2 session on H.R. 12517, May 21, 1936, 1–23; *Congressional Record,* 75 Congress, 1 session (1937), 184–86, radio address of B. C. Clark of Missouri, February 8, 1937.

[24]U.S. Congress, Senate, Committee on Irrigation and Reclamation, "Federal Reclamation of Arid Lands," hearing, 74 Congress, 2 session, relative to federal reclamation of arid lands, February 1, 1936, 1–10.

[25]*United States Statutes at Large,* 49:1570–97.

[26]Ibid., 1570–97; *Congressional Record,* 75 Congress, 1 session (1937), 567; 74 Congress, 2 session (1936), 4197–98; article in *New York Times,* March 22, by R. F. Wagner; 6315–16, radio address by C. Wallgen.

[27]Basil Rauch, *The History of the New Deal 1933–1938* (New York, 1933), 246–65; Dixon Wecter, *The Age of the Great Depression 1929–1941* (New York, 1948), 104.

[28]*Congressional Record,* 75 Congress, 1 session (1937), 74–75, editorial in *Washington Post,* January 26, 1937; 184–86, radio address by C. C. Clark of Missouri, February 8, 1937; 567–69, address by Orville Zimmerman of Missouri in St. Louis, Missouri, March 12, 1937, at Flood Control Conference of Mississippi Valley Association; 1179–81, address by Senator R. S. Copeland, New York, before the U.S. Chamber of Commerce, April 27, 1937, on "What Is Needed for Flood Control"; 1301–2, address by Bennett Clark of Missouri, May 27, 1937.

[29]Ibid., 5734–35, 5754–57, 9442–44; 1077, address by H. Overton, Louisiana; 1172, editorial from *St. Louis Star Times Editorial Research Report,* (Washington, 1937), 2(7):151–58.

[30]*Editorial Research Report,* (Washington, 1937), 2(7):151–58. Of new projects added authorization was given for a new T.V.A. dam near Gilbertsville, Kentucky, ultimately to cost $112 million (added to second Deficiency Bill by Senate vote of 46 to 29 and amendment accepted by House without roll call). The House increased a $3 million appropriation for Blue Ridge Parkway to $5 million and compromised with the Senate on $4.5 million. The Senate added to the Interior Appropriation Bill without record votes: $1.25 million for starting work on Gila reclamation project in Arizona ultimately to cost $19 million; $900,000 for starting work on Grand Lake Big Thompson transmountain diversion project, Colorado, ultimately to cost $24 million. (The House accepted Grand Lake Big Thompson project 174 to 154, rejected $1.25 million Gila 122 to 191, but compromised on $700,000, 160 to 147.) These results were brought through various trades of votes between southeastern members interested in obtaining federal funds for highway construction and western members desiring new reclamation projects.

[31]*Congressional Record,* 75 Congress, 1 session (1937), 567–69, address by Zimmerman of Missouri, March 12, 1937; 1179–81, address by Copeland of New York, April 27, 1937; 7822–88; 2437–39, remarks of William Lemke of North Dakota in House, August 16,

1937; 5754–57; 166–69, radio address by T. G. Bilbo of Mississippi, February 5, 1937; 950–53, address by W. M. Whittington of Mississippi before the National Rivers and Harbors Congress, April 26, 1937; 1336–40, address by Whittington before the American Forestry Association, May 31, 1937.

[32]*House Documents*, 140, 75 Congress, 1 session (1937), public works planning message from the president of the United States transmitting a proposed plan of a six-year program submitted by the National Resources Committee based on selection and priority of public works projects, February 3, 1937, letter from F.D.R. to Congress; *Congressional Record*, 75 Congress, 1 session (1937), Appendix 2465; 2 session (1937), Appendix 175–79; U.S. Congress, House of Representatives, Committee on Flood Control, *Hearings before the Committee on Flood Control*, 75 Congress, 3 session, on report of the chief of engineers, April 6, 1937, House Flood Control Committee, Document No. 1, 75 Congress, 1 session, and subsequent reports of the chief of engineers and amendments to the flood control acts of June 15, 22, 1936, August 28, 1937, March 30–April 18, 1938, "Comprehensive Flood Control Plans," 1–1147; U.S. Congress, House of Representatives, Committee on Flood Control, *Hearings before the Committee on Flood Control*, 75 Congress, 1 session, on levees and flood walls, Ohio River Basin, H.R. 7393 and H.R. 7646, a bill to amend an act entitled "An Act Authorizing the Construction of Certain Public Works on Rivers and Harbors for Flood Control and for Other Purposes," approved June 22, 1936, June 7–11, 15–18, 1937, 1–425; *Congressional Record*, 75 Congress, 1 session (1937), 2465, address of J. Buell Snyder of Pennsylvania before Western Pennsylvania Flood Control Committee in Pittsburgh, August 10, 1937.

[33]*House Miscellaneous Documents*, 1–369, 75 Congress, 1 session (1937), Document No. 261, creation of National Planning Board to provide for conservation and development of national resources, message from the president of United States transmitting the proposed creation of regional authorities or agencies to be known as the National Planning Board to provide for the regional conservation and development of national resources.

[34]*Congressional Record*, 75 Congress, 2 session (1937), 597–602, remarks by Edward T. Taylor of Colorado in the House of Representatives, December 21, 1937; *Congressional Digest*, 17:19–21 (January 1938), James Lawrence Fly, general counsel of the T.V.A., addressing American Bar Association, September 28, 1937, "National Approach to Water Conservation"; *Congressional Record*, 1169–72, 75 Congress, 1 session (1937), address by Sam Rayburn of Texas at Shreveport, Louisiana, April 24, 1937, and resolution adopted by Red River Improvement Association; U.S. Congress, Senate, *Hearings before a subcommittee of the Committee on Agriculture and Forestry*, 75 Congress, 1 session (1937), on S. 2555, a bill to provide for the creation of conservation authorities and for other purposes, June 21–July 7, 1937, 1–288.

[35]U.S. Congress, House of Representatives, Committee on Rivers and Harbors, *Hearings before the Committee on Rivers and Harbors*, 75 Congress, 1 session (1937), on H.R. 7365 and H.R. 7863, bills to provide for the regional conservation and development of the national resources and for other purposes, July and August 1937, 1–452.

[36]F.D.R. Papers, Group 13, OF 132, August 13, 1937, F.D.R. to the Senate; August 17, 1937, F.D.R. to McIntyre; August 20, 1937, F.D.R. to Ickes; *Senate Miscellaneous Documents*, 5–118, Document No. 95, 75 Congress, 1 session.

[37]*Editorial Research Report*, (Washington, D.C., 1937), 2:7151–58; *United States Statutes at Large*, 50:329.

[38]*Congressional Record*, 75 Congress, 2 session (1937), 597–602.

[39]Ibid., 3 session (1938), 306–8, address of W. M. Whittington at second annual meeting of the Mississippi Valley Flood Control Association, Washington, D.C., January 18, 1938;

3159–60, radio address by Peter J. DeMuth of Pennsylvania, June 25, 1938; 1043–46, Representative N. V. Mills, Louisiana, March 16, 1938; 2275–76, David I. Walsh of Massachusetts in Senate; 5501; 314–18, Whittington address before National Rivers and Harbors Congress, Washington, January 20, 1938; 3146–50, presidential message, March 9, 1938; *Public Papers and Addresses of Franklin D. Roosevelt: (1938) The Continuing Struggle for Liberalism* (New York, 1941), 144, Item 34, "The President Suggests a Comprehensive Congressional Study of the Forest Land Problem of the United States," March 14, 1938; *House Miscellaneous Documents,* No. 539, 75 Congress, 2–3 session (1938), 10,264, 1–4.

[40]*Congressional Record,* 76 Congress, 1 session (1939), 323–34, address by Whittington before Ohio Conservation and Flood Control Congress, West Virginia, January 27, 1934.

[41]Ibid., 75 Congress, 1 session (1937), 4172–80, remarks on water power by Rankin; 7822–88; 3 session (1938), 293–94, address by John L. McCellan of Arkansas, Washington, D.C., January 19, 1938, Appendix 347, radio address by Peter J. DeMuth of Pennsylvania, January 23, 1938.

[42]Ibid., 76 Congress, 1 session (1939), 5376, 5381, 5835, 5393–96; 1201–02, address by J. Randolph of West Virginia at 34 Conservation of National Rivers and Harbors Congress, March 24, 1939, 1913.

[43]Ibid., 1965–66.

[44]Ibid., 75 Congress, 3 session (1938), Appendix 325, "Nation Wide Forest Survey," 955, statement by Mr. Robertson on wildlife; 76 Congress, 1 session (1939), Appendix 325, 955; U.S. Congress, House of Representatives, Select Committee on Conservation of Wildlife Resources, *Hearings before the Select Committee on Conservation of Wildlife Resources,* 75 Congress, 3 session, pursuant to H.R. 11, a resolution to continue to select committee on wildlife authorized by House Resolution 337 of the 73 Congress and continued under authority of H.R. 44 of the 74 Congress to investigate all matters pertaining to the replacement and conservation of wild animal life with a view to determining the most appropriate method of carrying out such purposes, Washington, 1938, 1–342; U.S. Congress, House of Representatives, Committee on Appropriations, *Hearings before the Subcommittee of the Committee on Appropriations,* 76 Congress, 3 session, on the Interior Department Appropriation Bill for 1941, 1–1307; *United States Senate at Large,* 50:429, 329; *Congressional Record,* 76 Congress, 1 session (1939), Index Conservation cites proposed legislation.

[45]*Congressional Record,* 76 Congress, 3 session (1940), 86–87, Clare C. Hoffman of Michigan; Appendix 1510, John M. Coffee of Washington; 3505–7, J. Johnson of Oklahoma; Appendix 5187–88, Compton I. White of Idaho; Appendix 3367, Harve Tibbott of Pennsylvania; Appendix 1622, O. Brooks of Louisiana, speech delivered before Rivers and Harbors Congress, March 15, 1940, an N.B.C. broadcast; Appendix 1501–02, C. Ellis of Arkansas, address before Rivers and Harbors Congress, March 15, 1940; Appendix 3170–72, W. Cartwright of Oklahoma, statement before House Committee on Flood Control; Appendix 3505–7, J. Johnson Of Oklahoma; Appendix 5560, C. T. Curtis of Nebraska; Appendix 3142–43, N. V. Mills of Louisiana; Appendix 2550, M. Monroney of Oklahoma; 4802, J. Johnson; U.S. Congress, House of Representatives, Committee on Flood Control, *Hearings before the Committee on Flood Control,* 76 Congress, 3 session, on H.R. 9640, a bill authorizing the construction of certain public works on rivers and harbors for flood control and for other purposes, March 18–April 9, 1940, 1–1024.

[46]*Congressional Record,* 76 Congress, 3 session (1940), Appendix 671, E. C. Cathings of Arkansas; Appendix 250–51, letter by Lyle H. Brown of Oklahoma sent to members of Congress; Appendix 837–38, C. H. Leavy of Washington; Appendix 3505–7, J. Johnson of Oklahoma; Appendix 2570–71, H. D. Angell of Oregon.

[47]Ibid., Appendix 3367, Harve Tibbott.

[48]Ibid., Appendix 1622, speech delivered before Rivers and Harbors Congress, March 15, 1940, and N.B.C. broadcast by O. Brooks of Louisiana.

[49]Ibid., 77 Congress, 1 session (1941), Appendix 5117–21, address by W. Whittington before the special session of National Rivers and Harbors Congress, November 13, 1941; Appendix 1880, U. L. Burdick of North Dakota; Appendix 1745–46, statement of Frank Carlson of Kansas before Subcommittee on Appropriations, April 17, 1941; 8502, remarks by Wickersham of Oklahoma; 8537–38; 8684; Appendix 1521–22, address by R. R. Gardner of Wyoming, delegate to national convention of Izaak Walton League of America; Appendix 2591; Appendix 1248–49, remarks by C. Leavy of Washington.

[50]F.D.R. Papers, Group 13, OF 79, May 11, 1935, O. W. Bell, acting director, Budget Bureau, to F.D.R.; OF 149, May 14, 1935, F.D.R. to Bell; OF 132, July 20, 1935, Bell to F.D.R.; OF 79, April 23, 1936, Bell to F.D.R.

[51]Ibid., OF 149, April 10, 1941, Budget Director Harold Smith to F.D.R.; OF 79, May 27, 1941, Smith to F.D.R.; OF 149, August 21, 1941, Smith to F.D.R.

[52]Ibid., OF 79, July, 1933, Wallace to F.D.R.; OF 79, March 26, 1934, Wallace to McIntyre; National Archives, *General Correspondence—Conservation Secretary of Agriculture,* Record Group, No. 16, Folder, 1933, 1934, 1935, 1936, 1937.

[53]F.D.R. Papers, Group 13, OF 149, July 8, 1935, Wallace to F.D.R.; March 13, 1936, Wallace to F.D.R.

[54]Ibid., OF 1-C, July 30, 1936, Wallace to F.D.R.; Presidential Secretarial Files 1940, Interior Ickes, March 2, 1940, Wallace to F.D.R.; Group 13, OF 1-C, March 21, 1936, Wallace to F.D.R.; OF 1-F, March 14, 1937, Wallace to F.D.R.

[55]Ibid., Group 13, OF 114, Box 2, June 16, 1936, F.D.R. to Wallace; OF 1 Agriculture, May 5, 1939, Secretary Wallace to F.D.R.; Group 13, OF 1-C, March 13, 1937, Wallace to F.D.R.

[56]Ibid., OF 732, February 8, 16, 1937, Wallace to F.D.R.; Presidential Secretarial Files 1936, A.A.A., Box 16, 1936, Wallace to F.D.R.; *General Correspondence of the Secretary of Agriculture,* Conservation Folder 1933, Department of Agriculture, National Archives, Washington, D.C., Conservation Society, May, 1933; Annual Reports of the Secretary of Agriculture, 1933–1940; Henry Wallace, "The War at Our feet," *Survey Graphic,* 29:109–14 (February 1940).

[57]F.D.R. Papers, Presidential Secretarial Files 1937, Agriculture, Box 26, 1937, Wallace to F.D.R.

[58]Ibid., Group 13, OF 149, April 7, 1941, F.D.R. to Wickard; August 11, 1941, Wickard to F.D.R.; December 26, 1941, Wickard to F.D.R.; October 12, 1942, Wickard to F.D.R.; OF 446, October 23, 1942, Wickard to F.D.R.; October 29, 1942, Wickard to F.D.R.

[59]Interview with Harold L. Ickes, March 1949, Washington, D.C.; Annual Reports of the Secretary of Interior, 1933–1941; Harold L. Ickes, *The Autobiography of a Curmudgeon* (New York, 1943), 1–343.

[60]*New York Times,* February 27, 1934.

[61]Ickes interview.

[62]F.D.R. Papers, Group 13, OF 6, Box 1, December 21, 1933, Ickes to F.D.R.; OF 235, May 21, 1936, Ickes to F.D.R.; OF 132, August 20, 1937, F.D.R. to Ickes; OF 6, Box 45, March 7, 1941, Ickes to F.D.R.; OF 149, July 5, 1941, Ickes to F.D.R.; July 16, 1941, Ickes to F.D.R.; August 12, 1941, Ickes to F.D.R.

[63]Ibid., OF 402, September 7, 1934, Ickes to F.D.R.

[64]Ibid., OF 79, March 22, 1938, Ickes to F.D.R.

[65]Ibid., Presidential Secretarial Files 1939, Interior, Box 41, January 31, 1939, Ickes to F.D.R.

[66]Ibid., Presidential Secretarial Files 1940, Box 58, February 8, 1940, memo, F.D.R. to Ickes.

[67]Ibid., OF 732, February 2, 1937, Cooke to F.D.R.

[68]Ibid., February 28, 1938, Cooke to F.D.R.; OF 132, March 27, 1936, Cooke to Early; June 10, 1936, Cooke to Early; OF 114, June 30, 1936, Cooke to F.D.R.

[69]Ibid., OF 149, June 19, 1935, Tugwell, Resettlement administrator, to M. McIntyre; OF 144, June 19, 1935, McIntyre to David T. Mason; OF 1-F, July 2, 1935, J. Darling to F.D.R.; August 21, 1935, Morgenthau to F.D.R.; August 23, 1935, F.D.R. to Darling; August 26, 1935, Darling to F.D.R.; OF 1-C, August 26, 1935, Tugwell to F.D.R.; OF 1-R, August 26, 1936, Morgenthau to F.D.R.; OF 132, May 26, 1938, Clyde L. Seavey, acting chairman, Federal Power Commission, to F.D.R.

[70]*United States Statutes at Large*, 48:200–10; Donald C. Blaisdell, *The Growth of Federal Farm Aid* (Washington, 1940), 100–10, Blaisdell was former assistant to under-secretary of Agriculture; *New York Times*, January 28, 1934.

[71]*Congressional Record*, 76 Congress, 3 session (1940), Appendix 1444–45, Mississippi Valley Flood Control Association, March 13, 1940.

[72]Ibid., 74 Congress, 2 session (1936), 1026–29, "Soil Erosion and Its Control in United States," address presented by Dr. W. Lowermilk, at Third International Congress of Soil Science in London, England, on August 7, 1935.

[73]George W. Norris, *Fighting Liberal* (New York, 1945), 249–50.

[74]*United States Statutes at large*, 48:58–72.

[75]Norris, *Fighting Liberal*, 374–75.

[76]F.D.R. Papers, Group 13, OF 1092, May 6, 1938, Norris to F.D.R.

[77]Norris, *Fighting Liberal*, 372–73, 1–411.

[78]"Geologists' Conservation Warning," *Literary Digest*, 120:19 (July 13, 1935). Various national organizations guided the conservation movement by holding annual meetings devoted to conservation and by preparing and publishing material. These groups were: American Nature Association, Game Conservation Society, Izaak Walton League, National Association of Biology Teachers, National Audubon Societies, National Wildlife Federation, and Wildlife Management Institute.

[79]Asa Dickinson, *Best Books of the Decade 1936–1945*, H. W. Wilson (1948) list, and it appeared as fourth in the list of 11 of the most-distinguished general nonfiction of 1936 by the American Booksellers of North America.

[80]F.D.R. Papers, Group 13, PPF 38, January 23, 1933, Marshall N. Dana, associate editor, *The Journal*, Portland, Oregon, to F.D.R.; OF 149, March 3, 1939, James G. K. McClure, president of American Forestry Association, to F.D.R.; Catherine Glover, "Blue Ribbon Citizen," *Survey Graphic*, 29:180–81 (March 1940).

[81]F.D.R. Papers, Group 13, OF 149, February 28, 1934, C. Ben Ross, governor of Idaho, to F.D.R.; OF 402, June 13, 1934, Frank F. Merriam, governor of California, to F.D.R.; OF 149, July 15, 1935, Charles H. Martin, governor of Oregon, to F.D.R.; OF 132, May 8, 1936, Herbert H. Lehman, governor of New York, to F.D.R.; OF 1-C, April 9, 1937, Elmer A. Benson, governor of Minnesota, to F.D.R.; Alphabetical File, Langer, April 19, 1937, William Langer, governor of North Dakota, to F.D.R.; Group 13, OF 149, April 14, 1933, Ovid Butler, secretary of American Forestry Association, to F.D.R.; February 18, 1935, Francis H. Coope, Jr., Pennsylvania, Forestry Association, to F.D.R.; OF 132, March 20, 1935, Alf M. Landon to F.D.R.; April 11, 1935, Landon to F.D.R.; OF 732, April 19, 1935, Landon to F.D.R.; OF 132, July 13, 1935, McCook, Nebraska, *Daily Gazette*, to F.D.R.; PPF 1-P, Box 206, July 19, 1935, press conference, Number 222; OF 132, May 28, 1936, Harry H. Woodring, acting secretary of war, to F.D.R.; PPF 1-P, Box 208, April 9, 1937, press conference, Number 359.

[82]*New York Times*, March 12, 16, July 25, 1933, March 31, April 9, 1935; Theodore M. Knappen, "Operating On a Continent," *Reader's Digest*, 28:59–60 (March 1936); "Dust Bowl," *Literary Digest*, 121:9 (March 7, 1936); "Save Our Soil," *Colliers*, 97:86 (March 14, 1936); W. I. Drummond, "Dust Bowl," *Review of Reviews*, 93:37–40 (June 1936); D. C. Coyle, "Balance What Budget?" *Harper's Magazine*, 175:449–59 (October 1937); H. H. Bennett, "Emergency and Permanent Control of Wind Erosion in the Great Plains," *Scientific Monthly*, 47:381–99 (November 1938); Charles W. Collier, "At Last—A Soil Erosion Program," *New Republic*, 83:68–70 (May 29, 1935); A. W. Malone, "Desert Ahead," *New Outlook*, 164:14–17 (August 1934); F.D.R. Papers, Group 13, OF 1-R, August 31, 1936, James A. Farley to F.D.R.; OF 132, February 12, 1937, North Side Business Men's Association, Evansville, Indiana, to F.D.R.

[83]F.D.R. Papers, Group 13, OF 149, April 22, 1933, Early to Howe.

[84]Ibid., OF 1-Agriculture, December 13, 1933, Wallace to F.D.R.

[85]Ibid., OF 402, September 27, 1934, Water Resources Section of National Resources Board to Ickes, administrator, Public Works Administration.

[86]Ibid., OF 177, July 19, 1935, Paul Kelley, assistant director of North Carolina Conservation and Development Department, to F.D.R.

[87]Ibid., OF 1-Agriculture, June 27, 1936, Wallace to F.D.R.

[88]Publications such as the *Land Policy Review* pamphlets relating to national forests, Soil Conservation Service pamphlets, the *Soil Conservation Magazine*, National Park Service folder, Grazing Service pamphlets, Reclamation folders, and Soil Erosion Survey material, as well as departmental publications were numerous in volume. The Forest Service, Fish and Wildlife Service, Soil Conservation Service, Extension Service, Office of Education, and the T.V.A. all developed educational programs in conservation or resource use education. Representatives of these agencies assisted schools in their programs. The Office of Education called a conference in 1937 on Conservation Education, which resulted in the publication of a series of references and bibliographies. The Extension Service called a national conference of leaders of 4-H Clubs (Head, Heart, Health and Hand Clubs) in 1936 to promote conservation education; National Archives, *Soil Conservation*-631-Box, folder on Soil Conservation Education, and letters.

[89]*Congressional Record*, 76 Congress, 3 session (1940), Appendix 86–87; Conservation as a topic subject appeared in various magazines devoted to nature, such as *American Forests, American Fur Breeder, Field and Stream, National Nature News, National Sportsmen, Outdoor American, Outdoor Life, Southern Sportsman, Sports Afield, Living Wilderness, Forest News Digest, Recreation*, and the *American Lumberman.*

[90]"Our Better Ordering and Preservation," *Science ns*, 93:191–97 (February 28, 1941).

[91]*Congressional Record*, 76 Congress, 3 session (1940), Appendix 1572–73, "Farmer and Forest Service."

[92]Interview, Director Herman Kahn, the Franklin D. Roosevelt Library, June 1950; National Archives, *General Correspondence—Conservation Secretary of Agriculture*, 1933, 1936 (letters).

[93]*Congressional Record*, 75 Congress, 1 session (1937), 1173–74; 74.

[94]*New York Times*, December 27, 1934.

[95]Richard L. Weaver, program director, North Carolina Resources Use Education Commission (authority on conservation education); "Wisconsin Establishes Conservation Courses in Schools," *Bird Lore*, 38:39 (January 1936); "Legislative Action 1938," *School Life*, 24:146 (February 1938); H. A. Lawson, "New Federal Aid Bill—Harrison Thomas Fletcher Bill," *National Education Association Journal*, 27:130 (May 1938); "State Legislation Affecting Education," *School Life*, 23:107–8 (December 1937); F. S. Melcher, "Support the Education Bill, F. S. Fletcher," *Publishers Weekly*, 133:1748 (April 30, 1938); L. W. Ashby and B. A. Dawson, "Harrison-Black-Fletcher Bill," *National Education Association Journal*, 26:49–56

(February 1937); "First National Conference on Conservation Education," *School and Society*, 46:172–73 (August 7, 1937); E. G. Bathurst, "Progress of Teaching Conservation," *School Life*, 23:41–42 (October 1937); *Review of Educational Legislation 1935–1936* (U.S. Office of Education, 1937), 1–39, bulletin. Since 1929, Arkansas, Florida, Georgia, Kentucky, Maryland, North Dakota, Oklahoma, and Wisconsin had enacted legislation requiring the teaching of conservation in the schools. This initial step was furthered by additional state legislation. Oklahoma, in 1937, Arkansas in 1939, Mississippi in 1940, and many others passed state laws relating to conservation study in schools.

[96]M. L. Cooke, "New Step to Save the Land," *Survey Graphic*, 29:246 (April 7, 1940).

[97]"Conservation," *Nature Magazine*, editorial (April 1935).

[98]*Congressional Record*, 77 Congress, 1 session (1941), 4543.

✑ 4 ✑
The Objectives of Conservation during the Roosevelt Administration

The development of conservation policy in the 1930s has to be interpreted from a great complexity of programs with varying degrees of relevance. These programs emanated from the ideas and activities of a great number of people during a period of considerable historical change. Hence it is not easy to unravel the threads of what could be claimed to be the objectives of conservation under the Roosevelt administration. At least it is difficult to do so in very great detail. It is of interest, however, to examine some of the available evidence concerning the relative importance to this administration of temporary and longer-term objectives and of different long-term objectives. It is also desirable to consider how genuine President Roosevelt and his followers were in developing programs relating to conservation. Did they really seek as an independent objective the "protection, upbuilding and prudent use of our natural resources for the greatest good of the greatest number of our people?"[1] Were they inspired by individual or group motives of self-interest and bigotry and a consequent desire for power?

IMMEDIATE OBJECTIVES

The immediate objectives of the Roosevelt administration were relief and recovery. It was necessary to save the young from warped and idle years and to put courage in the hearts of parents who saw their families hungering. Accordingly, many conservation programs were formulated in terms of the contribution they would make to the relief of unemployment and poverty. This may be illustrated by the establishment and work of the Civilian Conservation Corps (C.C.C.), the Public Works Administration (P.W.A.), and the Works Progress Administration (W.P.A.). These will be discussed briefly.

Civilian Conservation Corps

Franklin D. Roosevelt promised his party members in his Democratic national convention speech of acceptance, July 2, 1932, a plan for converting millions of marginal and unused acres into timberland by a means that would provide relief both for the unemployed and for agriculture.[2] His inaugural words, "our greatest primary task is to put people to work,"[3] were followed soon after by a meeting of officials to discuss the new organization. Permissive legislation was swiftly passed for C.C.C. projects, by which the promise of relief became a reality. By July 1933, 300,000 young men enrolled under the scheme.[4] The objective was relief to the unemployed, not merely in the economic but also in the spiritual sense—conserving, restoring, indeed creating those human resources that are the seed and the fruit of a nation. For what end should a democratic nation exist except that the multitudes of persons who make it up have the best chance to mature as individuals? Mere occupation by "make work" does not make men, but these young men could see, if they could think at all, that what they did was a benefit not simply to themselves but to the land. Those who could be redeemed would, and did, face the future with hope and a new courage.[5]

The C.C.C. was voluntary, but it was conducted with a mildly military discipline and spirit, although drilling, saluting, and marching were taboo. The War Department directed the building of camps and also supervised health, morale, and welfare. The administration of the C.C.C., however, became wholly civilian before 1939. Each enrollee received a monthly wage of $30, part of it as a family allotment. At first, the needy were accepted from relief and nonrelief families, but in 1935 the latter were eliminated and the age range was set from 17 to 28. The organization's top enrollment of nearly half a million was reached in the autumn of 1935. At that time blacks comprised about a tenth of the enrollees and native Americans a small proportion. Some 2.75 million recruits served up to the end of 1941, and the majority of these were in their teens. Of these 400,000 were young men and 145,000 war veterans. The C.C.C. afforded employment not only to young men and war veterans, but also foresters, technicians, teachers, mechanics, and other groups serving in the organization and operation of the C.C.C.[6]

The rapid turnover of enrollees was caused by the desire for regular work, restlessness, or rebellion against discipline. All told, about one-half left the C.C.C. before finishing their terms of from six months to two years. The bulk of those who stayed, however, gained in experience. They learned regular habits, hygienic living, physical agility, and manual skill, all of which engendered ambition and self-confidence. Perhaps this teaching was expensive, because the C.C.C. proved the most costly form of relief per capita, averaging about $1,175 annually to maintain each enrollee. However, to offset this cost, in addition to gains in health and self-respect, roads and trails were built, forest fires checked or prevented, erosion prevented, wildlife preserved, and over 2 billion trees planted. Also, the enrollees serviced various projects such as the model projects set up under the Soil Erosion Service (later the Soil Conservation Service), which began to dot the map with an active partnership between farmers and their government.[7]

Public Works Administration

An attack on the economic emergency from another angle was the P.W.A., which was organized on June 16, 1933, with an appropriation of $3.3 million. The P.W.A. was designed to stimulate heavy industry by fostering public works that required huge quantities of material. President Roosevelt placed it in the hands of Harold L. Ickes, secretary of the interior, cautious and self-styled "curmudgeon," whose aversion to using federal funds "to hire grown men to chase tumbleweeds on windy days" infiltrated the whole workings of the organization.[8] Ickes was able to carry out P.W.A. work under contract with private concerns, and he insisted on careful inspection of projects before lending or giving funds to states and municipalities. The P.W.A. was conceived by the New Dealers as a "pump-priming" agency, best calculated to stimulate private employment in accord with the Keynesian theory of compensatory spending. This analogy was suggested by the old-fashioned pump into which water had to be poured before it drew properly and a steady flow of water emerged. Whether industry of the nation could be put into efficient operation by priming or whether the primed water simply returned occasioned dispute. Nevertheless, the P.W.A. kept an average of a half-million men steadily at work through 1934. By the time it began liquidation in the early 1940s, it had spent over $4 billion on more than 34,000 projects. Among them were projects that enabled the government to expand the work of conserving the nation's resources. The largest share of the work was through flood control, water power, and reclamation, to which the P.W.A. had contributed $262,535,655, in addition to the work of building forest roads and trails to open timberlands to fight fires and for recreation. P.W.A. allotments brought Boulder (later called Hoover) Dam to completion by day and night shifts two and one-half years ahead of schedule. The social usefulness and relief value of the P.W.A. projects admitted little question.[9]

Works Progress Administration

There were also immediate measures of direct relief or dole, which cannot be classed as conservation except in the fundamental sense that people were kept from starving. However, the W.P.A., which made its advent in the summer of 1935, divorced work relief from this direct relief, the latter being returned to the states and local agencies. Harry Hopkins was the head of the W.P.A., and the work of this new organization varied from the construction of airports, roads, bridges, the improvement of parks and playgrounds, the building of flood control and irrigation dams, to academic projects.[10]

Congressional Support of Conservation Relief

The faith of President Roosevelt in conservation as a relief measure was accepted by the American people and by Congress, whose members in both the House and Senate gave full support to his leadership, passing extensive legislation, whether it built a dam in Tennessee or established a C.C.C. camp in Montana. The public works and construction projects established by the National Industrial Recovery Act of June 16, 1933,[11] returned thousands of workers to the payroll. The belief of congressmen in the value of conservation projects for relief was clearly stated in the hearings held before the Committee on Flood Control in March and April 1935.[12] Further evidence was the decisive step on April 5, 1935, by which Congress approved conservation as relief by a House vote of 317 to 70 and a Senate vote of 66 to 13. A clear-cut majority vote gave approval to the largest relief bill in U.S. history, in which appropriations were granted for water conservation, soil erosion, reforestation, and the C.C.C.[13]

Thus it was that conservation and relief—a short-term objective—became linked. It was the president's opinion that should unemployment linger or recur, planned development of land and water resources would meet the threat effectively.[14] Such a belief he helped to pass on to posterity. Economists today both agree and disagree with a policy of public spending to offset depression and unemployment. Few would disagree that natural resource development and conservation are worthy media for transferring such expenditure to the economy.

PERMANENT OBJECTIVES

Although relief was the immediate objective, it is obvious that a good many of the conservation programs, such as the T.V.A., were substantially long-range undertakings. Further, many of the emergency measures would have influences far beyond their contribution to recovery—influences that would be felt for many years. Thus, there was ever present a large and important field of decision making, involving choices between projects clearly temporary—such as direct relief—and those of a more or less permanent nature. Among the latter were also many alternatives. The important point is that there was a need to formulate a more permanent policy toward conservation if the problem were to be comprehensively handled.

The Democratic administration did show an early awareness of this important issue. In February 1934 for instance, Secretary of the Interior Harold Ickes publicly stated that the Roosevelt administration had a "twenty-five or fifty-year plan" for the country's natural resources. He was a firm believer in the idea of making all projects a part of a permanent program.[15] In a similar vein, the National Resources Board in its report to the president in 1934 (made public December 17, 1934) emphasized the merits of more permanent public works programs.[16]

President Roosevelt's Commitment
to a Permanent Conservation Policy

Gradually, a need for permanent policy with respect to conservation was more explicitly stated and more generally recognized, becoming the subject of frequent statements by the chief executive. When signing the Soil Conservation and Domestic Allotment Act on March 1, 1936, Roosevelt declared he was approving a measure that would safeguard vital public interest not only for two days but "for generations to come." To him the act meant an attempt to develop, out of the far-reaching and partly emergency efforts under the Agricultural Adjustment Act (A.A.A.), a long-term program for U.S. agriculture. This was a program, then under development, to encourage farmers throughout the nation to learn and practice techniques for retaining their fertile soil.[17] His concern for durable results shows also in his review of the summary of the Great Plains Drought Area Committee's preliminary report, submitted August 27, 1936, during a drought inspection trip. The trip and the report made it evident that the American people were confronted here with no mere short-term relief problem.[18] H. H. Bennett supported the president's belief that an enduring policy was essential to protect the fertility of the Great Plains.[19] In 1937, the president put this point of view explicitly to the Congress:

> During the depression we have substantially increased the facilities and developed the resources of our country for the common welfare through public works and work relief programs. We have been compelled to undertake actual work somewhat hurriedly in the emergency. Now it is time to develop a long range plan and policy for construction—to provide the best use of our resources and to prepare in advance against any other emergency.[20]

He did not speak to minds unwilling or unprepared. Two years before, representatives had urged that something lasting be undertaken to circumvent the dangerous erosion. It was evident then that continued effects called for continuing activity.[21] In 1937 the House held hearings on a permanent system of flood control.[22] On this matter there was evident accord with the administration in the legislative branch of the government. During the following years, the president continued to plead this cause. When, in 1940, the giant rumble of approaching war rolled through the American consciousness, the chief executive urged the people not to let the widening peril distract them from the conservation plans for a better America.[23] On January 11, 1940, he told Congress that "the provision for the wise use and conservation of our national resources must necessarily be one of the primary responsibilities of the Federal Government at all times."[24] Congress, for its part, continued to grant appropriations for conservation measures, guiding its action by an awareness of the need for permanence.[25]

Economic Improvement:
A Part of Conservation Policy

Permanent and general economic improvement was implicit in the development of conservation policy under Roosevelt. This was evident even at the beginning of the New Deal. Under the N.R.A. the government regulated 500 million acres of forest land with the intention of preventing destructive competition.[26] Farm studies were carried out to use natural resources to better advantage, and to aid farm families to move from unsuitable land to areas better adapted to furnish a livelihood.[27] President Roosevelt in a message to Congress on January 4, 1935, declared that one of his desires for the people of the United States was to obtain "the security of a livelihood through the better use of the national resources of the land in which we live."[28]

Conservation's relationship to the standard of living was acknowledged by many government officials. Congressmen testifying at hearings held before the Committee on Irrigation and Reclamation in June 1935, expressed belief that the conservation of natural resources was necessary to maintain prosperity.[29]

Economic Objectives

Economic objectives in conservation were seen in various phases of conservation work. Harold Ickes considered electric energy, although subsidiary to the large conservation program, an important and economically inseparable part of it.[30] Confidential reports of the federal government concerning conservation projects pointed to the economic benefits of the work.[31] Reports on the conservation of wildlife showed the economic benefits to the fish and fur industries.[32] Governmental reports on forest resource conservation stressed the economic significance of contributions being made to employment and business.[33]

Perhaps no one more aptly stated the economic goals of conservation on the agricultural front than Clyde L. Herring (Democrat) of Iowa on May 17, 1937, in a radio address:

> . . . The interest which the government has taken in agriculture has not been for the sake of agriculture alone. The larger aim has been national recovery.
> . . . The soil conservation program has demonstrated its value, and is, in my opinion, here to stay. It is the foundation of an economically sound national farm policy.[34]

It will be remembered that conservation provided the means to continue the production control feature of the A.A.A. even after the Supreme Court in 1936 adjudged the A.A.A. to be unconstitutional. Scarcely had the decision been rendered when the original Soil Conservation Act was amended to permit the government to make direct payments for practices to conserve the soil. Each major political party endorsed government payments as an important plank in its agricultural program at the time of the 1936 election. The switch to emphasis on conservation and its economic benefits received larger nonfarm support than the original production control schemes of 1934–35. The 1936 Conservation Domestic Allotment Act recognized the need to promote conservation and the profitable use of agricultural land resources by temporary aid to farmers and by providing for a permanent policy of federal aid to states for such purposes. Stress on this tie-up continued during the following years. In 1939 the secretary of agriculture reported that the A.A.A. program for 1940 sought the twofold objective of soil conservation and crop adjustment. The 1940 A.A.A. program put increased emphasis on soil conservation and provided increased opportunities for participation by small farmers.[35]

The President's Emphasis on the Economic Value of Conservation

Roosevelt capably inspired Congress to recognize the economic value of conservation and to develop the national resources with that goal in view. He also kept such benefits before the U.S. public from the outset of his administration. At press conferences and in memoranda he explained how scientific forestry practices would yield valuable lumber crops, how labor of C.C.C. enrollees would establish new national forests, how the Grand Coulee Dam could be used for power and a basin, and how food for the armed forces could be raised on reclaimed western land. The federal conservation policy was to pay off in dollars and cents, plus help to solve the country's economic ills.[36]

Social Improvement: Tennessee Valley Authority, An Example

Economic improvement was, however, too narrow an objective to fit Roosevelt's conservation policy. Social improvement, which would almost of necessity include economic considerations, was more nearly the goal. And social improvement could not be gained except through the cooperative advance of all members of society. The T.V.A. provided a good example of this. The stated objective of the T.V.A. was to promote flood control, navigation, electric power production, the proper use of land and forest, and the economic and social well-being of the people in the area. The new agency was to deal with all natural resources as factors in one big problem.[37]

Though the T.V.A. could invoke the power of eminent domain in matters like flood control, the essence of its program was voluntary cooperation and a democratic enlistment of the people's understanding. It was recognized that the program would serve the general welfare best if it ignited the spark of willing cooperation among the ordinary men and women affected. Under a planning council, six divisions (representing agriculture, forestry, industry, engineering and geology, land use, and social and economic aspects) maintained "demonstrative units," which became the chief means of individual persuasion. While still engaged in building locks and dams and power plants, the T.V.A. developed means to secure the retirement of submarginal lands, to inculcate ways to conserve the soil, to encourage afforestation, together with the introduction of better farm machinery, the fostering of local manufacturers, and the improvement of public health and education. In all cases the emphasis was on mutual understanding and cooperation. The once-backward region became the second largest producer of power in the United States, with municipalities and cooperatives in partnership with the T.V.A. supplying electricity to consumers at 3 cents a kilowatt-hour instead of 10 cents. Freezing lockers, electric pumps, hay driers, motors to grind feed and to cut wood—these were the practical markers on the scale to measure plenty. They meant efficiency in work and a new joy in living.[38]

President Roosevelt told Congress on April 10, 1933, that the T.V.A. "will be a laboratory for the Nation to learn how to make the most of its vast resources for the lasting benefit of the average man and woman."[39] By the mode of its development, the Authority enabled the people of the valley to help themselves.[40] Their social and economic improvement was one of the benefits named by Roosevelt in 1940 when he hailed the T.V.A. as one of the "great social and economic achievements of our time."[41]

Improvement could be rapid and obvious in an area like the Tennessee Valley, where there was initially a great lack of modern techniques in soil and forest management together with a ready source of inexpensive power. However, the objective of social improvement was not found only in the T.V.A.; Harold Ickes saw it as proper to all conservation projects. "If we are alive to our own interests and care anything about our own normal and legitimate pleasures, we will make the conservation of our natural resources a common objective."[42] Henry Wallace, in his annual report of 1938, also stated that though conservation as a public policy had to do overtly with trees, its underlying purpose was social. In the same year this view was reiterated by the chief of the Forest Service. Human welfare was fundamental to conservation as the administration viewed it.[43]

Social Value of Recreational Facilities

Recreational facilities provided through the National Parks Program had direct social value on a very broad basis. President Roosevelt believed that the concentration of responsibility for the parks under the National Park Service justified, as a permanent policy, their development as a great recreational and educational project, the definite objective being human happiness.[44] Official reports in 1942 show this. The Departments of Agriculture and Interior submitted, in January 1942, to the National

Resources Planning Board a report on a national program of public works for forest conservation that was devoted to recreational gains. Simultaneously, another such joint report to the same committee dealt wholly with a national program of public works for recreational land.[45] So firmly rooted became the respect for this social value that even the fierce threat of war did not wrench it loose. President Roosevelt included the conservation of natural resources as one of the social objectives from which the current emergency of May 1940 did not justify retreat.[46]

Conservation Objectives

When conservation is considered in the light of a permanent policy, it may well claim a meaning independent of the objectives already discussed. That is, it is possible for principles of conservation, such as, for example, an aim of maintenance without depletion of forest resources, to become so firmly established that few conceivable changes in economic conditions would be felt to warrant a deviation from it. In other words, the principle may come to be considered more important than related economic conditions of a single generation. The comments immediately following illustrate that the Roosevelt administration envisaged a wider application and acceptance of such principles of conservation.

The dust storms of 1934 and 1935 provided a dramatic opportunity for directing full attention to long-term conservation needs. The clouds of dust swirling about the heads of farmers and nonfarmers alike made United States citizens realize the value of enduring conservation policy. It was forcibly drawn to their attention by the soil erosion problem.[47] In fact, the seriousness of the situation caused the states of Kansas and Oklahoma to appeal to the federal government for aid.[48] The least that can be said is that the Roosevelt administration took advantage of this opportunity to present to the nation programs involving conservation of the nation's resources. Roosevelt himself capitalized on the opportunity in press conferences by warning the people against continued exploitation and mining of the soil that would cause but future dust storms. The maintenance of the soil had become an urgent necessity. The Soil Erosion Service, set up under the N.R.A. in the latter part of 1933, received a $10 million allotment for the purpose of demonstrating the practical possibilities of curbing erosion and allied evils.[49] A correction of past evils with their desolate harvest could be realized only by scientific soil practices. Conservation was the answer.[50]

By 1936 the importance of conservation was recognized in wildlife, forestry, and soil erosion projects. The president valued forest planning as a means of fulfilling social and economic objectives and also as a contribution to long-range conservation—meaning extension of resources—through scientific forestry.[51] He withdrew public lands to be used for the planned development of natural resources.[52] Particularly in wildlife did the administration stress the value of long-term conservation. For example, in calling a wildlife conference from February 3 to 7, 1936, President Roosevelt stated that one of the purposes of the conference was to develop a North American program for the advancement of wildlife restoration and conservation.[53] The National Works Program for Wildlife Conservation laid emphasis on this objective. Projects were to conserve an adequate seed stock of wild animals in nature and to restore, develop, and protect a satisfactory environment to ensure their preservation.[54]

The Roosevelt administration was very fortunate also in its development of a water resources conservation policy in having a dramatic opportunity to claim the necessity of conservation practices. The extensive flooding during 1936–37 warranted immediate attention, plus offered proof that floods were everrecurring happenings that demanded a long-term approach. Congressmen offered concrete proof of their conviction by passing flood control legislation in 1936 and additional legislation in succeeding years. They voiced a need for scientific practices in using the nation's wealth.[55] An editorial in the *New York Times,* January 26, 1937, which discussed the flood problem, declared that "the physical preservation of the United States is the actual issue."[56] Conservation was no longer an idealistic goal—it had become a necessity.[57]

Permanency of Conservation by 1939

Conservation had clearly come to a position of predominance by 1939 when all government departments took constructive steps to get more conservation into their programs.[58] Secretary Ickes of the Department of the Interior declared that "there can be no question about the advance we have made upon the conservation front."[59] Appropriations to long-range programs were voted even during the dire period of 1940–42, which pivoted on Pearl Harbor. At this time the administration continued to emphasize conservation of range lands. The broad objective of this program, to rehabilitate, develop, maintain, and manage the resources of the range land, was to go on.[60] Likewise, the National Program of Public Works in 1942 stated that forestry conservation was to continue. The nation's forest lands were to be used to meet current and future needs.[61] United States land was not to be exploited to make war-time profits, as had been feared by Secretary Ickes and others in high office.[62] Not even a major catastrophe was to disrupt seriously or end the conservation aims of the Roosevelt administration.

MULTIPLE OBJECTIVES
AS ILLUSTRATED BY STATUTES

An attempt has been made to focus attention on important broad groups of objectives in the formulation of conservation policy under President Roosevelt. Each of these objectives and their component parts were tied together in legislative acts, and examination of the statutes shows that more than one objective was ofttimes contained within a single act. Herein is illustrated the temporary—relief and recovery—and the permanent economic, social, and conservation objectives of the natural resources policy. A chronological examination of the national statutes relating to conservation perhaps shows best the multiplicity and changing emphasis of the objectives as well as the conscious effort of the administration to include them all in a general policy. A summary presentation of this legislation is hence presented, even at the risk of repetition, in amplification of the foregoing comments.

Emergency Conservation Work Act (March 1933)

The first piece of conservation legislation, "An Act for the Relief of Unemployment through the Performance of Useful Public Works and for Other Purposes," was approved by President Roosevelt on March 31, 1933.[63] This act, usually referred to as the Emergency Conservation Work Act, gave the president blanket authority to restore the country's depleted resources and advance a program of useful public works whereby the acute conditions of unemployment in the nation would be relieved.[64] The Democratic administration lost no time in attempting to lessen the unemployment rolls, and as part of its solution immediately tied up relief with the restoration of the national resources. Acting promptly upon the authority vested in him, the president made the Emergency Conservation Work Act effective by issuing an executive order on April 5, 1933,[65] that appointed a director and advisory council and provided a fund to establish the C.C.C. The C.C.C. was established as the Emergency Conservation Work Organization, or E.C.W.; however, at its very beginning it was known as the Civilian Conservation Corps (C.C.C.). The popular name of C.C.C. was officially adopted as the legal designation of the organization by an act approved on June 28, 1937.[66] Its purpose, as stated earlier, was to give immediate relief, to provide physical and moral well-being, and to conserve the nation's resources.[67]

National Industrial Recovery Act (June 1933)

Relief, however, was not a problem to be dismissed with one major piece of legislation. Further provision for employment was seen in the act of

June 16, 1933, "To Encourage National Industrial Recovery, to Foster Fair Competition and to Provide for the Construction of Certain Public Works. . . ." Again conservation was to be used. The law specifically stated that an administrator under the direction of the president should prepare a comprehensive program of public works that should include:

> (b)conservation and development of natural resources, including control, utilization, and purification of waters, prevention of soil and/or coastal erosion, development of water power, transmission of electrical energy, and construction of river and harbor improvements, and flood control. . . .[68]

The National Industrial Recovery Act (N.I.R.A.) of June 16, 1933, clearly illustrated the relief objective of the conservation provision just as the March 31, 1933, act had done. However, here too the value and need to conserve the natural resources quickly came to the foreground. Under authority of the June 16 act, the Federal Emergency Administrator of Public Works made a grant of $5 million to be used for erosion work. In October 1933, the Soil Erosion Service was established to administer this grant of money. The objectives of the Soil Erosion Service were: to demonstrate that the impoverishment and destruction of the remaining areas of good agricultural land by continuing erosion could be controlled; and to lay the foundation for a permanent national erosion control program of adequate scope to meet the acute land crisis by wasteful methods of land utilization.[69]

Tennessee Valley Authority Act (May 1933)

The early legislation showed that conservation work was directed toward permanent reform as well as emergency relief. This was also illustrated in the projects and services adopted. Multiple purposes and goals were apparent within a single agency or act. An excellent example of the latter is the Tennessee Valley Authority Act of May 18, 1933. This act created the T.V.A., which had the power to acquire, construct, and operate dams in the Tennessee Valley, manufacture fertilizers, generate and sell electric power, carry out flood control through reforestation, withdraw marginal lands from cultivation, develop the Tennessee River for navigation, and advance the economic and social well-being of the people in the river basin. The T.V.A. was a long-range plan to improve a vast area. It included all of the temporary and permanent objectives of the conservation policy.[70]

Wildlife Acts (1934)
and Taylor Grazing Act (June 1934)

The desire to conserve the natural resources and to derive the benefits thereof was exemplified in the conservation legislative acts of 1934. Relief as an objective was still emphasized, but the conservation objective received more and more attention. Specific acts dealing with wildlife conservation were passed by Congress. An act "To Promote the Conservation of Wildlife, Fish, and Game, and for Other Purposes" became effective March 10, 1934. It provided for the cooperative promotion of conservation of wildlife and studies to be made on the effects of polluting substances on wildlife. On the same date, March 10, 1934, "An Act to Establish Fish and Game Sanctuaries in the National Parks" was approved. This act gave the president blanket authority to set aside certain areas of the national forests as fish and game sanctuaries.[71] On June 28, 1934, the Taylor Grazing Act became law.[72] The objectives of the act were: to conserve the natural resources; and to stabilize the livestock industry on the range. The act provided for a wide variety of range restoration projects.[73]

Conservation Acts of 1935

The conservation acts of 1935 afforded relief, a permanent conservation policy, and conservation practices that would promote the welfare of United States citizens by enhancing social values and by aiding in solving economic ills. The complexity of the conservation program was clearly apparent. The Bituminous Coal Conservation Act, August 30, 1935, was related to economic problems in that provision was made to stabilize the bituminous coal-mining industry and to promote its interstate commerce. The act also provided for the conservation of bituminous coal in the United States.[74] On February 22, 1935, an act was approved "to Regulate Interstate and Foreign Commerce in Petroleum and its Products. . . ." This act was to encourage the conservation of deposits of crude oil available in the United States.[75] The Soil Erosion Act of April 27, 1935, provided for the conservation of soil as well as relief.[76] The act recognized that the wastage of soil and moisture resources on farm, grazing, and forest land of the nation resulting from soil erosion was a menace to national welfare. The act declared it to be a policy of Congress to provide permanently for the control and prevention of soil erosion, and thereby to preserve natural resources, control floods, prevent impairment of reservoirs, and maintain navigability of rivers and harbors, protect public health and public lands, and relieve unemployment. The secretary of agriculture was directed to coordinate all federal activities in this direction. In order to begin this policy, he was authorized to conduct surveys and research to carry out preventive measures, and to enter into agreements with any agency to further the purposes of the act. The Soil Erosion Act also authorized the secretary of agriculture to establish an agency known as the Soil Conservation Service.[77]

Emergency Relief Appropriations Act (April 1935)

Further conservation activity was permitted by executive order on May 1, 1935, when President Roosevelt by virtue of authority in the Emergency Relief Appropriations Act, April 8, 1935, established an agency known as the Resettlement Administration. The functions and duties of this agency were to initiate and administer a program of approved projects with respect to soil erosion, stream pollution, seawash erosion, reforestation, forestation, and flood control.[78]

Flood Control Act (June 1936)

In 1936 Congress passed a major piece of water resource legislation by the adoption of the Flood Control Act on June 22, 1936. The act authorized the construction of certain public works on rivers and harbors for flood control.[79] Section 1 of the act contained its declaration of policy:

> It is hereby recognized that destructive floods upon the rivers of the United States, upsetting orderly processes and causing loss of life and property, including erosion of lands . . . constitute a menace to national welfare; that it is the sense of Congress that flood control on navigable waters or their tributaries is a proper activity of the Federal Government in cooperation with States. . . .[80]

Soil Conservation and
Domestic Allotment Act (February 1936)

The Flood Control Act was a clear-cut conservation measure with many ramifications that touched all phases of life. On the other hand, the Soil Conservation and Domestic Allotment Act of February 29, 1936, which took the form of an addition to the Soil Erosion Act of 1935, had political and agricultural aid purposes as well as conservation.[81] It was designed to continue the invalidated Agricultural Adjustment Act of 1933 as well as to promote conservation. Here, conservation was used as a vehicle to continue a program the Supreme Court had declared unconstitutional.

The deceased A.A.A. reappeared under a cloak of soil conservation emphasis.[82] The purpose of the Soil Conservation and Domestic Allotment Act as passed in 1936 was "to Promote Conservation and Profitable Use of Agricultural Land Resources by Temporary Federal Aid to Farmers and by Providing for a Permanent Policy of Federal Aid to States for Such Purposes." The purposes of the act were: preservation and improvement of soil fertility; promotion of the economic use and conservation of land; diminution of exploitation of wasteful and unscientific use of national soil resources; and protection of rivers and harbors against the results of soil erosion in aid of maintaining waters and water courses and in aid of flood control.[83] The act as it appeared on the statute books was to promote conservation, which it did. Without a doubt, however, its primary purpose was to continue part of the unconstitutional A.A.A.[84] President Roosevelt, when commenting on the act, frankly stated that although it was addressed primarily to the serious and long-neglected problem of soil conservation, the establishment and maintenance of farm income were also major objectives.[85]

Legislation in 1937

Legislation by 1937 had firmly established the temporary and permanent objectives of the national resources policy. As has been shown, some acts were clear-cut in their intent and others contained multiple purposes. Also, some of the acts by their very general wording enabled the Roosevelt administration to apply them in such a way as to serve many goals. Hence, conservation served many purposes and at the same time stood rightly on its own value. The Democrats were not just using conservation, but, as discussed previously, aimed at establishing a permanent conservation policy on the grounds that it was justified and essential to the welfare of the nation. The conservation of resources as a relief measure had been proved. It was superseded by the other goals. During 1937 acts were passed that extended the period of time of the Soil Conservation and Domestic Allotment Act and granted appropriations to carry out provisions of the act.[86] An act on July 19, 1937, granted appropriations for flood control.[87] An act "to Promote Conservation in the Arid and Semiarid areas of the United States by Aiding in the Development of Facilities for Water Storage and Utilization" was approved on August 28, 1937.[88] The secretary of agriculture was authorized to carry out projects. The national resources policy objectives were also furthered by the authorization of the Bonneville project on August 20, 1937. The purpose of this project on the Columbia River was to improve navigation and develop hydroelectric power.[89]

Conservation Objective Emphasized
in Legislation, 1938–42

The legislation passed between 1938 and 1942 was concerned primarily with the conservation objective. An act "Authorizing the Construction of Certain Public Works on Rivers and Harbors for Flood Control", passed on June 28, 1938,[90] amended the Flood Act of June 22, 1936, which made it apply to all flood control projects, except as otherwise specifically provided by law. An attempt to make the public more aware of floods was illustrated by an act of June 29, 1938, requesting the president of the United States to proclaim the week of May 31, 1939, National Flood Prevention Week.[91] The Reclamation Project act of August 4, 1939, made it possible to adjust many difficulties of the water users, to draft new contracts gearing payments to the year-by-year ability of farmers to make payments, to reclassify lands from time to time, and to accomplish other needed reforms. The act recognized the importance of power in determining the feasibility of a project. It provided that any sale of electric power or lease of power privileges should be for a period not longer than 40 years and at such rates as would cover an appropriate share of the annual operation and maintenance cost as well as the construction investment. The act established a broad foundation for the conservation and economic development of the water resources of the west.[92] On August 11, 1939, an act was approved authorizing construction of water conservation and utilization projects in the great plains and arid and semiarid areas of the United States. The act was continued by legislation on October 14, 1940, and subject to an amendment on March 7, 1942, which added figures to be allowed in individual projects.[93] Thus, conservation laws continued to be added to the federal statute books.

A final question, raised at the beginning of this chapter, was whether Roosevelt and his supporters were inspired by individual or group motives of self-interest and bigotry and a consequent desire for power.

Was Roosevelt, the conservationist, impelled by a desire for fame? It would be difficult to establish the truth of such a claim. But even if it were true, as human motives go, this is not ignoble, and fame would not result except from public benefits of great magnitude, long continued to illuminate a name. Rather, was it not love of country to be shocked by the display of inordinate waste that had been rife for generations and threatened, in no short time, to make a Yellow River of the Mississippi and reduce the Southwest to a Sahara? Was it not public spirited to try to cure this cancerous disease of his country? From a historical view of available evidence, Roosevelt's loyalty to the nation had depth.

The desire simply to be reelected, nevertheless, could have motivated the advocates of conservation if they thought that that measure, implementing related policies, might awaken a large popular enthusiasm. Although such an argument can hardly be used to discredit an administration in a democracy, obviously the Roosevelt administration did not limit its activities to the passive role of reflecting popular opinion; as was shown in Chapter 3, the administration claimed a need to instigate an extensive program of education for conservation, in addition to whatever public support may have already existed. Perhaps, then, the Roosevelt conservation policy, though laudable in itself, may have merely screened a dangerous bureaucratic drive for power. There were those who said so, plain, loud, and long. There were those who said worse: that a planned economy was being forced upon the nation; that the state was encroaching upon the realm of private enterprise, whose existing autonomy was basic to democracy; that a blueprint was being laid for the management of the United States that would put all persons from the cradle to the grave in the place ordained for them by the government. This charge was more than a taunt. The various sections of the vast and revolutionary New Deal program were so correlated in their working, by the very nature of the situation, that this argument did not sound implausible. It is, in fact, too grave a charge and too importantly aligned with the temper and the movements of the modern world to dismiss here with a phrase; it receives a separate treatment in Chapter 7.

It remains for the record of accomplishments to indicate how well the Roosevelt administration realized its temporary and permanent objectives. Conservation as a method of providing relief and recovery, as a vehicle to aid in economic problems and to provide for economic betterment, and as a means to enhance social values—all were used in conservation work completed. But it is clear that behind these objectives was the objective of conservation for its own sake; with the Roosevelt administration there had developed a real appreciation of a need for defining general rules under which the nation's resources henceforth should be exploited. Where was a net depletion acceptable? Where should there be, at least, maintenance? Where should there be a building up of resources? It was on the basis of its answers to these questions that the Roosevelt administration shaped and directed a national resources policy in the critical years of the 1930s. Subsequent administrations will determine its future as events prove or disprove the adequacy of the policy passed on to them in the face of changing conditions.

NOTES

¹Definition given by Harold Ickes during an interview in March 1949, Washington.

²*Campaign Book of the Democratic Party: Candidates and Issues* (Democrat National Committee, 1932), pamphlet.

³*Congressional Record,* 73 Congress, special session of Senate (1933), 5.

⁴*The Public Papers and Addresses of Franklin D. Roosevelt; 1933* (New York, 1938), 80–84, "Unemployment Relief," March 31, 1933; *New York Times,* March 11, 12, 1933, October 17, 1934; *The Public Papers and Addresses; 1933* (New York, 1938), 67–72, third press conference, March 15, 1933, Item 101, "The Simple Purposes and the Solid Foundation of Our Recovery Program," July 24, 1933.

⁵F.D.R. Papers, Group 13, OF 268, October 10, 1933, F.D.R. to Howe; December 12, 1941, J. J. McEntee, director of the C.C.C., to McIntyre; April 5, 1935, R. S. Fechner to F.D.R.; *Public Papers and Addresses; 1933* (New York, 1938), 160–68, "What We Have Been Doing," May 7, 1933; "Essentials for Unemployment," March 21, 1935; "Democracy: Its Essentials and Its Problems," *Scholastic,* 35:18S–20S (December 11, 1934).

⁶*Summary Report of the Director of Emergency Conservation Work: April 1933 to June 30, 1935,* (Washington, 1941), 5; see Chapter 6.

⁷*Civilian Conservation Corps* (Washington, 1941), not paged; *Work Experience Counts* (Washington, 1941), not paged.

⁸Harold L. Ickes, *The Autobiography of a Curmudgeon* (New York, 1943), 1–343; Harold L. Ickes, *Back to Work: The Story of P.W.A.* (New York, 1935), 5–50.

⁹*America Builds the Record of P.W.A.* (Washington, 1939), 1–291, Public Works Administration, July 1, 1939, publication; Ickes, *Back to Work,* 5–50.

¹⁰Robert E. Sherwood, *Roosevelt and Hopkins: An Intimate History* (New York, 1948), 49–106, 200–10.

¹¹*United States Statutes at Large,* 48:90; F.D.R. Papers, Group 13, PPF 1-P, Box 204, press conference, Number 156, November 7, 1934; Box 210, press conference, Number 449A, April 8, 1938; "Soil Erosion," *Science ns,* 78:Supplement 9 (August 4, 1933); A. W. Malone, "Desert Ahead," *New Outlook,* 164:14–17 (August 1934); "Relief of Unemployed through General Land Reclamation Interests in Italy," *Monthly Labor Review,* 37:836–39 (October 1933); "Democracy: Its Essentials, Its Problems," *Scholastic,* 35:18S–20S (December 11, 1939).

¹²U.S. Congress, House of Representatives, Committee on Flood Control, "Bill to Authorize Funds for the Prosecution of Works for Flood Control and Protection against Flood Disasters," hearings, 74 Congress, 1 session, on H.R. 6803, Washington, March 22, 23, April 2, 1935, 1–38.

¹³*United States Statutes at Large,* 49:115; *New York Times,* April 6, 9, 1935; *Congressional Record,* 73 Congress, 2 session (1934), 10,311–12; 76 Congress, 3 session (1940), Index— Conservation projects bills.

¹⁴F.D.R. Papers, Group 13, PPF 191, February 14, 1933; editorial, "Jobs on Trees," clipping from *Illinois Republican News;* OF 177, September 25, 1934, Burton K. Wheeler to F.D.R., *New York Times,* October 17, 1934.

¹⁵*New York Times,* February 27, 1934; Ickes interview, March 1949, Washington; Harold Ickes, "A Department of Conservation Broadened," *Vital Speeches,* 3:693–95 (September 1, 1937), broadcast August 29, 1937.

¹⁶*New York Times,* December 17, 1934; *Congressional Record,* 73 Congress, 2 session (1934), 10,311–12.

¹⁷*Congressional Record,* 74 Congress, 2 session (1936), 3098; F.D.R. Papers, Group 13,

PPF 316, January 25, 1934, F.D.R. to W. Winston; PPF 191, September 7, 1935, F.D.R. to C. L. Pack; *Congressional Record*, 74 Congress, 2 session (1936), 1584–85.

[18]*The Public Papers and Addresses of Franklin D. Roosevelt: (1936) The People Approve* (New York, 1938), 301–5, summary of Great Plains Drought Area Committee's presidential report.

[19]H. H. Bennett, "Emergency and Permanent Control of Wind Erosion on the Great Plains," *Scientific Monthly*, 77:381–99 (November 1938).

[20]*House Document* 140, 75 Congress, 1 session, public works planning message from the president of the U.S., transmitting a proposed plan of a six-year program submitted by the National Resources Committee based on selection and priority, public works projects, February 3, 1937, V.

[21]*Congressional Record*, 74 Congress, 1 session (1935), 3350–53, 4770–71; 75 Congress, 1 session (1937), 166–69.

[22]U.S. Congress, House of Representatives, Committee on Flood Control, "To Provide for a Permanent System of Flood Control and Other Purposes," hearings, 1933–38, 74 Congress, 2 session, on H.R. 12517, Washington, May 21, 1936.

[23]F.D.R. Papers, Group 13, PPF 1-P, Box 210, April 8, 1938, press conference, Number 449A; PPF 993, September 5, 1940, F.D.R. to O. S. Warden, president, National Reclamation Association; OF 268, Box 8, February 8, 1937, F.D.R. to state governors; *Public Papers and Addresses; 1936* (New York, 1938), 167–70, Item 49, address at the dedication of the new Department of Interior Building, Washington, April 16, 1936.

[24]*The Public Papers and Addresses of F.D.R.; 1940* (New York, 1941), 36–37.

[25]*Congressional Record*, 76 Congress, 3 session (1940), Appendix 1501–02, 250–51.

[26]F.D.R. Papers, Group 13, PPF 97, November 13, 1934, F.D.R. to M. C. Roosevelt; *New York Times*, June 24, 1933.

[27]*Report of the Secretary of Agriculture, 1934* (Washington, 1934), 1–111.

[28]*Congressional Record*, 74 Congress, 1 session (1935), 96.

[29]U.S. Congress, House of Representatives, Committee on Irrigation and Reclamation, "To Provide for the Impounding, Conserving and Making Use of the Unappropriated Waters of the Eastern Slope of the Rocky Mountains and for Other Purposes," hearings, 74 Congress, 1 session, on H.R. 5533, Washington, June 12, 13, 1935, 1–47.

[30]*Congressional Record*, 75 Congress, 2 session (1937), 187–89, "Conservation Phases of Government's Power Program," article by Harold Ickes.

[31]National Archives, *Economic Effects of Federal Public Works Experience, 1933–1938* (Washington, 1939), mimeographed, not for public inspection, 1–150, records of National Resources Planning Board and its predecessor agencies, report of Subcommittee on Economic Public Lands to Public Works Committee of National Resources Planning Board.

[32]Ibid., *Evaluation and Long Time National Public Works Program for Wildlife Conservation* (Washington), mimeographed, 1–28, records of National Resources Planning Board.

[33]Ibid., *Forest Resources Conservation: National Significance and Objectives*, mimeographed, 1–75, records of National Resources Planning Board and its predecessor agencies.

[34]*Congressional Record*, 75 Congress, 1 session (1937), 1228.

[35]*Report of the Secretary of Agriculture, 1938* (Washington, 1938), 1–158; W. Wilcox, "Economic Aspects of Soil Conservation," *Journal of Political Economy*, 46:702–13 (October 1938); *United States Statutes at Large*, 49:1148; "Agriculture Conservation in 1938—Why?" (Washington, 1938), General Information Series issued October 1937, U.S. Department of Agriculture, A.A.A.; *Report of the Secretary of Agriculture, 1939* (Washington, 1939), 1–107.

[36]F.D.R. Papers, Group 13, PPF 1-P, March 15, 1933, press conference, Number 3; Box 202, August 11, 1933, press conference, Number 43; Box 204, November 28, 1934, press conference, Number 161; Presidential Secretarial File 1940, Interior Department,

Box 58, December 21, 1939, F.D.R. to Ickes; PPF 993, October 21, 1943, F.D.R. to O. S. Warden, president, National Reclamation Association; *Economic Effects of the Federal Public Works Experience 1933–1938* (Washington, December 20, 1939), mimeographed, 1–150, (confidential, not for public inspection); National Archives, *National Program of Public Works for Range Conservation* (Washington, January 1942), mimeographed, 1–105; *Evaluation of Public Works for Land Protection and Development* (Washington, January 1941), mimeographed; *Congressional Record*, 74 Congress, 1 session (1935), 94–97, 865–80; 75 Congress, 1 session (1937), 705–7; 80–81; *The Public Papers and Addresses of F.D.R.: (1935) The Court Disapproves* (New York, 1938), Item 10, "A Presidential Statement, January 29, 1935," 64–65.

³⁷*Public Papers and Addresses; 1933* (New York, 1938), 160–68, "What We Have Been Doing and What We Are Planning to Do," May 7, 1933; George W. Norris, *Fighting Liberal* (New York, 1945), 260–78.

³⁸*House Document 565*, 76 Congress, 3 session, recreation development of the Tennessee River System (Washington, 1940), 1–99; *Federal Power Commission Report on Review of Allocation of Costs at the Multiple Purpose Water Control System in the Tennessee River Basin* (Washington, 1949), 1–90; D. E. Lilienthal, *Democracy on the March* (New York, 1944), 1–191; C. J. Green, *Analysis of the Real Cost of T.V.A. Power* (Washington, 1948), 1–91, Chamber of Commerce, U.S. Natural Resources Department; *Annual Report of the T.V.A.* (Washington, 1948), 211; Stuart Chase and Marian Tyler, *Men At Work* (New York, 1945), 134–36; J. Ranameier, *Tennessee Valley Authority* (Vanderbilt University Press, Nashville, Tenn., 1942), 486; *T.V.A. Its Work and Accomplishments* (Washington, 1940), 1–64; A. Taylor, "Celebrate Decade of T.V.A. Benefits," *Christian Century*, 66:1429 (November 30, 1949); Bruce Bliven, "Human Welfare in the T.V.A.," *New Republic*, 113:340–42 (September 17, 1945); L. Larisch, "States and Decentralized Administration of Federal Functions," *Journal of Politics*, 12:3–12 (February 1950); J. Dombrowski, "Some Social Aspects of T.V.A.," *American Scholar*, 14(4):479–84, (October 1945); Ernest Kirschten, "T.V.A. the First 15 Years," *Nation*, 166:656–59 (June 12, 1948).

³⁹F.D.R. Papers, Group 13, PPF 5850, May 17, 1933, F.D.R. to the editor of *Knoxville* (Tennessee) *Journal; Public Papers and Addresses; 1933* (New York, 1938), 122–29.

⁴⁰Victor Weybright, "The Valleys and the Plains," *Survey Graphic*, 26:145–49 (March 1937); George C. Stoney, "A Valley to Hold To," *Survey Graphic*, 29:391–99 (July 1940); *Congressional Record*, 76 Congress, 3 session (1940), 11,524–25, address of the president at Chickamauga Dam.

⁴¹*Congressional Record*, 76 Congress, 3 session (1940), 11,525.

⁴²Ibid., 75 Congress, 1 session (1937), Appendix 475, speech delivered by Harold Ickes before the N.Y. Rod and Gun Editor's Association in Commodore Hotel, N.Y.C., February 23, 1937, broadcast by N.B.C.

⁴³*House Miscellaneous Documents*, 75 Congress, 2–3 session, 10,264, 1–4 House of Representatives Doc. No. 539, immediate study of the national forest problem; *Report of the Secretary of Agriculture, 1938* (Washington, 1938), 1–156; *Annual Report of the Chief of Forest Service* (Department of Agriculture, 1938); *Annual Report of the Chief of Forest Service, 1937;* Henry A. Wallace, "The War at Our Feet," *Survey Graphic*, 29:109–14 (February 1940); National Archives, *A National Program of Public Works for Range Conservation* (Washington, January 1942), 1–105.

⁴⁴*New York Times*, August 6, 1934, presidential address on parks, March 4, 1934; *Annual Report of the Secretary of Interior, 1935* (Washington, 1935), 1–439.

⁴⁵National Archives, *Report of the Departments of Agriculture and Interior* (January 1942), mimeographed, submitted to Land Committee of the National Resources Planning Board, 1–214.

⁴⁶*Public Papers and Addresses, 1940* (New York, 1941), 237–38, Item 52, "At This Time

When the World Is Threatened by Forces of Destruction, It Is My Resolve and Yours to Build Up Our Armed Defense," May 26, 1940; National Archives, *Evaluation and Long Time National Public Works Program for Wildlife Conservation*, (Washington), mimeographed, 1–28; *Forest Resource Conservation National Significance and Objectives* (Washington), 1–75.

[47]*Report of the Secretary of Agriculture, 1935* (Washington, 1935), 1–120; Owen P. White, "Land of the Pilgrim's Pride," *Colliers*, 96:12–13 (July 27, 1935); *New York Times*, March 31, 1935; F.D.R. Papers, Group 13, PPF 1-P, Box 206, October 25, 1935, press conference, Number 243.

[48]*New York Times*, March 24, 26, April 14, 1935.

[49]*United States Statutes at Large*, 48:200–10; H. H. Bennett, "Soil Erosion—A National Menace," *Scientific Monthly*, 39:385–404 (November 1934), H. H. Bennett, director of Soil Erosion Service, Department of Interior.

[50]F.D.R. Papers, Group 13, PPF 1-P, Box 297, January 10, 1936, press conference, Number 265; Box 206, October 25, 1935, press conference, Number 243; Box 207, January 24, 1936, press conference, Number 269.

[51]*Public Papers and Addresses, 1936* (New York, 1938), 66–67, 431–39, campaign address, Omaha, Nebraska, October 10, 1936; *Report of the Secretary of Agriculture, 1936* (Washington, 1936), 1–115; *United States Statutes at Large*, 48:22–23,58–72; *The Civilian Conservation Corps* (Washington, 1941), not paged; *Annual Reports of the Director of the C.C.C.; Monthly Labor Review*, 36:1039 (May 1936); *Public Papers and Addresses, 1933* (New York, 1938), 160–68; *New York Times*, July 25, 1933.

[52]*The Public Papers and Addresses of F.D.R.: (1934) The Advance and Recovery and Reform, 1934* (New York, 1938), 477–79, a typical Executive Order, Number 6910, on withdrawal of public lands, November 26, 1934.

[53]*Congressional Record*, 74 Congress, 2 session (1936), 1150–52.

[54]National Archives, *Evaluation of Long Time National Public Works Program for Wildlife Conservation*, mimeographed (Washington), 1–28, Division—Natural Resources Record.

[55]*United States Statutes at Large*, 49:1570; *Congressional Record*, 75 Congress, 1 session (1937), 173–74.

[56]*New York Times*, January 26, 1937.

[57]Morris Llewellyn Cooke, "Is the United States a Permanent Country?" *Forum*, 99:236–40 (April 1938); *Annual Report of the Secretary of Agriculture, 1936* (Washington, 1936), 1–115; *Report of the Department of Interior, 1939* (Washington, 1939), 1–430.

[58]National Archives, General Correspondence, secretary of agriculture, conservation folder, letter to Mr. E. R. Henson, coordinator, Southern Great Plains, Amarillo, Texas, from C. W. Collier, executive assistant, December 22, 1939.

[59]*Report of the Department of Interior, 1939* (Washington, 1939), 1.

[60]National Archives, *A National Program Public Works for Range Conservation* (January 1942), mimeographed, 1–105, prepared by representatives of the Departments of Interior and Agriculture, Natural Resources Division.

[61]Ibid., *A National Program of Public Work for Forest Conservation* (February 1942), mimeographed, 1–198, prepared by representatives of the Department of Agriculture and Interior, Natural Resources Division.

[62]*Report of the Department of Interior, 1939* (Washington, 1939), 1; National Archives, *A National Program Public Works for Range Conservation* (January 1942), mimeographed, 1–105, Natural Resources Division.

[63]*United States Statutes at Large*, 48:22–23.

[64]*The Civilian Conservation Corps* (Washington, 1941), not paged.

[65]Executive Order 6101, April 5, 1933, "Relief of Unemployment through the Performance of Useful Public Work," in Executive Orders 6071–6299, (Washington, 1933).

[66]*U.S. Government Manual* (Washington, 1948), 625.

[67]The purposes of the C.C.C. are stated in the *Annual Reports of the Director of the Civilian Conservation Corps*, government publications of leaflet and bulletin form; articles in periodicals as *Monthly Labor Review*, 36:1039 (May 1936), *Congressional Digest*, 16:2 (January 1937); Floyd Anderson, "Unemployment and the C.C.C.," *America* (March 16, 1935), reprinted in *Congressional Record*, 74 Congress, 1 session (1935), 3620.

[68]*United States Statutes at Large*, 48:200–10.

[69]Ibid., *Government and Agriculture: The Growth of Federal Farm Aid* (Washington, 1940), 100; *Annual Report of the Secretary of Interior, 1934* (Washington, 1934), 353.

[70]*United States Statutes at Large*, 48:58–72; *Public Papers and Addresses, 1933* (New York, 1938), 160–68, "What We Have Been doing and What We Are Planning to Do," May 7, 1933; Norris, *Fighting Liberal* (New York, 1945), 260–78.

[71]*United States Statutes at Large*, 48:401, 400.

[72]Ibid., 1269–75.

[73]Ibid., *Annual Report of the Secretary of the Interior, 1935* (Washington, 1935), 11–43.

[74]*United States Statutes at Large*, 49:991–1011.

[75]Ibid., 30–33.

[76]Ibid., 163.

[77]Ibid.

[78]Executive Order 7027, May 1, 1935.

[79]*United States Statutes at Large*, 49:1570–79.

[80]Ibid. 1570.

[81]Ibid., 1148–52; James Magee, Wallard Atkins, and Emanuel Stein, *The National Recovery Program* (New York, 1933), 32–53.

[82]*U.S. v. Butler et al., Receivers of Horace Mills Cor.;* 297 U.S. 1. Invalidation of the agricultural adjustment act of 1933 in the Supreme Court's *Horace Mills* decision handed down January 6, 1936, led to emphasis upon soil conservation as the core of the agricultural control program. The Agricultural Adjustment Act (A.A.A.) attempted to reestablish equality between agriculture and industry by raising the level of agricultural commodity prices and easing the credit and mortgage load. When this legislation was declared unconstitutional, the production control idea of the A.A.A. was tied to the broader objective of soil conservation through the Soil Conservation and Domestic Allotment Act.

[83]*United States Statutes at Large*, 49:1148–52.

[84]Ibid., Magee, et al., *National Recovery Program* (New York, 1933), 32–53.

[85]*Public Papers and Addresses; 1936* (New York, 1938), 135–39, Item 39, "The President Suggests Cooperation by Farmers on the Soil Conservation Program in Their Individual and National Interest"; *Congressional Record*, 74 Congress, 2 session (1936), 3098.

[86]*United States Statutes at Large*, 50:329, 429.

[87]Ibid., 517–18.

[88]Ibid., 869.

[89]Francis W. Laurent, *Tennessee Valley Authority* (March 15, 1938), 1–108 (legal authority).

[90]*United States Statutes at Large*, 52:1215.

[91]Ibid., 1248.

[92]Ibid., 53:1187; J. R. Mahoney, *National Resources Activity of the Federal Government* (Washington, 1950), 131.

[93]*United States Statutes at Large*, 53:1418; 54:1119.

ᗡ· 5 ᗡ
Conservation
Accomplishments

The conservation accomplishments during the Roosevelt administration far surpassed those of any previous presidential administration. The conservation work of Franklin D. Roosevelt's predecessors was continued, but there was, in addition, an extensive development of new projects and policies. Abundant funds were poured into erosion and flood control, dam construction, power development, reclamation, such social and economic experiments as the T.V.A., and the care of the forest, mineral, and wildlife resources. In these fields the Democratic administration of the 1930s paid attention to the importance of the individual in carrying out a conservational policy for natural resources. By education, by subsidy, by demonstration, by regulative law, the government emphasized the conservation responsibilities of the private citizen. At the same time, the United States citizens saw the application of planning and research in the adoption of conservation measures. This policy channelled the desire for long-range natural resource development in relation to long-term human needs. In all of this, emphasis was placed upon the cooperation of the government with the individual in promoting the ends of conservation.

The government also emphasized cooperation within its own administrative machinery in carrying out conservational activity. Earnest attempts were made to coordinate work of the various governmental departments and bureaus in every phase of the use of natural resources. The government recognized the significant interrelationship of the natural resources and the wisdom of practicing conservation procedures that would be of mutual benefit in obtaining conservation goals. For example, the scientific planting and cutting of trees would preserve forests, prevent soil erosion, and help control floods, protect wildlife, and increase recreational facilities. In a similar way, every aspect of the conservation of natural resources was integrated. Hence, to discuss forest or soil conservation per se during Roosevelt's presidency would present a misleadingly incomplete account. Conservation activity extended to every phase of the use of natural resources. All conservation projects incorporated various aspects of the conservation movement. However, for analysis and discussion it is necessary to break down the conservation accomplishments into six major sectors: forests, soil, water, minerals, wildlife, and recreational resources.

FOREST RESOURCES

The conservation of forest resources, which had been the primary concern of the original conservation movement, continued to enjoy priority in the 1930s, a policy justified by the vastness of the forests and their relation to other resources. A third of the United States land area, or 630 million acres, was forest land (as of 1940). This was half again as much as the total cropland. This tremendous forest acreage served at least five major purposes: timber production, watershed protection, recreation, support of wildlife, and forage production. Usually it could further two or more purposes simultaneously, and sometimes all five. Of the 630 million acres, for example, nearly three-fourths (462 million) could be cropped for commercial timber, nearly three-fourths had watershed value, more than half (342 million) was grazed by domestic livestock, practically all was suited for wildlife, and a very large percentage was used for recreation.[1]

The value of the forest land received recognition in 1933 by the initiation of the Emergency Conservation Work Organization (later known as the C.C.C.) and the allotment of more than $60 million to acquire land and improve the national forest. This grant of money and the labor of the C.C.C. made it possible to accomplish within a short term of months what, as matters had gone in the past, would not have been completed within many years. It produced a tremendous stimulus to the forestry activities of the Department of Agriculture.[2]

Expansion of Government Forest Holdings

A definite part of the New Deal forest plan was to expand the governmental forest holding. Until 1911, land had been only set aside from the public domain, but the Weeks Act in that year authorized direct purchase.[3] However, prior to 1933, federal acquisition of forest lands never exceeded 550,000 acres in any one year. The total area approved for purchase was 4,727,680 acres in the first 22 years of the program. In 1933, by the congressional authorization of accelerated activity, the area acquired in the three-year period ending June 30, 1936, exceeded 11.4 million acres. The national forest system in 1936 covered more than 170 million acres in 37 states and two territories.[4] The government continued to acquire land until by June 30, 1941, the national forests included 177,497,531 acres within 42 states and two territories.[5]

In conjunction with the plan for expansion of national forest acreage, the federal government sponsored the expansion of state forests by the passage of the Fulmer Act in 1935. This act extended federal aid to the states in purchasing land for state forestation.[6] As of June 30, 1937, 36 states had met the requirements of the Fulmer Act, which enabled the federal government to cooperate in promoting state forests.[7] By 1940 the states owned 19 million acres of forest land.[8]

Even though the government made substantial gains in ownership of forest lands, the major share of the acreage remained in private hands. The 630 million acres of forest land in 1940 were held as follows: 29 percent (185.5 million acres) by farmers, of the 70 percent (433.8 million acres) by private owners, and 30 percent (196.3 million acres) by public bodies. Most of the best commercial forest land was privately held.[9] To encourage such owners to practice conservation, Congress set up a program of cooperation involving the use of federal government research, better fire protection, and the establishment of Divisions of State and Private Forestry in the Federal Forest Service.[10]

Copeland Report on Forestry

The government expressed a progressive attitude and critical approach to the handling of the forests by reviewing the entire field of policy toward forest resources. On March 27, 1933, the Department of Agriculture submitted to the U.S. Senate a report of the Forest Service prepared in response to Senate Resolution 175 (72nd Congress, 1st session, 1932) introduced by Senator Royal S. Copeland of New York. Entitled "A National Plan for American Forestry" and popularly known as the Copeland Report, this recommended a dual solution of the nation's forest problem: a large extension of public ownership of forest lands, and more intensive management on all forest lands. The report was critical of private forestry practices and contemplated assumption by the private owner, with suitable help, of a substantial part of the national undertaking to obtain all of the benefits, economic and social, that the forests could render under a plan, wisely devised and rightly applied, for their best use.[11]

Comprehensive Forestry Policy

Public attention was again directed to the need of a comprehensive forestry policy by a message to Congress on March 14, 1938, in which the president recommended immediate study of the forest problem. A Joint Committee on Forestry was authorized by Congress to conduct such a study.[12] The Committee received directives with particular reference to:

(a) The adequacy and effectiveness of present activities in protecting public and private forest lands from fire, insects, and diseases, and of co-operative efforts between the Federal Government and the States.

(b) Other measures, Federal and State, which may be necessary and advisable to insure that timber cropping on privately owned forest lands may be conducted as continuous operations, with the productivity of the lands built up against future requirements.

(c) The need for extension of Federal, State, and community ownership of forest lands, and of planned public management of them.

(d) The need for such public regulatory control as will adequately protect private as well as the broad public interests in all forest lands.

(e) Methods and possibilities of employment in forestry work on private and public forest lands, and possibilities of liquidating such public expenditures as are or may be involved.

(f) The need for additional legislation, authorizations, appropriations, research, and other measures to insure adequate administration and development of the forest lands in Federal ownership.[13]

The Committee conducted hearings in all important forest sections of the nation and heard testimony by federal, state, and local officials and other interested parties. After a three-year study, the Joint Congressional Committee on Forestry, under the chairmanship of Senator John H. Bankhead of Alabama, issued a report on "Forest Lands of the United States," which cited deplorable conditions in the forest areas of many sections of the nation, and recommended "the establishment of a real forest economy in this country which . . . will put to constructive use one-third of our total land area." The report recommended various cooperative aids to private forest land owners, expansion of public ownership, and a federal–state system of regulation of forestry practices. These recommendations were not received without some controversy, and it remained for Congress to formulate new organic legislation that would satisfy the complex tangle of interests.[14]

SOIL

The depressed condition of agriculture plus serious erosion and the exhaustion of soil fertility caused the Roosevelt administration to view soil conservation as the single most urgent problem facing the United States conservation policy. It meant attacking the problem of production and price control through the A.A.A. and launching the first broadly conceived and widespread practical program ever undertaken in the United States for permanent protection of its land resources.[15]

Soil erosion was no new problem. Its evil had been manifest since the early settlement of the country. It was estimated that the erosion of the soil cost the United States about $3,844 million a year.[16] A survey of 1,907 million acres, which the Department of the Interior conducted in 1934 as a reconnaissance, indicated that only 578,167,670 acres were relatively unaffected by erosion. In an area of 857,386,922 acres, the sheet erosion ranged from slight damage to complete destruction. Wind erosion had affected a total area of 322,961,231 acres, principally in the middle-western states. Gully erosion had caused severe damage in approximately 337 million acres, with about 4 million acres so seriously cut up as to be unfit for practical cultivation.[17]

The Soil Erosion Service, 1933

The gravity of the erosion problem in the United States received attention in the early months of Roosevelt's administration. A Soil Erosion Service was established in October 1933, as an emergency agency in the Department of the Interior, to administer a grant of $5 million made by the Federal Emergency Administration of Public Works for erosion work. An additional $5 million was allocated for the same purpose at a later date and became available for expenditure in late March 1934.[18]

Soil Erosion Control

The Soil Erosion Service inaugurated a nationwide program of soil erosion control and at the same time helped to relieve unemployment by putting people to work on the conservation of the country's resources. A series of experimental and demonstration projects was developed. These projects were located within different major geographical and agricultural regions of the country where destructive erosion prevailed. Staffs of specialists manned the projects and adopted practical programs of erosion control. This was the first attempt in the history of the country to attack the erosion problem on a widespread scale.[19] As early as April 1934, 24 projects were established. Twenty of these were demonstration watershed projects and varied in size from 25,000 to 200,000 acres.

Larger projects were on federally controlled land. That on the Navajo Indian Reservation encompassed an area of 15 million acres, whereas one on the Gila River Watershed in Arizona and New Mexico covered an area of 8.2 million acres. In addition to these projects, there were two experimental and erosion-survey survey projects, one in New York and one in Pennsylvania.[20]

The Soil Conservation Service

The urgency of erosion control work was reemphasized by a giant dust storm sweeping eastward from the Great Plains to the Atlantic Ocean in 1934. This swirling cloud of dust and subsequent dramatic storm awakened large numbers of people to the dangers of erosion and lost soil wealth.[21] As a consequence, Congress declared in the Soil Conservation Act it adopted in 1935:

> ... That the wastage of soil and moisture resources on farm, grazing, and forest lands of the Nation, resulting from soil erosion, is a menace to the national welfare and that it is hereby declared to be the policy of Congress to provide permanently for the control and prevention of soil erosion. . . .[22]

By this act, soil erosion control became a permanent part of national policy. The temporary Soil Erosion Service was put on a permanent basis and was transferred to the Department of Agriculture as the Soil Conservation Service (S.C.S.), which was enlarged to include those erosion control functions already existing in the Department of Agriculture.[23]

This newly created service worked in cooperation with state experiment stations and other federal agencies in directing a national movement to protect and conserve the land from accelerated erosion. It developed practical and effective methods of erosion control through research and experience, and demonstrated the methods under varying conditions. The practical control measures were: the adaptation of thick-growing vegetation to practical farm operations; the use of engineering structures, such as terraces and dams; and the retirement of excessively eroded land from cultivation.[24]

By 1940 the S.C.S. had carried on work in more than 1,200 research, demonstration, land utilization, and watershed projects, S.C.S. nurseries, farm forestry projects, C.C.C. camps, water facilities areas, and soil conservation districts. These work areas were located in 47 states and Puerto Rico, and covered approximately 400 million acres.[25]

Individual Cooperation

In the various work areas, individual cooperation was stressed by the encouragement and preparation of farm conservation plans covering more than 29 million acres of land in private ownership or under lease to farmers and ranchers.[26] (See Appendix A, Table A-1.) Approximately 110,000 cooperators were represented in the service operations on these lands. (See Appendix A, Table A-2.) On an additional area of 21 million acres of public land, the Service had worked or was working under comprehensive conservation plans. At the same time, more than 10,000 conservation plans covering 2 million acres had been developed by Service technicians cooperating with other bureaus and agencies. These plans provided for erosion control treatment on S.C.S.-Extension Service demonstration farms, Farm Security Administration farms, drought relief farms, roadside erosion control projects, and state institutional farms.[27]

Examination of this work proved that its primary objective—better protection and use of land in order to promote the welfare of the people—had been accomplished. Where detailed plans were prepared for conservation operations, significant changes in land use had resulted. The plan was to convert more than 1.6 million acres, which was formerly cultivated to other uses, to acreage less conducive to erosion. This involved a reduction of approximately 15 percent in total acreage as previously cultivated. Permanent hay land was increased approximately 150 percent. Additional acreage was provided for pasture, range, and farm woods. Approximately 78,900 acres was especially treated to provide food and habitat for wildlife.[28] (See Appendix A, Table A-3, showing the land use changes on farms and ranches where conservation operation was adopted.)

In addition to actual results achieved on the land, there was a growing public appreciation of the soil conservation objective. Whereas there was no measurable public interest in the subject in the 1920s, there was general and enthusiastic support of the soil conservation principle by 1940.[29]

Production Control

The soil conservation program was not centered entirely within erosion control work. Wise land use, prevention of soil depletion, and individual cooperation in carrying out sound agricultural practices were all a part of the national land policy. The pronouncement of the unconstitutionality of the Agricultural Adjustment Act of 1933 in the Supreme Court's *Horace Mills* decision handed down in 1936 led to emphasis on soil conservation as the core of the agricultural control program. Production control was incorporated in the broader objective of conservation by the passage of the Soil Conservation and Domestic Allotment Act in 1936. This act permitted payments to individual farmers that were based primarily upon the substitution of soil-building for soil-depleting crops and the adoption of soil-conserving farm practices. The provisions were continued and strengthened in the Agricultural Adjustment Act of 1938.[30]

Soil Conservation Districts

Soil conservation on both an individual and group basis also received a boost by the formation of special local government units known as soil conservation districts, first organized in 1937. They were local public agencies established under state laws by a majority vote of land users in a given area, governed by a board of supervisors consisting primarily of locally elected farmers. As public bodies, the soil conservation districts enabled the federal and state governments to enter into cooperative agreements to provide technical help in surveying soil conservation problems and to work out methods for the better use of land. In the districts the S.C.S. did not cooperate with individual farmers as in the demonstration projects, but with locally organized groups of farmers who were working out conservation problems on their own initiative. The activity was a new farmer–government working alliance. By 1940 laws providing for the establishment of soil conservation districts had been enacted in 38 states. Under these laws 314 districts were organized that embraced a total area of 190 million acres.[31]

These statistics tell only part of the story. Figures do not reveal how thousands of farmers changed their thinking about the land. Figures cannot depict the growing philosophy that land should be husbanded as a continuously productive resource. A new cooperative attitude developed between the federal and state governments and the farmer. The joint responsibility of society and the individual landowner in the condition of the land became more clearly apparent.[32]

Shelterbelt

Perhaps one of the most novel and colorful of the soil conservation projects was the "shelterbelt." An executive order on July 11, 1934, allocated $15 million for the planting of a belt of trees, 100 miles in width, from Canada to Texas to break the force of the wind and to conserve moisture.[32] One hundred twenty-five miles of shelterbelt plantings had been established by 1935.[34] However, although many agriculturalists approved the wisdom of this plan and the shelterbelt idea caught the public imagination, political ridicule hampered and ultimately curbed the program by cutting appropriations. Nevertheless, by 1940 there were 13,684 linear miles of shelterbelt on 22,130 farms. Men from Russia and Arabia came to study it with a view to setting up similar projects in their countries. In contrast, it was a debatable project in the United States, that was later heralded as a success and publicly revived in the 1980s.[35]

Taylor Grazing Act, 1934

Another phase of soil conservation involving important action on public land arose from overgrazing on the western ranges. Until 1934 the unappropriated areas in the public domain were held as grazing common, without public control. The consequence was misuse and injury to the land. The Taylor Grazing Act of 1934 boldly attacked this abuse by authorizing the organization of grazing districts, withdrawing for this purpose 80 million acres from entry. This was increased to 142 million acres in 1936. The Department of the Interior was given authority to control grazing practices in such districts, which were to be used to protect the land and improve it as a range. By 1939 the 50 grazing districts established included practically the whole area authorized by the act. The Pierce Act of 1938 authorized the government to leave state, county, corporation, and private lands in grazing districts so as to give these areas the protection provided under the Grazing Act. By 1941 the grazing districts embraced nearly 260 million acres of federal and non-federal land.[36]

Livestock owners were permitted to use the grazing lands upon application and upon renewal of licenses and permits, designed to limit grazing to what the natural forage could support without injury to the range. At the same time, the government carried on projects of fire control, reseeding, water control, and range surveys, a conservation effort that enlisted active cooperation by stockers.[37]

WATER

Water control was vital to the whole soil conservation activity. Optimum distribution of the limited water supply in the arid and semiarid areas of the West was essential to the proper use of the land. Heavy rainfall on deforested areas in eastern regions also produced soil erosion and floods. Hence, there was a general, necessary relation between land and water conservation.

The husbandry of water included the promotion of navigation, protection against floods, development of power, checking of soil erosion, abatement of pollution, recreational development, irrigation, and the protection of fish and wildlife. The American people have been concerned with one or another phase of water conservation since our national history began. It remained, however, for the Democratic administration of the 1930s to adopt a unified water policy that took into account the interrelated purposes of water control. The principle was that the federal government had a responsibility for these major assets, but could effectively conserve them only by vigorous local co-operation.[38]

Flood Control

The extension of the principle of federal support for flood control was embodied in the comprehensive Flood Control Act of 1936. Local authorities were still to provide the land and rights-of-way, but the bulk of the financial burden was now placed on the federal treasury. Congress authorized construction of 270 flood control projects located in 31 states.[39] Thus, flood protection became a matter predominantly of national concern and an important part of the large-scale federal public works program. Congress annually appropriated large sums for flood control, reaching in 1940 a peak of $172.8 million. The appropriations for flood control show a fluctuating but generally upward trend after the adoption of the Flood Control Act of 1936:[40]

1936	$ 38,811,730
1937	27,924,487
1938	86,123,330
1939	120,110,008
1940	172,800,000

The increased national awareness of a great need to control the destructive floods was reflected in the flood legislation passed by Congress. More progress was made during the administration of Franklin D. Roosevelt in flood control than in all the preceding presidential administrations.[41]

Technical progress in flood protection demonstrated that the best control usually resulted from dams and reservoirs on the tributaries of major streams. Adding these devices to the older ones of levees, flood walls, and floodways made it possible to promote other objectives of water conservation jointly with flood control. One of these was the development of power. Harnessing the rivers meant construction of such enormous national projects as the Hoover, Grand Coulee, and Bonneville dams. These also helped to control floods and reclaim land. The Flood Control Act of 1938 assigned to the Federal Power Commission certain duties in determining what facilities should be installed for future power development in dams and reservoirs to be constructed primarily for flood control. Thus the dam projects created in the 1930s served a multiple purpose.[42]

Hoover Dam (Boulder Dam)

The Boulder Canyon or Hoover Dam was authorized in 1928, and work was begun on it in 1930. With its completion in 1936, humans had succeeded at last in controlling the Colorado River. The Hoover Dam existed as a versatile multiple-purpose giant with achievements in hydropower production, irrigation, flood control, city water, recreation, and wildlife preservation. It supplied the principal source of energy that enabled Los Angeles to increase its population by a million people and build more than 1,800 new industrial plants. Practically a half-million arid acres in southern California and Arizona depended on the dam for irrigation water. Its hydroelectric power and irrigation waters permitted the founding of a highly developed economy that created a market for products of farms, mines, and factories of the entire nation. At the same time, it stood as a bulwark against the great mainstream floods that once ravaged the lower reaches of the Colorado River.[43]

Bonneville Dam

The purposes of the Bonneville Dam were to improve navigation and to generate hydroelectric power. Begun in September 1933, it was largely complete in 1937. In August of that year, an act of Congress created a provisional agency set up for the transmission and sale of Columbia River hydroelectric power. By 1941 the Bonneville Administration had furnished enough power to assume a major stature as a utility enterprise and a regional institution.[44]

Grand Coulee Dam

Underway also in the 1930s was the great Columbia Basin project, the Grand Coulee Dam. Construction began in 1934 under the W.P.A. Its purposes were to irrigate 1.2 million acres of land, generate hydroelectric power, and provide for river regulation and improved navigation. The principal features were the construction of the dam proper, the creation of Lake Roosevelt (a 151-mile storage reservoir behind the dam), the building of a powerhouse on each side of the central spillway at the dam, and the erection of the world's largest hydroelectric generating units. Such an enterprise was indeed spectacular in its conception and in the scope of its achievement. In the Northwest it opened vast frontiers for development.[45]

Irrigation

An important phase of water conservation is irrigation. In the 17 states lying wholly or partially to the west of the 100th meridian, successful farming was virtually impossible, except in limited areas, without an artificial water supply to supplement the scanty rainfall. Even grazing often required supplemental water for stock subsistence. The need of large-scale irrigation was not new in 1933. A Reclamation Service established by act of Congress on June 17, 1902, became the Bureau of Reclamation, which had as its responsibility water resource development in the West. The bureau's work was continued and expanded under the Roosevelt administration. Reclamation's primary purpose was irrigation. In 1934 there were 32 federal reclamation projects in 14 western states, and five Indian reclamation projects. By 1941 work was in progress on 37 projects in 14 states. There were 73 reservoirs in operation containing 13,000 billion gallons of water. With the expansion of its irrigation and power activities, the Bureau of Reclamation was serving more than 4.7 million people in 1941. The year before it was able to serve irrigation water to 4,168,168 acres, which was the largest area since its operation began. Government operations varied in size from small garden patches in Indian reservations to the spectacular Boulder, Grand Coulee, and Central Valley projects. For example, the Central Valley project in California was to benefit 2 million acres of rich highly cultivated land in addition to providing protection from floods, repulsing salt water intrusion from San Francisco Bay, and generating hydroelectric power.[46]

Planning: The Tennessee Valley Authority

With the intervention of government in different areas of water conservation, there developed a growing recognition of the close interrelation of water problems and of the subsequent need of coordinated planning. The various federal agencies concerned with the control and use of water worked through the Water Resources Committee of the National Resources Committee. The Committee, at the request of President Roosevelt, studied the drainage basin problems and programs, which brought into focus an integrated pattern of water development. Subsequent studies and reports encouraged the development of a national water policy.[47]

An example of coordinated planning and the adoption of an integrated water program is the T.V.A. authorized May 18, 1933.[48] It was created to promote flood control, navigation, electric power production, proper use of land and forest, and the "economic and social well-being of the people." The T.V.A. encompassed territory that made it necessary to work cooperatively with seven state governments and scores of local areas. It meant the use of regional planning on a large scale.[49] The work of the T.V.A. was carried on by a planning council of six divisions representing agriculture, forestry, industry, engineering, land use, and social and economic aspects. Each maintained demonstration units. These units became the chief means of individual persuasion. The essence of the T.V.A.'s program affecting the people's daily life was voluntary. While still building dams, power plants, and locks, the T.V.A. began retirement of submarginal lands, soil conservation, the introduction of better farm machinery, public health, and education. In all of this work, the natives of the area were gradually converted to the T.V.A. program and sold its ideas not only to each other but the nation. They became ardent converts in spreading the gospel of the T.V.A.[50]

The T.V.A proved to be a successful venture in public ownership. It raised the economic and social level of a region of the United States and operated at a profit as a business venture in the selling of power. Another important effect was its regulating impact upon the conduct and policies of privately owned utilities in other parts of the nation. The very fact that the T.V.A. could invite comparisons in rates and operation and might be imitated in other parts of the country caused the privately owned companies to pursue rate and service policies calculated to dispel dissatisfaction with private ownership. Indeed, the T.V.A. served the dual role of benefactor and disciplinarian.[51]

MINERALS

The American people use more energy per capita than any other people, and scientists predict that their demand for energy will continue to increase. The energy to service industry, homes, and national defense comes mainly from coal, oil, gas, and water power. The last was a resource actively guarded and developed under the Roosevelt administration. The others, however, also came under the sage policy of conservation, the chief agencies concerned being the Geological Survey, the Bureau of Mines, the Petroleum Conservation Division, and the Bituminous Coal Division.[52]

Geological Survey

The Geological Survey, as an old agency, established in 1879, continued its field, laboratory, and office work with increased emphasis on the wise husbandry of these natural resources, a service that it could do well by reason of the accurate scientific information it had gathered. An example is the examination and classification of lands for mineral deposits, water, and power—information indispensible for any sensible use. During 1941 the Geological Survey made more than 8,100 reports on mineral resources, water power, and storage possibilities of public lands, at the same time safeguarding the governments's ownership of great reserves of coal, oil, gas, potash, phosphate, and other minerals.[53]

Bureau of Mines

The responsibility of the Bureau of Mines was to conduct inquiries and scientific and technologic investigations with a view to conserving resources. In 1940 there were 14 experiment stations and many field offices throughout the mining centers of the United States where such inquiries were conducted. The Bureau of Mines also proved an invaluable aid to the oil industry by giving technical assistance designed to prolong the producing life of wells through the application of better engineering practices.[54]

Oil and Gas Resources

The federal government promoted the conservation of mineral resources on public as well as private lands. National policy had permitted uncontrolled exploitation of mineral resources of public lands by private interests. To correct the adverse effects, the act of August 21, 1935, inaugurated a leasing policy for oil and gas that materially reduced speculative operations based on the public reserves. It also provided for a more businesslike development of oil and gas resources on public lands.[55] In order to promote a wise use of oil reserves, the government established the Petroleum Conservation Division in 1936. This sought to secure cooperation with the states in the conservation of oil and to help secure the passage of uniform state oil conservation laws. The agency also had enforcement responsibilities under the Connally Hot Oil Act of February 22, 1935, which was designed to assist state conservation efforts by prohibiting the shipment in interstate and foreign commerce of oil produced in violation of state laws. The success of the Connally Act was proved by Congress' extension of its legislative authority on two different occasions.

Bituminous Coal Division

The Bituminous Coal Division was established in 1939 to administer the Bituminous Coal Act of 1937, which Congress passed to stabilize the bituminous coal industry and thereby conserve coal. This was achieved by helping to eliminate conditions that bred unfair competition, compelling mines to produce only the more cheaply mined coal and waste the rest. The act steadied the bituminous coal markets by establishing minimum price and marketing rules and regulations.[56]

WILDLIFE

In addition to the more material lines of action, the president's interest in the more personal welfare of the United States citizens was manifest in the government's wildlife and recreation projects. An adequate program for conserving the various species of wildlife provides a suitable environment for the growth and propagation of each species. Although such growth would proceed most rapidly under conditions of complete protection, it was impractical for the federal government to acquire and administer sufficient areas to produce optimum wildlife populations throughout the country. A more rational plan consisted in focusing special attention upon areas set aside exclusively for wildlife use, where nucleus stocks of all species would be preserved as a source for restocking the surrounding territories. A basic requirement was a system of protected refuges, located and developed on a scale sufficient to maintain wildlife. The federal government sought such a goal, and in 1941 there were 267 national wildlife refuges under the jurisdiction of the Fish and Wildlife Service. The refuges are classified in Table 5-1.

TABLE 5-1. Wildlife refuges under jurisdiction of the Fish and Wildlife Service

	No.	*Acres*
For migratory waterfowl	178	3,554,356
For other migratory birds, small upland game, fur animals, and other wildlife	25	3,436,131
For colonial nongame birds	50	107,679
For big game	14	6,642,1338
Total	267	13,740,304

Source: Note 57.

The work of improving the refuges to make them as attractive as possible to the wildlife was done through the use of C.C.C., W.P.A., and National Youth Administration labor.[58]

To make the federal wildlife projects most effective, the program was supplemented by similar programs undertaken by the states and by the adoption of improved land utilization and wildlife conservation practices by individual owners. The provisions of the Pittman-Robertson Federal Aid to Wildlife Restoration Act authorized the secretary of the interior to cooperate with the states, through their respective game and fish departments, in wildlife restoration projects to include the selection, restoration, rehabilitation, and improvement of areas of land and water adaptable as feeding, resting, or breeding places for wildlife. By 1941 all states with the exception of Georgia and Nevada had enacted assent legislation taking advantage of the benefits offered by the Pittman-Robertson Act.[59] The bulk of the population of valuable wildlife, however, was still produced in agricultural lands through the use of practices that did not interfere with normal crop production. In this phase of conservation of wildlife resources, the Fish and Wildlife Service Survey assisted state and federal agencies and cooperated with individual landowners in the development of wildlife conservation plans and projects.

RECREATION

Conservation of natural resources was not directed entirely toward dollar-and-cents saving or practical and wise use of existing materials for economic reasons. True, the wildlife conservation program did have economic objectives, but it also aimed to provide recreation and human pleasure. The Roosevelt administration realized the hunting, fishing, and camping value of the nation's natural resources. The American people's growing awareness of the need for recreation gave a substantial boost to the federal government's support of recreational projects. The government adopted a campaign in 1934 to make it an outstanding park year. Appeals were made to citizens to visit their national parks. Transportation systems, oil companies, chambers of commerce, and civic organizations aided in distributing printed propaganda. The press supported the movement universally, and radio companies were exceedingly generous in donating free time for national park broadcasts. As a result, travel to the scenic national parks during the period from October 1, 1933, to June 30, 1934, increased 38 percent over the same period the previous year. This campaign to use the national parks became increasingly effective until over 21 million persons used the parks in the travel year ending October 1, 1941.[61]

The National Park Service

The National Park Service was charged with reserving, or acquiring and caring for, land for the preservation of natural scenery, natural formations of scientific value, and monuments of historic interest. In this work the Service was able to use the money and labor of the emergency activities of the federal government.[62] National legislation enabled the service to enlarge its national park area, and in 1937 the area embraced

17,086,671.31 acres. This was increased to 21,609,289.63 acres by 1941. The acreage was divided into 164 separate units administered by the National Park Service.[63]

Lands acquired by the Park Service for inclusion in the national park system varied from rugged mountain tops to level valleys. In many instances, such as in the Florida Everglades park project and the Hatteras seashore in North Carolina, previous use of the areas had been for purposes so unsuited to their character that ultimately their usefulness, even as parks, would have been destroyed. Lands acquired by the Service were restored to their original condition.[64]

The National Park Service cooperated with other governmental agencies in carrying on recreational projects. It supplied information, scientific research, and interpretive service in developing projects of recreation. The Service worked with state and county park authorities through the C.C.C. camps. All effort was directed toward preserving a vast American playground for the use and enjoyment of the nation's citizens.[65]

All the conservation work of the federal government had as its goal the wise use of the nation's natural resources in terms of present and future human use. The following tables attest that insofar as expenditure measures such an attempt to develop and promote a nationwide conservation, the government's policy is vindicated. See Appendix B for the following tables: Table B-1: summary of expenditures of federal public works classified by function and years 1933–41; Table B-2: water use and control; Table B-3: public land development; Table B-4: summary of expenditures for federal grants for public construction classified by function and years 1933–40; Table B-5: water use and control; Table B-6: public land development; and Table B-7: summary of federal expenditure, corporation outlays, grants, loans, and guarantees for new construction classified by function and years 1933–40.

Monetary figures give added proof of the Roosevelt administration's record of conservation accomplishments. This chapter has already shown, however, that examination of any one of the major sectors of conservation work gives resounding evidence of the great strides made in the conservation of natural resources in the decade of the 1930s. The record is such that it would be extremely difficult to rate advances in one field of conservation above another. The approach to conservation of the Roosevelt administration was a comprehensive one. Far more important than any proof that might be presented as to a greater emphasis on, say, soil conservation than water conservation, or vice versa, is the fact that there are no notable examples of resources or regions overlooked in the overall scheme. More important, too, is the fact that the Roosevelt administration offered a more spectacular record of advance than any previous administration in every field of conservation discussed, namely, forests, soil, water, minerals, wildlife, and recreation.

During the 1930s many conservation activities acquired a new meaning in the minds of the American people. Even if soil erosion control, water conservation, the preservation of wildlife, and the other fields of conservation mentioned cannot be claimed to be inventions of the Roosevelt administration, these activities did, for the first time, become a part of the everyday thought and action of a greatly increased proportion of citizens. The magnitude of the work was new and in itself inspiring. What is also certain is that many new concepts were introduced in the planning for the wise use of natural resources: the planned development of a whole river basin; a multipurpose approach to the conservation of water; large-scale government supervision and, indeed, competition in the field of public utilities; national planning for the coordinated use of natural resources and the coordinated action of diverse governmental agencies in conservation work; and finally the concept of development by the people for the people through decentralized planning. All of these were largely new ideas.

Conservation projects were related to many different resources. They also stemmed from a great variety of needs, interests, and pressures. Likewise, the facilities used to conduct the project work varied from local to federal government participation, individual to governmental labor, relief, and emergency funds to permanent funds. Projects that might be claimed to relate to specific resources were, in fact, intertwined. This cannot be overemphasized. While it has proved practicable for purposes of exposition in this chapter to classify conservation work into major sectors on the basis of resources, no part of the federal conservation policy was an entity in itself. It must be viewed as a whole to be viewed properly.

Having placed the overall policy of conservation in its correct perspective, it remains to examine how single projects and single agencies operated in day-to-day work. Such factual data are essential background material for a real appraisal of the overall policy. However, complete coverage is an immense task and, carried to its logical conclusion, obviously outside the scope of this book. It will be possible only to present a detailed account of the work of one agency. Perhaps no better example exists than that of the C.C.C.

NOTES

[1]*Farmers In a Changing World,* Agriculture Year Book (Washington, 1940), Annual Reports of Forest Service 1933–40, pamphlets relating to National Forests; National Ar-

chives, "A National Program of Public Works for Forest Conservation" (Washington, February 1942), mimeographed, 1–198.

²*Annual Report of the Secretary of Agriculture, 1933* (Washington, 1933), 80–81; *New York Times,* March 12, 1933.

³*Public Land* (Washington, 1940), 14, National Resources Board publication. The federal government had sponsored the setting aside of forest reservations from public lands by the passage of legislation on March 3, 1891, and June 4, 1897. Under these basic authorizations, approximately 135 million acres was set aside from the public domain. However, the realization grew that forest conservation objectives could not be accomplished solely through reserving parts of the public domain. Subsequently, the Weeks Act of 1911 permitted the purchase of land in water sheds of navigable streams and the Clark-McNary Act of 1924 authorized further purchases.

⁴*Annual Report of the Secretary of Agriculture, 1936* (Washington, 1936), 1–115.

⁵"Forests and People," *Report of the Chief of the Forest Service* (Washington, 1941), 27.

⁶"Highlights in the History of Forest Conservation" (Washington, January 1948), 13, mimeographed, Forest Service. Hearings were held discussing the proposed Fulmer Act and its objectives—"Program of Forest Land Management"; U.S. Congress, House of Representatives, *Hearings before a subcommittee on Commission on Agriculture,* 74 Congress, 1 session, on H.R. 6914, April 12, 1935 (Washington, 1935), 1–39; House Reports on Public Bill II 528–1058, 74th Congress, 1 session, Report No. 830, "Progress of Forest Land Management," May 6, 1935.

⁷*Report of the Secretary of Agriculture, 1937* (Washington, 1937), 4.

⁸*Report of the Chief of Forest Service* (Washington, 1940), 20.

⁹*Farmers in a Changing World,* Agriculture Year Book (Washington, 1940), 38; *Report of the Chief of Forest Service* (Washington, 1940), 20.

¹⁰*Annual Report of the Secretary of Agriculture, 1937* (Washington, 1937), 7. The Norris-Doxey, or Cooperative Farm Forestry Act (50 stat, 188), was passed on May 18, 1937. It provided for increased technical aid for farm owners in the sound management of their woodlands; "Forests to Farmers," *Land Policy Review,* 1:8–11 (1938–40).

¹¹"Highlights in the History of Forest Conservation" (Washington, 1948), 12, mimeographed; *Annual Report of the Secretary of Agriculture, 1933* (Washington, 1933), 83.

¹²*House Miscellaneous Documents,* 75 Congress, 2–3 session, 10, 264, 1–4, House of Representatives, Document No. 539; "Highlights in the History of Forest Conservation" (Washington, 1948), 14.

¹³U.S. Congress, Joint Committee on Forestry, hearings on forest lands of the United States, 75 Congress, 3 session (1939), Part 1, 4.

¹⁴"Highlights in the History of Forest Conservation" (Washington, 1948), 1–21.

¹⁵*Annual Reports of the Department of Agriculture and Interior, 1933–41; Soils and Men,* Agriculture Year Book (Washington, 1938); *Report of the Chief of the Soil Conservation Service* (Washington, 1940), 1–30; see citations of periodical and National Archives material in following footnotes.

¹⁶*Annual Report of the Secretary of the Interior Department, 1934* (Washington, 1934), 353–55; *Report of the Chief of Soil Conservation Service* (Washington, 1940), 1.

¹⁷*Annual Report of the Secretary of Agriculture, 1935* (Washington, 1935), 63.

¹⁸*Annual Report of the Secretary of the Interior, 1934* (Washington, 1934), 353; *National Resources Board, 1934* (Washington, 1934), 15–17; U.S. Congress, House of Representatives, Committee on Public Lands, 74 Congress, "Soil Erosion Program," *Miscellaneous Senate and House hearings, Hearing before a subcommittee of the Committee on the Public Lands,* 74 Congress, 1 session, on H.R. 7054, reported March 20, 21, 22, 25, 1935, 1–106; U.S. Congress, Senate, Committee on Agriculture and Forestry, 74 Congress, "Protection of Land Resources against Soil Erosion," *Miscellaneous Senate Hearings, 1935–1936, Hearings*

before a subcommittee of the Committee on Agriculture and Forestry, 74 Congress, 1 session, on S. 2149, S. 2418, and H.R. 7054 bills to provide for the protection of land resources against soil erosion, April 2, 3, 1935, 1–78.

[19]*Annual Report of the Secretary of Interior, 1934* (Washington, 1934), 353–60; *Chief of Soil Conservation Service* (Washington, 1940), 4.

[20]*Annual Report of the Secretary of Interior, 1934* (Washington, 1934), 357–59.

[21]*Report of Chief of Soil Conservation Service* (Washington, 1940), 4–5; H. H. Bennett, "Soil Erosion—A National Menace," *The Scientific Monthly,* 39:385–404 (November 1934); *New York Times,* March 22, 23, 1935.

[22]*Report of Chief of Soil Conservation Service* (Washington, 1940), 5.

[23]Ibid.; *Annual Report of the Secretary of Agriculture, 1936* (Washington, 1936), 1–115; *Progress,* Agriculture Year Book (Washington, 1938), 26–29.

[24]*Annual Report of the Secretary of Agriculture, 1935* (Washington, 1935), 1–120; *Report of Secretary of Agriculture, 1936* (Washington, 1936), 1–115; National Archives, *Soil Conservation—General Files, 1933–1935* (Box S-CS.100-100.9), Department of Agriculture.

[25]*Report of the Chief of the Soil Conservation Service, 1940* (Washington, 1940), 1–30.

[26]Ibid., 9.

[27]Ibid.

[28]Ibid., 9–13.

[29]Ibid., 13; National Archives, Records of Soil Conservation Service, 1933–43.

[30]*Annual Report of the Secretary of Agriculture, 1937* (Washington, 1937), 31–33; *Annual Report of the Secretary of Agriculture, 1938* (Washington, 1938), 1–156; National Archives, correspondence of commissioner of agriculture and secretary of agriculture, 1933–34.

[31]*Annual Report of Secretary of Agriculture, 1936* (Washington, 1936), 21; *Annual Report of Secretary of Agriculture, 1939* (Washington, 1939), 50; *Farmers in a Changing World,* Agriculture Year Book, 1940, 432–43; *Report of the Soil Conservation Service, 1940* (Washington, 1938), 29; *Progress,* National Resources Board (Washington, 1938), 28.

[32]*Report of the Chief of the Soil Conservation Service, 1941* (Washington, 1941), 9, 37–40; *Report of the Chief of the Soil Conservation Service, 1940* (Washington, 1941), 29–30; *Farmers in a Changing World* (Washington, 1940), 421–45; *National Resources Committee Progress Report, 1938* (Washington, 1938), 28–30. A part of this philosophy was expressed in the authority of the Resettlement Service of the federal government. The Service acquired poor farm land and promoted its development for other uses. It also aided farm people in some areas to find better locations; *Annual Report of the Secretary of Agriculture, 1936* (Washington, 1936), 1–115; Charles W. Collier, "At Last a Soil Erosion Program," *New Republic,* 83:68–70 (May 29, 1935); John E. Lodge, "New Federal Service to End Destruction of Our Farms," *Popular Service Monthly,* 124:38–39 (January 1934); "Work of the S.C.S.," *Fortune,* 22:68–69 (July 1940); W. Wilcox, "Economic Aspects of Soil Conservation," *Journal of Political Economy,* 46:702–13 (October 1938); L. C. Gray, "Our Land Policy Today," *Land Policy Review,* 1:3–8 (May–June 1938); *Save Your Soil,* pamphlet of the S.C.S.

[33]Executive Order, Official Files 1-C (Hyde Park), July 17, 1934; Executive Order 6793, July 11, 1934, "Allocating Funds from the Appropriation to Meet the Emergency and Necessity for Relief in Stricken Areas"; F. A. Silcox, *Report of the Forester* (Washington, 1934), 5–6.

[34]Silcox, *Report of the Forester, 1935;* "President approves Plan for National Reforestation," *Literary Digest,* 118:39 (July 28, 1934); "The Establishment of a Forest Shelter Belt," *Science,* 80:91 (July 27, 1934); "Planting a Shelter Belt Through Middle America," *Literary Digest,* 118:15 (August 11, 1934).

[35]National Archives, "A National Program of Public Works for Forest Conservation" (Washington, February 1942), mimeographed, 1–214, prepared by representatives of Department of Agriculture and Interior for Land Commission of National Resource Planning

Board; "Highlights in History of Forest Conservation," (Washington, January 1948); *Congressional Record*, 74 Congress, 2 session (1936), 2941; 77 Congress (1941), Appendix A1351–52; Zen Raphael, "Shelterbelt—Futile Dream for Workable Plan," *Science*, 81:391–94 (April 26, 1935); Jonathan Mitchell, "Shelter Belt Politics," *New Republic* 80:69–71 (August 29, 1934); National Archives, *Shelterbelt Project*, mimeographed; Wilmon H. Droze, "The New Deal's Shelterbelt Project, 1934–1942," *Essays on the New Deal*, edited by Harold M. Hollingsworth and William F. Holmes (Austin: University of Texas Press, 1969), 24–48; Thomas R. Wessel, "Roosevelt and the Great Plains Shelterbelt," *Great Plains Journal*, 8:57–74 (Spring 1969); Edgar B. Nixon, ed., *Franklin D. Roosevelt and Conservation, 1911–1945*, Vol. I, Franklin D. Roosevelt Library, Hyde Park, New York (U.S. Government Printing Office, Washington, 1957), Item 291.

[36]*Annual Report of the Secretary of the Interior, 1935* (Washington, 1935), 11; 1937, 1; 1939; 1941, 247–61.

[37]*Annual Report of the Secretary of the Interior, 1937* (Washington, 1937), 1; 1941, 247–61; National Archives, "A National Program of Public Works for Range Conservation" (January 1943), mimeographed, 1–105.

[38]National Archives, correspondence on flood control, 11 boxes, Group 551; Flood control clippings, Box 551, 431–552.4; National water policy, 578 (January 1940); Abel Wolman, "Highlights of the National Water Resources Study," mimeographed; "Water Committee Minutes" (January 1940), 106–31; "Water Resources Committee—Committee on National Water Policy" (October 25, 1939), mimeographed, 1–4.

[39]*Annual Report of the Secretary of Agriculture, 1937* (Washington, 1937), 32; *U.S. Statutes at Large*, 688:1570; *Congressional Record*, 75 Congress, 1 session (1937), 547–52; 76 Congress, 3 session (1940), Appendix 1450–52.

[40]*Congressional Record*, 76 Congress, 3 session (1940), Appendix 2857, "Harness Our Rivers Is to Store Up Prosperity for All Time to Come," J. B. Snyder of Pennsylvania, Representative, address before National Rivers and Harbors Congress.

[41]Ibid., Appendix 1450–52; *Conservation Program of the U.S. Government* (Washington, July 1939), 1–22, mimeographed; U.S. Information Service, "Flood Control in the Mississippi Valley"; *Miscellaneous House Hearings 1935–36*, flood control in the Mississippi Valley, *Hearings before the Committee on Flood Control*, House of Representatives, 74 Congress, 1 session, on a plan to modify and extend the project for flood control and improvement of the Mississippi River authorized by the Flood Control Act of 1928," April 1–13, 1935, 1–832.

[42]"Federal Government and Water Power," *Congressional Digest*, 14:227–29 (October 1936); *Congressional Record*, "Conservation Phases of Government's Power Program," 75 Congress, 2 session (1937), 188–89; National Archives, excerpts from "Conservation Progress of the U.S. Government" (Washington, May 1939), Box 631–636, Folder 635.1; "The New Deal Program for Electric Utilities," *Congressional Digest*, 15:230–31 (October 1936); *Public Papers and Addresses, 1933* (New York, 1938), 325–28; Executive Order 6521, August 19, 1933.

[43]"Hoover Dam," U.S. Department of Interior Bureau of Reclamation folder; A. R. Roberts, "Certain Aspects of Power Irrigation and Flood Control Projects," *Water Resources Project*, prepared for the Commission on Organization of the Executive Branch of Government (Washington, January 1949), 1–62; *Reclamation Era*, 25:193–94 (October 1935) (Washington, 1941).

[44]*Annual Report of the Secretary of the Interior, 1941* (Washington, 1941), 50–76; 1938, 84; *Annual Reports of the Bonneville Power Administration, 1938, 1939, 1940*.

[45]"Soil and Water Conservation in the Pacific Northwest," *Farmers Bulletin*, 1773:1–59 (1937); "The New Deal Program for Electric Utilities," *Congressional Digest*, 15:230–31 (October 1936); *Annual Report of the Secretary of Interior, 1941*, 20–22 (Washington, 1941);

"The Columbia Basin Project," *Department of the Interior* (Washington, 1949), folder; Roberts, "Aspects of Power Irrigation and Flood Control," *Water Resources Projects,* prepared for the Commission on Organization of the Executive Branch of Government (Washington, 1944), 3–5; Harold Ickes, "Balancing Our Resources Budget," *The Reclamation Era,* 27:257 (November 1937).

[46]"The Resources Use Board," Department of Interior (Washington, 1940), 2–3; *Report of the Secretary of the Interior, 1941* (Washington, 1941), 1–49; *1849 A Century of Conservation 1949,* facts and background about the Reclamation Program, Department of the Interior, mimeographed; "Central Valley Project Approval," *The Reclamation Era,* 25:201 (October 1935); John C. Page, "The Challenge of the Drought," *The Reclamation Era,* 27:253–55 (November 1937); Harold Ickes, "Balancing Our Resources Budget," *The Reclamation Era,* 27:257 (November 1937).

[47]*National Resources Committee Progress Reports, 1939* (Washington, 1939), 12; *National Resources Committee Progress Reports, 1938* (Washington, 1938), 29–31; "Drainage," *National Resources Board* (Washington, 1938), 2–52; *Drainage Basin Problems and Programs, 1937* (Washington, 1938), 9; John C. Page, commissioner of Reclamation, "Water Construction and Control," *The Reclamation Era,* 27:46–47 (March 1937); Morris L. Cooke, "Upstream," *Survey Graphic,* 25:300 (May 1936).

[48]*United States Statutes,* 32:58–72.

[49]*U.S. Tennessee Valley Authority* (Washington, 1941), 1–40; *Public Papers and Addresses; 1935,* "A Suggestion for Legislation to Create the TVA," April 10, 1933, 122–29.

[50]*Congressional Record,* 76 Congress, 3 session (1940), 11, 524–25, address by the president at the opening of the Chickamauga Dam; George C. Stoney, "A Valley to Hold To," *Survey Graphic,* 29:391–99 (July 1940); F.D.R. Papers, Group 13, OF 42, October 17, 1933, David O. Lilienthal, director and general counsel of the T.V.A., address before the Rotary Club of Memphis.

[51]*Congressional Record,* 75 Congress, 1 session (1939), 4172–80; 77 Congress (1941), A1396; 75 Congress, 2 session (November–December 1937), 187–89; "The New Deal Program for Electric Utilities," *Congressional Digest,* 15:230–31 (October 1936).

[52]*National Resources Committee Progress Report, 1938* (Washington, 1938) 36–37; *Conservation,* Department of the Interior (March 1940).

[53]*Annual Report of the Secretary of the Department of Interior, 1937* (Washington, 1937), XVI; *Annual Report of the Secretary of Interior, 1938* (Washington, 1938), XI.

[54]*Conservation,* Department of Interior (Washington, 1940); *Annual Report of the Secretary of the Interior, 1941* (Washington, 1941), XIX–XX; 1940, 1–528.

[55]*Report of the Secretary of the Interior, 1936* (Washington, 1936), 1–385.

[56]*Conservation,* Department of Interior (Washington, 1940); *Annual Report of the Secretary of the Interior, 1941* (Washington, 1941), XXVIII–XXXIX.

[57]*Annual Report of the Director of the Fish and Wildlife Service to the Secretary of the Interior* (Washington, 1941), 372, table.

[58]*Public Land* (National Resources Board, 1940), 15–16; *Annual Report of the Director of Fish and Wildlife, 1941* (Washington, 1941), 329–406; *Annual Report of the Secretary of the Interior, 1941* (Washington, 1941), XVIII–XIX; *Congressional Record,* 74 Congress, 2 session (1936), 1150–52.

[59]*Annual Report of the Director of Wildlife* (Washington, 1941), 379; 1942, 217; *Public Land* (National Research Board, 1940), 15–16; *Conservation* (Washington, 1940), 8–9.

[60]*Public Land* (National Resources Board, 1940), 15–16; *Report of Fish and Wildlife Director* (Washington, 1941), 329–406; 1942, 185–232; *Conservation* (Washington, 1940), 8–9; *Annual Report of the Secretary of the Department of the Interior* (Washington, 1941), 329–406; 1940, 1–528; *Congressional Record,* 73 Congress, 2 session, 4035–36; 6709–11; National

Archives, *Evaluation and Long Time National Public Works Program for Wildlife Conservation,* mimeographed, 1–28.

[61]*Annual Report of the Secretary of Interior, 1934* (Washington, 1934), 164–65; 1941, XXV; *Conservation* (Washington, 1940), 11–13; *New York Times,* March 4, 1934; National Archives, "A National Program of Public Works for Recreational Land" (January 1942), mimeographed, 1–44.

[62]*Report of the Secretary of Interior, 1934* (Washington, 1934), 165–66.

[63]*Annual Report of the Secretary of Interior, 1941* (Washington, 1941), 277–90; 1937, XIV; 1938, all pages.

[64]*Public Land* (National Resources Board, 1940), 13–14.

[65]*Annual Report of the Secretary of Interior, 1941* (Washington, 1941), 275–328.

6

The Civilian Conservation Corps

The Civilian Conservation Corps, though operated as a separate federal agency,[1] received assistance from the Departments of Labor, War, Interior, and Agriculture, partly by means of a representative from each. The group of representatives formed an advisory council that conferred with the director of the C.C.C. and helped in carrying out the program.[2] In addition, all these departments were directed to cooperate actively. Thus, the Department of Labor was charged with selecting junior enrollees[3] for the Corps; the War Department was actually to enroll the men selected and to transport, feed, clothe, house, and care for them; whereas the Departments of the Interior and Agriculture were responsible for the work itself.[4] They designated, planned, and supervised the projects by means of experienced technicians of the various agencies and bureaus of these two departments.[5] As the types of projects varied during the final years of the Corps, these cooperating bodies varied somewhat, but a sample will show the specific sort of linkage.[6] From July 1, 1940, through June 30, 1941, the projects of the Department of the Interior were the National Park Service, Grazing Service, Bureau of Reclamation, Fish and Wildlife Service, General Land Office, and Office of Indian Affairs. Those of the department of Agriculture were the Forest Service, Soil Conservation Service, Bureau of Entomology Plant Quarantine, Bureau of Plant Industry, Bureau of Animal Husbandry, and the National Agricultural Research Center.[7] For this integrative channeling of service from these diverse federal instruments and from similar agencies of the states, the C.C.C. was held to be unique. It utilized them not only in its work program, but also in its administrative system, as is abundantly

128

illustrated by Figure 6-1, which analyzes the organization for its fiscal year 1941.

CONSERVATION WORK OF
THE CIVILIAN CONSERVATION CORPS

The tie-in with the Departments of Agriculture and the Interior will be clearly evident from an examination of their activity in more detail, because from its beginning on April 5, 1933, the Corps, by supplying men and money, was a real boon to their conservation efforts.[8] The great bulk of its activities was directed toward the protection of "vast forest areas of the country from fire and tree-attacking diseases and insects, soil erosion control, and the improvement of areas for recreational use."[9]

FORESTRY

Though popular thought associated the C.C.C. with tree planting, this was indeed far from being the whole of its vast program; even within the area of forestry where it involved existing forests, work included the protection, improvement, and betterment of forest administration. It may be well, therefore, to deal with these aspects in that order before concluding with a survey of the work in reforestation. All of the operations were under the primary auspices of the Forest Service Bureau. During the fiscal year 1940, it had general supervision over 177 state forestry camps and 99 privately owned forest land camps, directed field work on 18 T.V.A. camps, and in addition supervised the work of 323 camps on national forests. The activity of these camps, in turn, was under the general supervision of the Department of Agriculture.[10]

Fire Protection

Forest protection comprised action against fire and action against destructive insects. That against fire was important, extensive, and diverse. Each year the fires swept over some 40 million acres of the nation's timberland, an area almost as large as the state of Washington. Somebody's carelessness started nearly all of them (about 75 percent): carelessness in smoking, carelessness with handling campfires, carelessness in miscellaneous other ways connected with the use of forests. Therefore, all of these fires were preventable. Lightning was responsible for only 7 percent of the total number, although including some of the largest

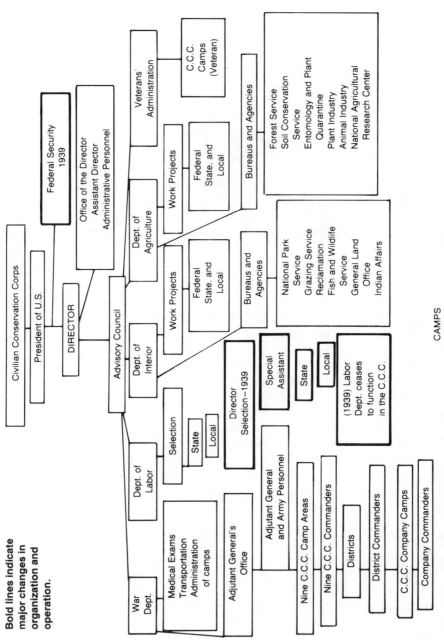

Bold lines indicate major changes in organization and operation.

FIG. 6-1. Administrative System of the Civilian Conservation Corps.
Source: **Based on reading material.**

130

recorded. The C.C.C. tried to keep fires from starting and to put out any fires promptly while they yet were small.

This protective work was varied. For one thing, the very presence of the camps near forests reduced the number of incendiary fires in certain parts of the country. People were evidently more careful when aware of being watched. Active work was even more effective. Patrol crews often prevented big blazes starting from campfires built by picnickers and other forest users.[11] The enrollees also did much to educate the public toward the prevention of forest fires by informal counseling and organized C.C.C. publicity.[12] Fires were further prevented by certain physical techniques, notably the construction of roads and trails, telephone lines, and lookout towers, all to extend the efficient range of detecting fires, alerting personnel, and putting men and tools on the spot in time. Time is a crucial factor in fighting any fire, so great a factor in fighting fires in forests that a loss of time alone may be fatally decisive. The value of swift communication between units and facilities for mobilizing rapidly upon the blaze with all requisite supplies and equipment needs no elaboration.[13] During its first eight years of work, the C.C.C. constructed over 118,490 miles of new truck trails and roadways to facilitate such movement and improved more than 509,130 miles of old trails and roadways. It strung more than 84,730 miles of new telephone lines to connect the lookout stations with mobilization points, and improved 243,460 miles of line.[14] The enrollees also constructed 3,108 new lookout towers and continued the maintenance of 1,767, as well as constructing 1,147 new lookout houses for fire detection and maintaining 859 old ones.[15]

Another protective activity was their removal of such fire hazards as dead trees, slash, and similar material that burns like tinder during the dry season. During its eight years, the Corps removed dead trees and underbrush from 2,075,970 acres of land. The roadside and trailside cleanup for fire prevention amounted to 78,140 miles[16]

The construction of firebreaks, which were cleared strips through woodlands designed to halt the spread of fire or to be used in backfiring, amounted to 66,215 miles. An example was the work done by the California camps in constructing the Ponderosa Way—a firebreak some 600 miles long, which separated the lower brush-covered foothills, where fires often start, from the valuable timber higher up on the slopes of the North-South chain of forested mountains.[17]

The C.C.C. made two other unique contributions to a fire control system. One was the construction of water storage basins and ponds convenient to roadsides in strategically selected spots throughout the New England forest areas to provide a ready supply of water for firefighting tanks and pumps. The second was the development of motorized well-digging units manned by C.C.C. enrollees in Michigan, Minnesota, and Wisconsin forest areas for the quick provision of water near potential fire zones.[18]

Fire Fighting

Aside from the protective facilities of the C.C.C., one of its most valuable contributions to forest preservation was actual fire fighting. The Corps devoted 6,273,220 man-days to this.[19] They fought in many ways, but tried to follow a rule as basic for battling a blaze as for battling an army, summed up in General Bedford Forrest's rule: "Git thar fustest with the mostest men." Catching a fire in its feeble youth prevented its rapid growth to a devouring giant. The techniques used were those developed over a long period of years by federal, state and local protective units, and the C.C.C. personnel fought fires under the direct orders of regular forest and park professionals.

In serving as forest fire patrol crews (for example, in the Lake States' forests), the enrollees covered forest routes by truck, by foot, by canoe, and by airplane. Throughout the nation they were used to a certain extent as lookouts during fire seasons. In areas of great recreational use, some served as special guards and patrollers or as checkers at forest entrances.

For big fires, such as those experienced in 1936 in upper Minnesota, Michigan, and Wisconsin, large concentrations of Corps members were rushed to the fires by truck caravans and trains. Fourteen hundred were thus mobilized on the fireline within a few hours during the big Los Angeles conflagration in 1934, and more than 1,000 at the Olympic fire in Washington in 1938.[20] In the fire fighting the enrollee supplied labor with grub hoe, ax, and saw in order to halt the fire at ground level by removing fuel from its path. They manned pumps, bulldozers, tractors, and other heavy equipment to build fire lanes. Some also operated short-wave radio sets, which had become a part of modern forest fire-fighting communication technique.[21]

Combatting Tree Diseases

The other major protective activity was the combatting of tree diseases like the pine blister rust and such destructive insects as the gypsy moth. To combat the rust, the men grubbed out or pulled up by hand the currant bushes and other plants that served as an "alternate host" whereby the disease spread from tree to tree. To control the gypsy moth, crews scouted through the forest to locate and destroy the egg clusters. In some areas, tree stands were thinned of undergrowth and of the particular tree species that the gypsy moths preferred for food. Other insect pests were also kept down vigorously. To guard young seedlings from grasshoppers, for instance, crews spread poison bait. To prevent fungus from spreading, they destroyed trees infected by it.[22]

Tree Improvement

A second phase of their forestry work was improvement. The timber stand was bettered by removal of dead, defective, and worthless trees; thinning overcrowded stands; making inventories or estimates on timber stands; and preparing surveys and forest cover maps.[23] The "weeding" not only reduced the fire menace, but also opened a more natural growth for younger trees.[24] The forest land thus improved came to the impressive total of 3,979,280 acres.[25] The timber estimate surveys under the guidance of experienced foresters and timber cruisers covered 35 million acres. They actually measured tree sizes and computed species on a percentage of any typical tract, calculated to determine the amount and kind of timber in a given area.[26]

Administrative Improvement

The third phase of C.C.C. forestry work was administrative improvement. The numerous ways and lines for transport and communication of such obvious protective value also provided for better forest management, as did the structural additions, the warehouses and garages for storage of trucks, tractors, road building machinery, and fire control equipment. Ranger and guard stations and houses were built and overnight cabins and shelters put up in various parts of the forest where rangers inspecting trails or grazing areas or on other forest business could remain overnight and be able to keep in touch with supervisors' offices by telephone. Tool houses and boxes were installed throughout forest areas at points at which equipment was hard to transport, serving as useful depots for road and trail repair and fire control crews. Sign shops in C.C.C. camps turned out attractive, durable route markers, which were of use to officials and the general public traveling through federal and state forests and parks.[27]

Reforestation

Reforestation, the fourth phase of forestry work of the C.C.C. enrollees, was probably the best known.[28] From 1933 through 1940, the C.C.C. reforested more than 2 million acres, which required the planting of about 2 billion trees. In 1932, before the C.C.C. was created, the puny extent of about 25,000 acres was all that the pitifully scant resources would cover for planting trees in national forest areas. The establishment of C.C.C. camps was mainly responsible for enabling the Forest Service to raise the total to 70,000 acres in 1933; to 74,000 in 1934; to 140,000 acres in 1935; and to a peak of 238,075 in 1936. From 1937 on, the average annual planting of about 150,000 acres was also largely the work of the C.C.C. The planting in 1940 brought the total acreage planted in the national forests to 1,333,000 acres, of which about 1,110,000 had been planted since the establishment of the C.C.C.[29]

The C.C.C. planted seedlings in spring and in fall, with crews usually made up of two man units. One with a grub hoe or mattock dug the hole and prepared the soil for planting, and the other placed the seedling in the hole and packed the earth around it. Most of the national forest planting was done by the one-man method.[30]

The seedlings were obtained from tree nurseries. Owing to the Corps' reforestation program, the total nursery production in the United States jumped more than 100 percent between 1932 and 1941. The Corps supplied great quantities of labor needed to create the 22 new forest nurseries that existed by 1941, and their labor enabled established nurseries to increase their production. The U.S. Forest Service had 26 nurseries in operation in 1941 and the states had 76. Two big nurseries were built and operated by the C.C.C. for the production of seedlings used by the T.V.A. in its reforestation and soil erosion control programs.[31]

Enrollees from forest camps were used in all phases of the nursery work. The work consisted of dozens of tasks, including the operation of various machines and specialized planting tools. In addition to the nursery work as part of reforestation, there was the collection of hardwood seeds, nuts, and pine cones. Enrollees detailed to seed collection usually worked in small crews. After gathering the seeds, they dried them, hulled some, screened and ran them through a fanmill, threshed and cleaned them, then packed and stored them until they were needed for sowing. Coordinated with seed collecting was the work of preparing seedbeds, laying pipe for winter seedlings, building lathing shades over seedbeds, sowing of the seeds, care of the seedlings, and their transplantation into locations where reforestation was necessary.[32]

Extent of Forestry Work

Two examples of the forestry work will indicate both its emergency value and the magnitude of effort: the New England Forest Emergency Project and the work in the T.V.A. The hurricane of September 1938 in New England left wind-thrown timber lying in large and small bodies on some

15 million acres of forest land. A large portion of the material was white pine, and in many places inflammable branches and needles were piled to a height of 30 feet. So tremendous a fire hazard had to be reduced. On January 1, 1939, a total of 40 state and private C.C.C. camps in New England was assigned for administration by the New England Forest Emergency Project, U. S. Forest Service. Of these camps 32 were located within the hurricane area. By opening roads and trails, clearing debris, and reestablishing fire towers and fire communication systems, the young men reduced the fire hazard significantly and helped stop fires that started.[33]

The C.C.C. supplied labor for the T.V.A. program over a period of years.[34] For the fiscal year 1940, 18 forestry camps were alloted to the T.V.A. The field work was supervised by the Forest Service under the plans and specifications prepared by the T.V.A. technicians, the effort being centered on erosion control, reforestation, and forest protection. When either control of erosion itself or demonstration of control methods was needed, and when erosion was too heavy for the private landowner to handle alone, the C.C.C. provided the manpower. By the end of the fiscal year 1940, more than 62 million young trees had been planted by the enrollees on 40,000 eroded acres on 8,500 farms within the watershed.[35]

SOIL CONSERVATION

Demonstrations

The C.C.C. played an important part in the federal government's conservation policy to protect the nation's soil by carrying out work of the Soil Conservation Service (S.C.S.) under the Department of Agriculture.[36] The first C.C.C. camps used by the S.C.S. set up large-scale demonstrations throughout the country where farmers could see and study them. The need they disclosed caused an increase the next year in C.C.C. camps assigned to the S.C.S. to permit more extensive demonstration. In 1937, several state legislatures passed enabling acts providing for the formation of state conservation districts, and in the early months of 1938 the first agreement was signed by the S.C.S. and a state district. At first, the assistance offered by the S.C.S. to the district was supervisory. However, during the fiscal year 1939, 64 agreements involving C.C.C. labor were signed between state districts and the S.C.S. acting for the Department of Agriculture. The number of these agreements increased in succeeding years,[37] and C.C.C. contingents helped farmers to stop the erosion of their soil.

Erosion Control

Such direct and plainly effective demonstration convinced thousands of farmers that the cost of erosion was measurable in steadily decreasing crop yields, and that the ruinous trend could be checked. The large-scale effort of the C.C.C. Soil Conservation Service camps bore substantial fruit. The gully control operations, terrace outlet construction and protection, planting of trees and shrubs, running of lines for contour furrows and terraces, and the building of structures for streambank protection not only added substantially to the soil erosion accomplishments but proved to be of educational value.[38]

Drainage

Another part of the C.C.C. effort under the S.C.S. dealt with drainage. At the beginning of its fiscal year 1940, operation of 38 C.C.C. camps engaged in drainage was transferred from the Bureau of Agricultural Engineering to the S.C.S. Working with drainage organizations existing under state laws, these camps rehabilitated ditches and drains in order to produce channels of adequate capacity. They also built water control structures to prevent erosion and repaired levees and tile drains. The practical results of this activity were illustrated in areas where the run-off from heavy rains had been carried without overflow by the ditches rehabilitated by the C.C.C. camps, while in adjacent areas where enrollees had not yet worked, overflows from the same rains resulted in heavy crop losses. In addition, public health benefited by the improved drainage, especially in areas where malaria was prevalent.[39]

Indeed, the C.C.C. camps contributed varied labor to the care of the nation's land in its assistance in the S.C.S. program.[40] The contributions ranged from the demonstrational erosion control to actual participation in soil erosion practices and to drainage and roadside care.[41]

WATER

The activity of the Corps forwarded the government's water policy. Maintaining the forests, building them up, and protecting them from fire conserved ground water. Also, the major stream engineering project work of building dams, clearing woods from land to be flooded, and establishing erosion control measures on watersheds proved invaluable. In addition, the Corps built levees, diversion channels, and other waterworks, thus furthering the national flood control program. In times of flood distress and crisis situations, the C.C.C. was a boon to the United

States citizens. This on-the-spot aid proved as valuable as the long-range labor.[42]

CIVILIAN CONSERVATION CORPS
UNDER THE DEPARTMENT OF AGRICULTURE

Certainly, C.C.C. conservation under the auspices of the Department of Agriculture was extensive and comprehensive. The Department of Agriculture had, from the beginning in 1933, the larger percentage of C.C.C. camps. The department had general supervision over national forest, wildlife and big game refuges (until July 1, 1939), soil erosion control projects, the project work of the T.V.A., and, under the Clarke-McNary Forest Cooperation Act, protection of and certain other functions for state and private forest lands. On July 1, 1933, the Department of Agriculture had 1,264 camps of a total of 1,468. Then peak came in September 1935, when it had 1,907 camps of a total of 2,635. By July 1, 1941, it had 793 camps of a 1,234 total of camps.[43]

CIVILIAN CONSERVATION CORPS
UNDER THE DEPARTMENT OF THE INTERIOR

Under the Department of the Interior, projects carried on included the development of recreational facilities in national, state, and local parks; broad conservation in the development of irrigation and hydroelectric power programs; protection and improvement of federal grazing lands and Indian reservations; protection and propagation of wildlife; and rehabilitation of the human and natural resources of the islands and territorial possessions. From July 1, 1940, through June 30, 1941, six agencies of the Department of the Interior supervised the operation of an average of 492 C.C.C. camps, 71 C.C.C. Indian camps, and 10 groups of enrollees in Hawaii, Alaska, and the Virgin Islands.[44]

Recreational Work

The recreational work of the C.C.C. was carried on by the National Park Service of the Department of the Interior.[45] In the fiscal year 1941, the National Park Service operated in the United States an average of 304 C.C.C. camps, comprising 50,000 enrollees, 190 camps in state, county, and metropolitan parks and monuments, 2 camps on military areas, and 22 camps on recreational areas. In the islands and territories, the National Park Service supervised the activities of nine C.C.C. units.[46]

Historical Sites and Campgrounds

The recreational projects carried on by C.C.C. labor were varied. One type was historical restoration. An example is the Bandolier National Monument in New Mexico, which preserved the ruins of a prehistoric culture. In decided contrast were the public campground development projects. At Jenny Lake in Grand Teton National Park, C.C.C. forces made 50 new camp locations available, including parking spaces, fireplaces, and tent sites. A water system and sewer line extension were also completed for this area as well as table and bench combinations and campground signs. Very similar projects were carried on in the nation's forests by the enrollees there who developed picnic camping grounds, built outdoor stoves, roads, bridges, and guard rails, and constructed water supply systems.[47]

State and Local Developments

Work of this kind also improved the state, county, and local park recreational areas by providing picnic, camping, swimming, and hiking facilities.[48] Between 1939 and 1940, the state park acreage increased 100 percent, almost entirely because C.C.C. manpower and funds for development were available. Indeed, several states had no such parks in 1933, whereas by 1940 the administration of their park areas was cooperating in the nationwide program for coordinated recreational planning. Other states added to their existing areas and brought new parks into their systems.[49]

General Land Office Camps

During the fiscal year 1941, the General Land Office of the Department of the Interior operated five camps in Oregon, one in Wyoming, and a fire control project in Alaska. The Oregon camps did conservation work on the 2.5 million acres of revested Oregon–California railroad grant lands, by work planned to protect the commercial timber in this area and further facilitate its sustained yield management. The Wyoming Camp handled the control of out-crop fires and saved from destruction an inestimable amount of the nation's coal resources in the vicinity of Little Thunder Basin, Wyoming.[50] During the fiscal year of 1940, the Corps' personnel worked on 13 separate coal bed fires. Those not too large they combatted by digging them out and covering the face of the coal seams with a layer of pulverized earth. Others they isolated from the main body of coal by encircling the affected areas with earth-filled trenches to block the spread of fire.[51] The General Land Office was charged with the administration of approximately 325 million acres of public domain in Alaska; here, projects were those most beneficial to the natives.[52]

BUREAU OF RECLAMATION CAMPS

The development of irrigation and hydroelectric power projects were carried on under the Bureau of Reclamation. The C.C.C. camps assigned to the Bureau of Reclamation worked in connection with the rehabilitation of Federal Reclamation projects, the development of supplemental water supplies, the construction of new reclamation projects, and the development of recreational facilities at irrigation reservoirs. The construction program of the Bureau of Reclamation aimed to conserve water to irrigate millions of acres of western land. This necessitated numerous artificial waterway systems, leading from large federal storage dams that required hundreds of permanent concrete structures to control and measure the irrigation water. Members of the C.C.C. annually built hundreds of these structures, and assisted in flood protection by supplying labor for such control projects as earth embankments, reservoir areas, channels, and dams.[53]

FEDERAL RANGE WORK

The C.C.C. contribution to the protection and improvement of the federal range involved the reclaiming of thousands of acres of formerly unused public range land by their improvement for grazing. This work included the development and conservation of water through construction of tanks and reservoirs, the digging of wells, dam construction, revegetation, the control of erosion, and the construction of truck trails and driveways. In the actual use of the land as range for cattle, the enrollees built fences, eradicated poisonous plants, and exterminated rodent species that fed on or otherwise depleted the forage cover. The Division of Grazing with the aid of the C.C.C. made possible the steady improvement and rehabilitation of the range.[54]

WILDLIFE

In the protection and propagation of wildlife, the C.C.C. assisted by improving wildlife habitats and by providing the necessary facilities for administration of wildlife refuges.[55] In general, the labor fostered and protected wildlife. In particular, it involved the creation of fish-rearing ponds and wildlife shelters, the propagation of food and cover vegetation, the development of wells, springs, lakes, ponds, and streams, the direct feeding of animals and birds, and miscellaneous contributory activities.

The construction and maintenance of water control structures were, in part, designed specifically to aid wildlife, but in part were incidental to that end. Such work included clearing ponds and channels and building check dams and dikes to stabilize water levels and to store water. In conjunction with their water control work, the enrollees planted food plants where food for birds was lacking. They collected and treated sick birds and later released them on federal refuges. They carried on erosion work to prevent silting of waterfowl ponds.[56]

An example of the C.C.C. labor to make refuges more attractive to wildlife facilities for administration is the following. In October 1935, when a C.C.C. camp was established on the Savannah River Refuge in South Carolina, the wildlife values were negligible. The refuge consisted of a tract of marsh land over which water flowed with each tide. The marsh was choked with undesirable plants. At the end of fiscal year 1940, the C.C.C. had created 3,385 acres of duck ponds with permanent dikes and control structures that would ensure stable water levels, thus providing for growth of food and cover plants. Fence and boundary markers had been erected and roads and trails had been built to facilitate refuge patrol. Residences for refuge personnel, office, and several utility structures including a lookout tower, a boathouse, a marine shop, a marine railway, and a garage had been constructed to enable effective and economical administration.[57]

DIVERSIFIED WORK

Much activity within the Corps supported the diversified work on the projects. Members served as cooks, bakers, leaders, mess stewards, clerks, hospital orderlies, and in many similar, necessary supporting functions. This activity was of two kinds, that common to all camps and that varying with projects. The following jobs were common:

ambulance driver (part time)	cook, first and second
assistant leader for education	dispensary attendant (hospital orderly)
attendant of recreation hall and library	kitchen police
	leader, senior
	mechanic, helper

baker
blacksmith, helper
canteen steward
clerk (army)
clerk (supply)
clerk (technical service)
clerk (tool)

mess steward
night guard
orderly
truck driver
utility and maintenance
  worker

The varying jobs are illustrated by these:

bridge construction
bulldozer operation
cabin construction
carpentry
concrete construction
diesel engine operation
drafting
drag line operation
jackhammer operation
landscaping
logging
road and trail construction
road grader operation

sawmill operation
sign painting and sign making
small dam construction
stone masonry
surveying
telephone line construction
tool sharpening
tractor operation
tree nursery work
truck driving
welding
wildlife management[58]

TEMPORARY AND PERMANENT OBJECTIVE OF THE CIVILIAN CONSERVATION CORPS

The C.C.C. faithfully fulfilled the temporary and permanent objective of the federal government's conservation policy. Clearly, it well served the temporary objective of relief, and the permanent social, economic, and conservation objectives were also equally realized. The latter are difficult to evaluate. In no other period of eight year of the country's history was so much conservation done by a single agency. It was estimated that the Corp' activities set the conservation movement forward in the United States by 25 years.[59] Nelson C. Brown, professor at N.Y. State College of Forestry, said, in 1933, that the C.C.C. had given the conservation program the greatest forward impetus since the days of Theodore Roosevelt. He believed the Corps pushed the country's forestry program forward 20 to 50 years or more.[60] Some foresters believed that the C.C.C. advanced forestry 20 years.[61] In all phases of the nation's conservation policy, the C.C.C. manpower contributed constructively.

Table 6-1 illustrates the various types of C.C.C. labor and highlights the important work done by the Corps from April 5, 1933, to July 1, 1941:

TABLE 6-1.   C.C.C. labor from April 5, 1933, to July 1, 1941

Categories of labor	Unit of measurement	Quantity
Vehicle bridges	number	38,087
Fences	rods	26,368,296
New telephone lines	mile	85,548
New water sources	number	23,725
Truck trails and minor roads	mile	122,169
Erosion or check dams	number	5,875,578
Forest trees planted	number	2,246,100,600
Forest stand improvement	acre	3,998,328
Fighting forest fires	man-day	6,182,269
Tree and plant disease and pest control operations	acre	934,581
Rodent and predatory animal control	acre	39,039,711

[1] *Source*: Note 62.

MONETARY VALUE OF CIVILIAN CONSERVATION CORPS WORK

Attempted estimates of the monetary value of the work of the C.C.C. vary. It was stated that "the work of the C.C.C. has increased the national wealth of the Nation by hundreds of millions of dollars."[63] Director James J. McEntee, C.C.C., in 1941, said, "It is my estimate that the total future value of C.C.C. work completed will greatly exceed $1,500,000,000."[64] By future value he meant the future return to be expected on the C.C.C. investment in conservation work. He admitted, however, that it was impossible to furnish an exact and complete figure on the future values of the total of Corps accomplishments, such as protective activities in connection with forest fires and attacks of gypsy moth or white pine blister rust. He based his estimate on a study made of a number of major items of work completed. For instance, competent authorities in the lumber and manufacturing industries were asked to compute to the best of their ability the future value on maturity of the more than 2 million acres of forest land planted to commercial-type trees. The C.C.C. office was informed that, assuming an average mortality rate for trees and that the C.C.C. timber stands reached maturity and that lumber values did not deteriorate, the C.C.C. trees should have a value in some 40 years of $240 million. It was on a study of this type that McEntee based his conclusions.[65] Without a doubt, the C.C.C. wrote a vivid page in the history of conservation accomplishments in the 1930s of unchallengeable worth and impressive magnitude. Most professional conservationists today would agree that the work of the C.C.C. was invaluable.

NOTES

[1]By President Roosevelt's reorganization plan the C.C.C. became a part of the Federal Security Agency, 1939. *United States Statutes at Large*, 48:22–24; *Annual Report of the Director of Emergency Conservation Work: June 30, 1936*, 1; *Annual Report of the Director of the Civilian Conservation Corps: June 30, 1939*, 5.

[2]James F. Kieley, *C.C.C.* (United States Department of the Interior, processed, Washington, 1938) 6–7, a great amount of the basic material in the booklet was supplied by the Office of the Director of the C.C.C. and the various departments cooperating in the work of the Corps; *The Civilian Conservation Corps: What It Is and What It Does* (Washington, January 1941), 3, a mimeographed booklet published by the C.C.C.; Executive Order 6101, April 5, 1933, "Relief of Unemployment through the Performance of Useful Public Work," in Executive Orders 6171–6299, Washington, 1933.

[3]Junior enrollees refers to the bulk of the enrollees in C.C.C. camps, the other enrollees being war veterans, native Americans, and territorial enrollees each in their respective camps.

[4]*The C.C.C.: A Youth Program* (Washington, 1938), not paged.

[5]*The Civilian Conservation Corps: What It Is and What It Does* (Washington, 1941), 3.

[6]The annual reports by the director of the C.C.C. noted changes in the agencies and bureaus cooperating with the Department of Agriculture and the Interior. The Fish and Wildlife Service had been known as the Biological Survey previous to the fiscal year 1941, and the National Agricultural Research Center had been known as the Beltsville Research Center previous to the fiscal year 1941.

[7]*Annual Report of the Director of the Civilian Conservation Corps: June 30, 1941*, 76.

[8]*Activities of the Civilian Conservation Corps: July 1, 1938–June 30, 1939*, 10, 68.

[9]*The Civilian Conservation Corps (Washington, 1941)*, not paged.

[10]C.L. Pack, "Auditing the C.C.C. Ledger," *Review of Reviews*, 89:58 (January 1934); *Woodsmanship for the Civilian Conservation Corps* (Forestry Divisions, Washington, 1941), 13: *C.C.C. Workers Spent 1,801,907 Man-Days in the Control of Forest Fires* (Washington, 1936), not paged; *Objectives and Results of the C.C.C. Program* (Washington, 1938), 13, mimeographed; *Annual Report of the Director of the Civilian Conservation Corps: June 30, 1940*, 51.

[11]*Forests Protected by the C.C.C.* (Forestry Division, Washington, 1938), 1, 6.

[12]James F. Kieley, *C.C.C.* (Washington, 1938), 17.

[13]*Forests Protected* (Washington, 1938), 6.

[14]*The Civilian Conservation Corps* (Washington, 1941), not paged.

[15]*Civilian Conservation Corps: Work Completed All Services, April 1939–June 30, 1941* (Federal Security Agency, Washington, 1941), 8, a processed bulletin.

[16]*Forests Protected* (Washington, 1938), 7; *The Civilian Conservation Corps* (Washington, 1941), not paged.

[17]*The Civilian Conservation Corps* (Washington, 1941), not paged.

[18]*Forests Protected* (Washington, 1938), 5.

[19]Kieley, *C.C.C.*, 17; *The Civilian Conservation Corps* (Washington, 1941), not paged.

[20]*Forests Protected* (Washington, 1938), 5.

[21]Ibid., 6; *The C.C.C. At Work: A Story of 2,500,000 Young Men* (Washington, 1941), 44.

[22]*Forests Protected* (Washington, 1938), 11–12; *The C.C.C. At Work* (Washington, 1941), 44.

[23]*Summary Report of the Director of Emergency Conservation Work, April 1933 to June 30, 1935*, 13.

[24]*Activities of the Civilian Conservation Corps: July 1, 1938–June 30, 1939*, 71.

[25]*The Civilian Conservation Corps* (Washington, 1941), not paged.

[26]*Reforestation by the C.C.C.* (Forestry Division, Washington, 1941), 11–12.

[27]*Forest Improvements by the C.C.C.* (Washington, 1939), 4–5.

[28]*Woodsmanship for the Civilian Conservation Corps* (Washington, 1941), 13. Reforestation means to replace a growth of trees on an area once covered with a forest.

[29]*Reforestation by the C.C.C.* (Washington, 1941), 4.

[30]Ibid., 5.

[31]Ibid., 6; *The C.C.C. At Work* (Washington, 1941), 46.

[32]*Reforestation by the C.C.C.* (Washington, 1941), 7–9.

[33]*Activities of the Civilian Conservation Corps: July 1, 1938–June 30, 1939*, 75.

[34]The annual report by the director of the C.C.C. cites work done by the C.C.C. enrollees on the T.V.A. for the years of 1936, 1938, 1939, 1940, and 1941.

[35]*Annual Report of the Director of the Civilian Conservation Corps: June 30, 1940*, 55–56.

[36]Ibid., 56. The S.C.S. was established by the authority of Congress on April 27, 1935. The service was designated to operate under the Department of Agriculture.

[37]*Activities of the Civilian Conservation Corps: July 1, 1938–June 30, 1939*, 77–80; *Annual Report of the Director of the Civilian Conservation Corps: June 30, 1940*, 56.

[38]*Annual Report of the Director of the Civilian Conservation Corps: June 30, 1940*, 56–57. A very good explanation of the erosion control work done by the enrollees, that is, methods and types of erosion work, is given in *Hands to Save the Soil* (Soil Conservation Service, Washington, 1939), not paged.

[39]*Activities of the Civilian Conservation Corps: July 1, 1938–June 30, 1939*, 81; *Annual Report of the Director of the Civilian Conservation Corps: June 30, 1940*, 57, 81.

[40]*Annual Report of the Director of the Civilian Conservation Corps: June 30, 1940*, 57. A part of the C.C.C. labor under the S.C.S. was devoted to roadside erosion control.

[41]Ibid., *Hands to Save the Soil* (Washington, 1938), not paged; Edgar B. Nixon, *Franklin D. Roosevelt and Conservation, 1911–1945*, Franklin D. Roosevelt Library, Hyde Park (New York, 1957), Item 146.

[42]*The Work of the C.C.C. in Water Conservation* (Forest Service, Washington, 1936), 3–19; *Annual Report of the Director of the Civilian Conservation Corps: June 30, 1940*, 58.

[43]*Annual Report of the Director of the Civilian Conservation Corps: June 30, 1941*, 34.

[44]Ibid., 28.

[45]*The Civilian Conservation Corps and Public Recreation* (Washington, 1941), 3; *Recreational Developments by the C.C.C. in National and State Forests* (Forestry Service Division, Washington, 1936), 3–17. The enrollees under the Forest Service in the Department of Agriculture also aided in the expansion of the nation's recreational program.

[46]*Annual Report of the Director of the Civilian Conservation Corps: June 30, 1941*, 28.

[47]*Annual Report of the Director of the Civilian Conservation Corps: June 30, 1940*, 45; *Forest Improvement* (Washington, 1939), 7.

[48]*Annual Report of the Director of the Civilian Conservation Corps: June 30, 1940*, 44–46.

[49]James J. McEntee, *The C.C.C. and National Defense* (Washington, 1940), 4, a bulletin

reprinted from *American Forests* (July 1940); *Recreational Development by the C.C.C. in National and State Forests* (Forestry Service Division, Washington, 1936), 3–17.

[50]*Annual Report of the Director of the Civilian Conservation Corps: June 30, 1941*, 31–32.

[51]*Annual Report of the Director of the Civilian Conservation Corps: June 30, 1940*, 40.

[52]*Annual Report of the Director of the Civilian Conservation Corps: June 30, 1941*, 32.

[53]*Annual Report of the Director of the Civilian Conservation Corps: June 30, 1940*, 41–43.

[54]*Annual Report of the Director of the Civilian Conservation Corps: June 30, 1941*, 29; Kieley, *C.C.C.*, 29; *Activities of the Civilian Conservation Corps: July 1, 1938–June 30, 1939*, 66–67.

[55]*Annual Report of the Director of the Civilian Conservation Corps: June 30, 1941*, 30.

[56]*The C.C.C. and Wildlife* (Bureau of Biological Survey, Washington, 1939), 6–9.

[57]Ibid., 8; *Annual Report of the Director of the Civilian Conservation Corps: June 30, 1940*, 50.

[58]*Work Experience Counts* (Washington, 1941), not paged.

[59]*The Civilian Conservation Corps* (Washington, 1941), not paged.

[60]Nelson C. Brown, *The Civilian Conservation Corps Program in the United States* (Washington, 1934), 1, 6.

[61]H. R. Kylie, B. H. Huronymus, and A. G. Hall, *C.C.C. Forestry* (Washington, 1937), 55, book published by the Department of Agriculture.

[62]*Annual Report of the Director of the Civilian Conservation Corps: June 30, 1941*, 14.

[63]*Civilian Conservation Corps: Contributing to the Defense of the Nation* (Washington, 1941), not paged; G. H. Gilbertson, "Rehearsal for Defense," *Soil Conservation* 7:37–39 (August 1941).

[64]James J. McEntee, *Future Value of Civilian Conservation Accomplishment Over Past Eight Years Exceed $1,500,000,000* (Washington, 1941), 3. A statement of James J. McEntee, director, C.C.C., contained in a letter to the Honorable Malcom C. Tarver, chairman, Subcommittee on Labor, Appropriations Committee, House of Representatives,May 28, 1941, outlining the character and value of the work performed by the Corps. The figure of $1.5 billion was reached by estimating the future value of more than 2.5 billion trees planted, 118,500 miles of truck trails and minor roads constructed through forests, 85,000 miles of telephone lines laid, more than 4,000 fire towers constructed, close to 100,000 bridges and buildings built, forest areas developed into forest and recreational area, 3.9 million acres of forests improved to effect faster and sounder growth, range lands revegetated, reclamation and wildlife work done, drainage ditches rehabilitated, and many other kinds of work completed. No attempt was made to place an exact estimate on the future savings effected through trees saved by enrollee fire fighters who expended more than 6 billion man-days fighting forest fires.

[65]*Annual Report of the Director of the Civilian Conservation Corps: June 30, 1941*, 14.

⌒ 7 ⌒
Conservation and Planning

The conservation record of the 1930s with its array of accomplishments did not come into being by disconnected effort or by change. It came as part of a plan—American planning, which became an important concept in the New Deal, and was particularly stressed in relation to natural resources.[1] The leadership necessary to the integration of any comprehensive plan was supplied here by Franklin D. Roosevelt. Throughout his presidential terms, he insisted upon the need for thoughtfully devised plans that would carry out an overall conservation policy. Not that planning as such was a creation of the incoming Democratic administration in 1933. It had been used by agencies in the federal service and in state and city governments as well. Nor was the idea of a national Planning Board original with the Roosevelt administration. The report of President Hoover's Research Committee on Recent Social Trends, published early in 1933, suggested the desirability of organizing a National Advisory Planning Board.[2] It was rather that the gravity of the fast-moving events of 1933 lifted planning from the level of polite discussion to the stage of instant necessity. Hysterical, stop-gap random measures but invited a more consuming disaster than already faced the nation. The New Deal, under Roosevelt, with its gigantic public works program, extended federal planning to an unprecedented range of activity. A National Planning Board was set up in 1933 in the Federal Emergency Administration of Public Works to assist the administrator through preparation, development, and maintenance of plans for regional areas; surveys and research concerning distribution and trends of population, land uses, industry, housing, and natural resources, and social and economic

146

trends; and analysis of projects for coordination in location and sequence.[3]

Meanwhile, President Roosevelt advised the use of surveys, research, and planning within existing federal bureaus and agencies dealing with natural resources.[4] By executive order he empowered the board of directors of the T.V.A. to make such surveys, plans, experiments, and demonstrations as would be suitable to aid the proper use, conservation, and development of the natural resources of the Tennessee River drainage basin.[5] In press conferences he spoke of national planning, and as early as February 14, 1934, he discussed a permanent long-range commission that would put the physical development of the country on such an organized, sustained basis for the first time.[6] Action followed. On June 4, 1934, in compliance with its request of the preceding February, Congress received a report from the president on a comprehensive scheme for the control and development of water resources. In submitting this, however, he pointed out that the study could be only preliminary, in view of the short time he had had to prepare it. He requested an opportunity to complete the studies and "to outline to the next Congress a comprehensive plan to be pursued over a long period of years."[7] While thus dealing directly with Congress, he conferred with his Cabinet officers on the advisability of establishing a general administrative instrument to achieve this desired end, and, on June 30, 1934, through executive order he replaced the National Planning Board by the National Resources Board.[8]

THE NATIONAL RESOURCES BOARD, 1934

The first task of the National Resources Board was to prepare a report, to be ready by December 1, 1934, on water and land use. The immediate responsibility for preparing it devolved to two technical committees on water and land. The Mississippi Valley Committee, appointed by the administrator of public works in September 1933 to study the possibilities of a unified plan of development for the entire river basin, became the water planning committee of the newly created Board. Its report went forward to the president on December 1, 1934, with other reports of the National Resources Board. The land committee prepared its report and submitted it to the president on the same date. In this case a field staff of land planning consultants was utilized to secure field data in cooperation with state planning boards, agricultural colleges, experiment stations, and field offices of federal bureaus.[9]

The foreword of the December 1934 report states its objective clearly:

This report of the President's National Resources Board brings together, for the first time in our history, exhaustive studies by highly competent inquirers of land use, water use, minerals, and related public works in their relation to each other and national planning. The report lays the basis of a comprehensive long-range national policy for the conservation and development of our fabulous natural resources.[10]

When President Roosevelt submitted the report to Congress on January 24, 1935, he stressed that for the first time in our history we had made an inventory of our national assets and the problems relating to them. Now at last we had synthesized the individual insights and foresight of various planning agencies of the federal government into a comprehensive policy and method for the future. The president expressed the hope that the documents he submitted would constitute a foundation for a permanent policy of orderly development in every part of the United States. Indeed, the chief executive anticipated a permanent National Resources Board that would recommend yearly to the president and Congress priority of projects in national planning.[11]

NATIONAL RESOURCES COMMITTEE, 1935

In June 1935, another executive order converted the National Resources Board into the National Resources Committee. This planning committee enjoyed more stable footing than its two predecessors by receiving appropriations until June 30, 1937, which ensured its life for two years.[12] In addition to continuing such functions as the preparation of plans for the use of land, water, and other resources, it had two other duties:

(b) To consult and cooperate with agencies of the Federal Government, with the states and municipalities or agencies thereof, and with any public or private planning or research agencies or institutions, in carrying out any of its duties and functions.
(c) To receive and record all proposed Federal projects involving the acquisition of land (including transfer of land jurisdiction) and land research projects, and in an advisory capacity to provide the agencies concerned with such information or data as may be pertinent to the projects. All executive agencies shall notify the National Resources Committee of such projects as they develop, before major field activities are undertaken.[13]

F.D.R.'s COMMITMENT TO PLANNING

President Roosevelt did not merely sponsor the work of the National Resources Committee and its precedessors. He also gave his attention to planning at all levels. This included the planning of projects of the various federal bureaus, water works, water pollution (being critical of pollution he endowed surveys), and the activity of the technical committee (from which he requested reports).[14] Little in planning was too extensive for his grasp or so small as to elude his vigilant attention, as he had the utmost interest and faith in organized planning.

Nor did F.D.R. stand alone in his belief in the value of conservation planning. In the early years of the New Deal, favorable publicity approved his planning leadership. Periodicals and newspapers alike expressed favorable opinions on the work of the national planning boards and the conservation planning activity of the federal government.[15] Segments of Congress, the secretaries of agriculture and the interior, and other governmental office holders accepted the blueprinting with enthusiasm.[16]

PERMANENT PLANNING BOARD PROPOSED

So extensive was the public and political support for the president's faith that it warranted sounding out the feasibility of creating a permanent planning board. Though a bill incorporating this idea failed in Congress in 1935,[17] the concept remained vigorously alive. Hearings in the House of Representatives in February–March 1936, and press statements, resolutions, and editorials in 1935 and 1936 showed strong support for the establishment of a permanent national planning agency.[18] Secretary of the Interior Harold Ickes clearly favored it. The Honorable Maury Maverick, member of Congress from Texas, supported the proposal, praising the existing Board's work and urging its nonpartisan continuity. Senators Royal Samuel Copeland and Patrick A. McCarran of New York and Nevada, respectively, clearly expressed a friendly attitude.

National Support

Other support was expressed by national associations. These included the American Society of Planning Officials, American Farm Bureau Federation, American Society of Civil Engineers, American Library Association, American Institute of Architects, the American Federation of Labor, the Construction League of America, the International City Managers Association, the American Engineering Council, and the American Society of Landscape Architects. Governors of the states, state planning boards, universities, and institutions swelled the chorus.[19]

Newspaper Support
and Congressional Opposition

But perhaps the best evidence of the wide range of support is found in the nation's newspapers. From the *San Antonio Express* of Texas to the *Wall Street Journal* of New York to the *Christian Science Monitor* of Massachusetts, the *Lewiston Tribune* of Idaho, and the *Gazette* of Berkeley, California, editorials throughout the country favored a permanent national planning agency.[20] It was, therefore, with a seemingly diverse, extensive, and explicit approval that President Roosevelt took the matter to Congress in his message of January 24, 1935, recommending the establishment of a permanent board.[21] However, the appearance of general approval was misleading. The president did not find in Congress the backing that had been voiced in the hearings in which testimony had emanated mainly from ardent backers of planning. The opposition in Congress to the idea of a permanent board was strong enough to defeat the proposed legislation.

F.D.R.'s CONTINUED SUPPORT OF PLANNING

Yet this setback by no means disheartened the president and those who supported planning. As early as February 3, 1937, the president again urged Congress, in his public works planning message, to consider a permanent planning agency.[22] He also continued to encourage careful planning. During the year 1936–1937, he organized a special committee on farm tenancy, under the chairmanship of the secretary of agriculture, and requested a report to be prepared under the supervision of the National Resource Committee.[23] In August 1937, he requested his Cabinet members to meet with him to discuss a plan for the creation of a committee for the comprehensive study of a program for the conservation and utilization of water resources.[24] He directed the chairman of the National Resources Committee on August 30, 1937, to proceed with a review and revision of the report on *Drainage Basin Problems and Programs* that had been transmitted to him in December 1936. "In undertaking this revision," he wrote, "it is understood that the Committee will cooperate with and have the benefit of the activities of all the Government agencies concerned." In addition, he urged that reviews of state and local agencies interested in these problems be canvassed in connection with a revised program. The president emphasized the importance of a decentralized approach.[25]

PLANNING AT LOCAL, STATE, AND REGIONAL LEVELS

The desirability of planning at local, state, and regional levels was no new idea with the Roosevelt administration. As early as 1933, the Public Works administrator circularized the state governors with regard to the desirability of state planning boards. Within a year, favorable responses were received from 42 states, and by 1937 all the states but two had established some form of official planning agency.[26] In 1935 President Roosevelt again showed his interest in decentralization by expressing a desire that the National Resources Committee investigate further the possibility of regional planning.[27] On June 3, 1937, he sent a message to Congress requesting it to consider the creation of seven regional authorities. He explained the purpose as threefold: to carry out flood control programs within their respective jurisdictions; to assist in the development of power projects that would be by-products of the flood control work; and to conduct miscellaneous planning functions. When presenting his plan, the president reminded the national legislators of past dust storms, floods, and droughts that necessitated works to guard against these calamities, but he hastened to caution them that what was wanted more than repair of disaster was prevention of its recurrence. Roosevelt stressed that it was not wise to direct everything from Washington. National planning should start at the bottom, or, in other words, the problems of townships, counties, and states should be coordinated through large geographical regions and thence come to the Capitol— hence a need for regional bodies.[28]

Regional Proposal

The president's request for regional bodies became a congressional proposal when Representative Mansfield, chairman of the Committee on Rivers and Harbors, introduced on June 3, 1937, a House bill to provide for regional conservation and development of natural resources. A companion bill was introduced by Senator Norris of Nebraska.[29] Hearings were held before a Senate Subcommittee of the Committee on Agriculture and Forestry, and during the session the debate on the issue became vigorous. Opponents attacked the bills' overriding of state ownership and control of water, the curtailing or duplication of existing federal agencies, the lack of provision for a hearing of state views on plans to come before the president, the probability that dominant interests of western states or of the power authority would sacrifice some states to benefit others, and, in a grand climax of alarm, the evident centering of economic power in regional authorities directly subject to a succession of presidents and beyond any effective check by the people.[30] These criticisms did not go unchallenged. There were those who supported the seven regional authorities, and their views resounded through a favorable press. Nevertheless, the powerful opposition struck down the regional proposal.[31]

CHANGE IN ATTITUDE BY 1937

F.D.R. Continues to Support Planning

By 1937 the pendulum of the public mood was swinging back toward conservatism. Rebounding from the depression years, which nobody wanted to remember, people seemed to feel that all planning was emergency improvisation and that the brave cards of the New Deal had been played out. In political talk and its legislative reflection, the years of daring were denounced in favor of the ages of individual greed, disguised as freedom and common sense. Nevertheless, the president, undaunted, held to his objective of a national board of permanent status. He continued to launch projects utilizing planning to sponsor and push an overall water resources plan and to recommend additional forestry planning and specialized studies such as, for example, a study of phosphate resources.[32] He did not hesitate to make recommendations to Congress on the basis of the National Resources Committee reports. On February 16, 1937, he transmitted to Congress a comprehensive study of energy resources, submitted by the National Resources Committee, to be used in formulating future legislation. Therein he reminded Congress that the widening interest and responsibility on the part of the federal government meant continued study of the general needs of the people as a whole. It meant also devising plans to meet these needs on a continuing basis, not merely giving attention to the interests of particular regions and highly vocal groups.[33]

Congressional Opposition

By 1938, however, Congress had demonstrated its opposition to planning. Its stand was clearly against the establishment of any permanent planning agency. Probably the most important single objection was that the various proposed legislative acts failed to provide a strict definition of the functions and competence of the planning board. Another argument was that such an agency would only duplicate activity in other departments and agencies—particularly the Army Engineer Corps; furthermore, Congress would not get a fair return for money disbursed and authority delegated. Additional opposition stemmed from the sur-reptitious and inconsistent mode of seeking for the desired authority: the permanent board proposal was attached as a rider to bills concerned primarily with emergency action on specific matters such as flood control and water pollution control. In spite of the determination of a small minority, this congressional opposition by apathy, suspicion, and specific hostility was strong enough to defeat the establishment of a permanent national planning agency.[34]

NATIONAL RESOURCES PLANNING BOARD, 1939

In the spring of 1939, President Roosevelt showed concern over the continuance of the National Resources Committee's work after June 1, 1939. He had conferences on this matter with Charles E. Merriam and Frederick Delano who had been appointed to the National Planning Board in 1933.[35] The Committee was continued by congressional action. Under Reorganization Plan Number 1, made effective July 1, 1939 (Public Resolution 20, approved June 7, 1939), the powers of the Federal Employment Stabilization Office and the National Resources Committee were combined in the National Resources Planning Board.[36] The Board was established as part of the executive office of the president.[37] In Executive Order 8248 on September 9, 1939, the president described the Board's function as follows:

> (a) To survey, collect data on, and analyze problems pertaining to national resources, both natural and human, and to recommend to the President and the Congress long-time plans and programs for the wise use and fullest development of such resources.
> (b) To consult with federal, regional, state, local, and private agencies in developing orderly programs of public works and to list for the President and the Congress all proposed public works in the order of their relative importance with respect to (1) the greatest good to the greatest number of people, (2) the emergency necessities of the nation, and (3) the social, economic, and cultural advancement of the people of the United States.
> (c) To inform the President of the general trend of economic conditions and to recommend measures leading to their improvement or stabilization.
> (d) To act as a clearing house and means of coordination for planning activities, linking together various levels and fields of planning.[38]

In the same year that the National Resources Planning Board was established, rumblings expressing the desire for a permanent planning board were again heard. Frederic Delano, on November 7, 1939, forwarded to the president a note sent him by another board member, stating that if the National Resources Planning Board was "to achieve a permanent status by additional legislation the support of Senator Hayden and his group seems essential."[39] Far from securing this "essential" support, the national board was fortunate not to have its appropriation cut to the bone in 1940. Even so ardent a supporter of conservation and planned development as Congressman W. M. Whittington informed Roosevelt on February 16, 1940, that he would support the $710,000 appropriation for the National Resources Planning Board for 1941, but that he could not commit himself to supporting permanent legislation for the board.[40] Until 1940 the national planning agency had been financed out of the "blank check" that Congress had written each year for relief. Once the agency was transferred to the executive office of the president, however, and renamed the National Resources Planning Board, it was forced to go through the regular course that all agencies followed to get their money. Hence, the Board nearly fell victim to a Congress that was pulling tight the strings on the public purse. The House Appropriations Committee did, in fact, delete the $710,000 appropriation that the Board requested, but the Senate Committee on Appropriations subsequently restored it.[41]

F.D.R.'s TOTAL COMMITMENT TO PLANNING

Further dangers beset the National Resources Planning Board. The threat of war, the need to appropriate heavily for defense, and the general reaction against planning that had been growing combined to threaten even the temporary existence of the National Resources Planning Board. Secretary of the Interior Ickes in 1940 reminded President Roosevelt that it was imperative to get favorable publicity for the Board.[42] Throughout the critical period, the president showed clearly how conscious he was of the importance of reminding Congress that the Board deserved to continue. His message of January 11, 1940, pointed out that the work of the Board in the past six years had been one of democratic planning, that it was decentralized, that it was based on the wishes of the people. He reminded Congress that the accomplishments of the Board were, in large measure, the result of cooperation among federal and nonfederal planning groups. With resounding emphasis he declared it to be planning "from the ground up."[43] The danger that faced the Board, and the principle of planning itself, was clear to the administration. But the

Board was doomed, and on October 1, 1943, it died by legislative abolition.[44]

Nevertheless, its spirit lived on—the sturdy principle of an orderly development of natural resources according to their location, their characteristics, and the persistent requirements of the nation.[45] Between the first report of the Board in 1934 and the Resources Development report of 1943 stretched a long series of intermediate reports, bulletins, digests, memoranda, and technical papers that left a mark on the thinking of Americans and on their government. The array of reports might well be divided according to the three major lines of activity. First, it organized material as a ground for proposing conservational policy. It prepared studies, plans, and reports that brought together materials and experience, and it set forth lines of coordinated action for the president and Congress to consider. Second, it decentralized its activity. Through regional offices it promoted cooperative planning among local, state, and federal agencies. Third, it prepared long-range studies that the president requested from time to time.[46]

EXAMPLE OF BOARD WORK

1934 Report and Supplements

An example of the work of the Board is the major report issued in 1934 by the Land Committee of the National Planning Board, outlining long-range objectives for land use and conservation that would serve for many years to come. This report furnished the first comprehensive view of the land situation, produced a balanced and coordinated plan for action, and served to focus popular attention on the necessity for a departure from the practice of heedless land exploitation. Supplementary reports were made that included studies of land classification and land acquisition.[47] The Water Resources Committee of the National Planning Board helped to formulate drainage basin studies that provided the base for the Committee's report on a national water policy and a national six-year program of public works involving water resources.[48] A planning committee on mineral policy prepared a report dealing with exploitation and waste, domestic and international problems bearing on mineral and "submarginal" mines. Later reports dealt with energy resources as a whole.[49] A sampling of the long list of reports will show the width of the activity of the national planning agency.

(1) Annual progress reports. That of 1938 consisted of a statement of the Advisory Committee, summarizing the organization and work

of the National Resources Committee and its technical committees during the previous five years and suggesting activities for the future.

(2) Regional planning reports for specific areas. The Pacific Northwest study published May 1936, deals with immediate and urgent problems in the Columbia Basin, and particularly with the policies and organization that should be provided for planning, construction, and operation of certain public works in that area, Bonneville and Grand Coulee Dams in particular.

(3) Water pollution reports. The third report of the Special Advisory Committee on Water Pollution to President Roosevelt, which was transmitted to Congress February 1939, consisted of a statement of the status of water pollution in the United States and problems involved in abating pollution.

(4) The forest resources report of the Pacific Northwest, March 1938, contains the findings and recommendations relative to a forest program for the Pacific Northwest, material dealing with conditions and problems in the area, and a statement of the economic importance of the forest industries of the Pacific Northwest.[50]

EVALUATION OF PLANNING AND F.D.R.'s ROLE

Work so extensive, complex, and diverse in scope could not be done properly without planning. To effect it, both national and local agencies were invaluable to those individuals whose duty was to determine and shape a policy for national conservation. The National Planning Board (and its successors) recommended; it did not order. The service that it rendered was in the American tradition of democracy. Leadership, a part of this tradition, was exercised in significant measure by President Roosevelt himself, whose activity during the 1930s was largely responsible for the continuance of federal planning. Direction aimed to be not only comprehensive but thoroughly informed, including a close scrutiny of European efforts. Thus the land program of Italy, especially reclamation activities, was carefully studied.[51] A careful digest was submitted to the president on the reforestation project in Spain and on Sweden's program of national conservation for private lands.[52] Realizing the value of such foreign pioneering, Roosevelt obtained information on European community-owned forests.[53] He suggested in 1935 that someone be sent to Europe to find out about the relation of forest lands to labor.[54] The value of parallel effort abroad was such that it was suggested in 1938 that a special commission be appointed to visit Europe to study the ways in which conservation was tied into the administrative controls of government.[55] Certainly, no important experience was to be disregarded in developing a permanent U.S. policy and effort.

In addition to learning from foreign countries and incorporating their experience where applicable in the United States conservation planning and implementation of projects, President Roosevelt also thought of conservation on an international level as well as a national one. He actively supported the idea of a Conservation Conference of the nations of the world,[56] not only for conservation per se, but as a "basis of permanent peace with Churchill and Stalin."[57] His seriousness in the idea was evident when he recommended that Governor Pinchot and Mr. Hugh H. Bennett, chief of Soil Conservation, get together and work out something concrete. President Roosevelt was concerned that the reaction of the State Department was less than desired.[58] Pinchot responded to the idea of a World Conference with enthusiasm and submitted a rough plan prefaced with:

> Dear Mr. President: Before your brilliantly successful visit to Yalta, you were good enough to agree that a rough plan for a World Conference On Conservation as a Basis of Permanent Peace should be worked out during your absence. Here it is.
>
> T. R. [Theodore Roosevelt] introduced conservation to America. Nothing could be more fitting than that you, who have already done so much for conservation on this continent, should crown your good work by rendering the same great service to the rest of mankind.
>
> If you decide to call such a Conference, you will guide all Nations toward the intelligent use of the earth for the general good of men, and you will make the movement for permanent peace the most enduring contribution of all.
>
> The proposed meeting would assist powerfully in attaining the objectives of the Bretton Woods and Dumbarton Oaks Conferences. It is intended to fit easily into the pattern of the coming international organization.[59]

However internationally minded F.D.R. might have been, with his growing concern for peace during the war years, he never lost sight of national needs warranting thought and action. His undaunted struggle to have a permanent planning board and a permanent national conservation policy tied to intelligent planning was an ongoing objective for the president in spite of some disappointments.

It is quite obvious that though explicit planning authorities received a setback when Congress deliberately killed the National Resources Planning Board in 1943 by refusing appropriations, the broadened responsibilities of the federal government in this field were now generally organized. The T.V.A., a convincing demonstration of what intelligent planning could accomplish, was now thoroughly established as a permanent activity. In many other fields, such as flood control, forest and soil conservation, the protection of wildlife, and the provision of public recreational areas, there now existed an extensive record of planning within the United States system. This record could not be concealed; it was one of achievement. Branches and limbs of the planning tree might be injured, trimmed, lopped off, but the roots would remain. An overall policy or organized development of the nation's resources was now an established fact.

NOTES

[1] *Planning Our Resources* (Washington, March 1938), 1–35, National Resources Committee pamphlet; *Subject Index of Reports* (Washington, 1940), 1–76, National Resources Committee publication; National Archive planning material used, including the records of the National Resources Planning Board and its predecessor agencies as of April 1949.

[2] *A Report of National Planning and Public Works in Relation to Natural Resources and Including Land Use and Water Resources with Findings and Recommendations, December 1, 1934* (Washington, 1934), 80; Charles E. Merriam, "The National Resources Planning Board, A Chapter in American Planning Experience," *The American Political Science Review*, 38:1075–89 (December 1944).

[3] *Planning Our Resources* (National Resources Committee, Washington, March 1938), 1–27; *National Planning Board, Federal Emergency Administration of Public Works, Final Report, 1933–1934* (Washington, 1935), 1–119.

[4] F.D.R. Papers, Group 13, OF 132, November 21, 1933, F.D.R. to Ickes.

[5] Executive Order 6161, June 7, 1933.

[6] F.D.R. Papers, Group 13, OF 378, January 25, 1934; PPF 1-P, January 31, 1934, press conference, Number 93, 3; February 14, 1934, press conference, Number 97, 3, 5.

[7] *Congressional Record*, 73 Congress, 2 session (1934), 10,399; *Public Papers and Addresses of Franklin D. Roosevelt; Address of Recovery and Reform, 1934* (New York, 1938), 283–85, Item 99, "The President Submits to Congress Reports on a Comprehensive Plan for Control and Development of Water Resources."

[8] F.D.R. Papers, Group 13, OF 1092, June 26, 1934, Wallace, Ickes, Perkins, and Hopkins to F.D.R.; June 27, 1934; June 28, 1934, Cummings, attorney general, to F.D.R.; June 28, 1934, Ickes to F.D.R.; Lewis C. Gray, *Land Planning* (University of Chicago, 1936), 10, L. C. Gray was assistant administrator in charge of Land Utilization Division, Resettlement Administration, and in 1934 was director of Land Committee of the Natural Resources Board; D. C. Coyle, "American National Planning Board," *Political Quarterly*, 16:246–52 (July 1935).

[9] *Planning Our Resources* (National Resources Committee, Washington, March 1938), 15–20; *Energy Resources and National Policy* (National Resources Committee, Washington, 1939), 425–27; *Public Papers and Addresses; Advance of Recovery and Reform, 1934* (New York, 1938), July 3, 1938, F.D.R. White House statement on establishment of National Resources Board, 336–38; Gray, *Land Planning* (Chicago, 1936), 1–37; *National Resources Board: A Report on National Planning and Public Works in Relation to Natural Resources Including Land Use and Water Resources with Findings and Recommendations, December 1, 1934* (Washington, 1934), 1–452. Water planning was given a new importance and broader interpretation through the work of the Mississippi Valley Committee of the P.W.A. and the president's Committee on Water Flow. Land planning studies had similarly been carried on contin-

uously over many years, but new efforts were beginning to bear fruit in the Committee on National Land Problems and the A.A.A. Through the Land Planning Committee previously set up by the National Planning Board, the work was coordinated and a restatement of new and old policies submitted. Mineral planning studies were begun by the planning committee for mineral policy upon its appointment by the president and continued with assistance from the National Resources Board.

[10]*National Resources Board: A Report on National Planning and Public Works in Relation to Natural Resources, December 1, 1934* (Washington, 1934), V. The Water Resources Committee report emphasized an inventory of water resources and brought together data on rainfall, run-off, stream flow, underground waters, etc. A series of eight monographs, each covering a region or group of drainage basins, was prepared and issued as supporting data. Following the submission of these reports, the water planning committee attempted a first priority rating of construction projects concerning water use and conservation. The report of the Land Planning Committee outlined long-range objectives for land use and conservation. Retirement of submarginal areas, resettlement policies, programs for national parks and national forests, policies for drainage and irrigation, an attack on the problem of farm tenancy—these and many more plans for land use were suggested in the report.

[11]*Congressional Record,* 74 Congress, 1 session (1935), 865–66, message from the president of the United States to Congress, January 25, 1935.

[12]Landon C. Rockwell, "National Resources Planning" (Doctoral dissertation, Princeton University, May 1942), 24, 115. Authority for the president's action had come on April 8 from the Emergency Relief Appropriation Act of 1935. The following quote was taken from a letter from the Office of the National Resources Planning board, which offers an explanation of the change in name of the agency from Board to Committee. [Taken from Rockwell, "National Resources Planning" (Princeton, 1942), 25.]

"The reason for the change in the name in June 1935 we are unable to account for, but we do recall that the name was changed by the Bureau of the Budget. One of the functions of the Bureau of the Budget is 'to assist in the consideration and the clearance and, where necessary, the preparation of proposed executive orders and proclamations.' Perhaps the Bureau felt at that time that the name 'Committee' would represent better administrative practice as applied to a temporary organization."

[13]Executive Order, Number 7065, June 7, 1935; Rockwell, "National Resources Planning" (Princeton, 1942), 24–25.

[14]F.D.R. Papers, Group 13, OF 1-F, February 12, 1935, OF 114, July 2, 1935, F.D.R. to Ickes; OF 114-A, July 19, 1935, F.D.R. to secretary of commerce; OF 1092, September 9, 1936, F.D.R. to F. D. Delano; July 31, 1936, Ickes to F.D.R.; August 18, 1936, Ickes to F.D.R.

[15]"Soil Erosion," *Science ns,* 78:Supplement 9 (August 4, 1933); Harold L. Ickes, "Saving the Good Earth," *Survey Graphic,* 23:52–59 (February 1934); A. W. Malone, "Desert Ahead," *New Outlook,* 164:14–17 (August 1934); Harold L. Ickes, "Thought for the Morrow," *Colliers,* 94:10–11 (December 8, 1934); George Creel, "Plan or Perish," *Colliers,* 94:10–11 (December 11, 1934); Richard Lieber, "Our Inherited Wealth," *Review of Reviews,* 89:44–45 (May 1934); "Water Planning Committee," *The American City,* 50:9 (May 1935); Morris L. Cooke, "Twenty Years of Grace," *Survey Graphic,* 24:276–82 (June 1935); *New York Times,* March 11, 1933, August 6. October 17, December 17, 18, 1934, March 31, 1935; National Archives, *Statements, Resolutions and Editorials Supporting National Planning Legislation* (National Resources Committee, 1936), 1–26, mimeographed; Newspaper editorials favoring national planning: San Antonio Texas *Express* (November 2, 1935), Little Rock Arkansas *Democrat* (October 2, 1935), Fort Wayne Maryland *Gazette* (November 22, 1935), *Wall Street Journal* New York (November 2, 1935), *Christian Science Monitor* Massachusetts

(January 25, 1935), Davenport Iowa *Democrat* (October 12, 1935), Philadelphia Pennsylvania *Bulletin* (November 21, 1935), Washington *Post* (November 19, 1935), Fresno California *Bee* (October 15, 1935), Cincinnati Ohio *Enquirer* (November 24, 1935), Reno Nevada *Journal* (November 20, 1933), Fort Wayne Indiana *News Sentinel* (November 24, 1935), Buffalo New York *Courier Express* (November 21, 1935), Newark New Jersey (November 26, 1935), Concord New Hampshire *Monitor* (November 24, 1935), Terre Haute Indiana (November 18, 1935), Wheeling West Virginia, (January 15, 1936), Indianapolis Indiana (November 20, 1935), Lewiston Idaho *Tribune* (November 4, 1935), Birmingham Alabama *Age Herald* (April 16, 1935), Fort Smith Arkansas *Times Record* (July 21, 1935), Elgin Illinois *Courier News* (January 29, 1935), St. Louis Missouri *Post Dispatch* (January 25, 1936), Los Angeles California *Post Record* (November 18, 1935), Grand Junction Colorado *Daily Sentinel* (January 23, 1935).

¹⁶F.D.R. Papers, Group 13, OF 1092, December 19, 1934, J. J. McSwain, South Carolina, to F.D.R.; OF 378, January 25, 1944, T. H. Beck to Marvin McIntyre; OF 1092, June 26, 1934, Wallace, Ickes, Perkins, and Hopkins to F.D.R.; August 18, 1936, Ickes to F.D.R.; August 18, 1936, Ickes to F.D.R.; U.S. Congress, Senate, Special Committee on Survey of Land and Water Policies of the U.S., *Hearing before a Special Committee on Survey of Land and Water Policies of the U.S.*, 74 Congress, 2 session, pursuant to S. Res. 58, a resolution authorizing a survey of all land and water policies and projects of the various executive agencies and establishments of the government, August 21, 1935, Washington, 1935, 1–29; *Report of the Secretary of Agriculture, 1933* (Washington, 1933), 1–101; *Report of the Secretary of Agriculture, 1934* (Washington, 1934), 1–111; *Report of the Secretary of Agriculture, 1935* (Washington, 1935), 1–120; *Report of the Secretary of the Interior, 1933* (Washington, 1933), 1–327; *Report of the Secretary of the Interior, 1934* (Washington, 1934); 1–418; *Report of the Secretary of the Interior, 1935* (Washington, 1935), 1–439; *Land Use Planning Committee*, mimeographed, book of material on land use 1932–1934, National Archives; C. W. Eliot, "National Planning," address by Eliot, second executive officer, National Resources Board, before Graduate School of City Planning, Harvard University, January 11, 1935, mimeographed, National Archives.

¹⁷Rockwell, "National Resources Planning" (Princeton, 1942), 130–36.

¹⁸U.S. Congress, House of Representatives, Committee on the Public Lands, "Establishment of a National Resources Board," *Hearing before the Committee on the Public Lands*, 74 Congress, 2 session, on H.R. 10303, "Bill to Provide for the Establishment of a National Resources Board and the Organization and Functions Thereof," February 20, 21, 26, 28 to March 3, 1936, 1–95.

¹⁹Ibid.; National Archives, *Statements, Resolutions and Editorials Supporting National Planning* (National Resources Committee, 1936), 1–26, mimeographed.

²⁰Ibid., 1–12, mimeographed. See Note 15.

²¹U.S. Congress, House of Representatives, Committee on the Public Lands, "Establishment of a National Resources Board," *Hearing before the Committee on the Public Lands*, 74 Congress, 2 session, on H.R. 10303, February 20, 21, 26, 28 to March 3, 1936, 1–95.

²²*Public Works Planning Message*, February 3, 1937, House Documents 140, 75 Congress, 1 session.

²³*Planning Our Resources* (Washington, March 1938), 20, National Resources Committee.

²⁴F.D.R. Papers, Group 13, OF 132, August 12, 1937, F.D.R. to secretaries of war, interior, agriculture, treasury, and acting director of the budget.

²⁵U.S. National Resources Committee Water Resources Committee *Drainage Basin Problems and Programs*, Rev. Ed. 1937 Washington, February 1938, 2.

²⁶*National Resources Committee 1938 Progress Report* (National Resources Committee, 1938), 1–8; Alvin H. Hansen and Harvey S. Perloff, *Regional Resource Development* (Wash-

ington, 1942), 5–40, National Planning Association, Planning Pamphlets, Number 16; Merle Fainsod and Lincoln Gordon, *Government and the American Economy* (New York, 1948), 757.

[27]A technical subcommittee was set up to study the problem and report. *National Resources Committee 1938 Progress Report*, 9–13. John M. Gaus, Jacob Crane, Marshall E. Dunock, and George T. Renner, "Regional Factors in National Planning and Development (Washington, 1935), Report of the National Resources Committee.

[28]*Congressional Record*, 75 Congress, 1 session, 5280–81; *House Miscellaneous Documents*, 75 Congress, 1 session, Document No. 261, creation of National Resources Planning Board to provide for conservation and development of national resources, message from the president of the United States transmitting the proposed creation of regional authorities or agencies to be known as the National Planning Board to provide for the regional conservation and development of national resources; F.D.R. Papers, Group 13, PPF 1-P, Box 208, February 9, 1937, press conference, Number 343, 1–8; Presidential Secretarial File 1937, Conservation, Box 25, April 20, 1937, "Confidential Draft—April 20, 1937."

[29]*Congressional Record*, 75 Congress, 2 session (1937), 597–602.

[30]Ibid., U.S. Congress, Senate, Committee on Agriculture and Forestry, "Creation of Conservation Authorities," *Hearings before a subcommittee of the Committee on Agriculture and Forestry*, 75 Congress, 1 session, on S. 2555, "Bill to Provide for the Creation of Conservation Authorities and for Other Purposes," June 21–July 7, 1937, 1–288.

[31]*Washington Post*, January 26, 1937; *New York Times*, January 26, 1937; B. W. Allen, "Is Planning Compatible with Democracy," *American Journal of Sociology*, 42:510–20 (January 1937); Victor Weybright, "The Valleys and the Plains," *Survey Graphic*, 26:145–49 (March 1937); Karl T. Compton, "Engineering in an American Program for Social Progress," *Science ns.*, 83:301–2 (March 26, 1937); Stuart Chase, "Working with Nature," *Survey Graphic*, 26:624–28 (December 1937); James Lawrence Fly, "National Approach to Water Conservation," *Congressional Digest*, 17:19–21 (January 1938), Fly, general counsel of the T.V.A., addressing American Bar Association, September 28, 1937; *Congressional Record*, 75 Congress, 1 session (1937), 705–7; *House Reports* 1990–2369; 75 Congress, 3 session, Report Number 2030, "National Planning for Regional Conservation and Development of National Resources"; Dixon Wecter, *The Age of the Great Depression* (New York, 1948), 171–72.

[32]F.D.R. Papers, Group 13, PPF 1-P, Box 208, February 9, 1937, press conference, Number 343, 1–8; OF 1092, April 21, 1939, Roosevelt to F. Delano; December 1, 1938, Ickes to F.D.R.; December 3, 1938, F.D.R. to W. I. Meyers, chairman of Land Committee, National Resources Committee; *Congressional Record*, 75 Congress, 3 session (1938), 3149–50, 7216–17; 76 Congress, 3 session (1940), Appendix 1913–14.

[33]*Congressional Record*, 76 Congress, 1 session (1939), 1484–85, "Nation's Energy Resources," message from the president.

[34]Rockwell, "National Resources Planning" (Princeton University, May 1942), 130–55.

[35]F.D.R. Papers, Group 13, OF 1092, April 21, 1939, F.D.R. to Delano; Merriam, "National Resources Board," *American Political Science Review*, 38:1075–89 (December 1944).

[36]*National Resources Development Report for 1943, Part II: Wartime Planning for War and Post War* (January 1943, Washington), 2, National Resources Board.

[37]Merriam, "National Resources Board," *American Political Science Review*, 38:1075–89 (December 1944).

[38]Executive Order 8248, September 9, 1939.

[39]F.D.R. Papers, Group 13, Presidential Secretarial File, 1939, F. D. Delano, November 7, 1939, Delano to F.D.R.

[40]F.D.R. Papers, OF 1092, February 16, 1940, Whittington to F.D.R.

[41]Rockwell, "National Resources Planning" (Princeton, 1942), 1–218; *Summary History of N.P.B.*, mimeographed, National Archives.

[42]*Summary History of N.P.B.*, National Archives; F.D.R. Papers, Group 13, correspondence of H. Ickes to F.D.R.

[43]*Congressional Record*, 76 Congress, 3 session (1940), 269–70.

[44]Merriam, "National Resources Board," *American Political Science Review*, 38:1075–89 (December 1944); National Archives, *Summary History of N.P.B.*, mimeographed; *United States Statutes at Large*, 57:169.

[45]*Congressional Digest*, 17:14–17 (January 1938); "Energy Resources and National Policy," *Monthly Labor Review*, 49:1082–85 (November 1939); Robert H. Randall, "Conservation of Natural Resources," *Annals of the American Academy*, 206:142–46 (November 1939); *Congressional Record*, 76 Congress, 3 session (1940), Appendix 4944; 75 Congress, 1 session (1937), 1179–81; 950–53; 76 Congress, 1 session (1939), Appendix 1201–2; 3 session (1940), Appendix 1517; 250–51; 6833–34; *Summary Outline on National Land* (N.R.B., 1940), 1–29, mimeographed, National Archives; *A National Program of Public Works for Recreational Land* (January 1942), 1–44, prepared by representatives of the Department of the Interior and Agriculture for the Land Committee of the National Resources Planning Board, mimeographed, National Archives; *A National Program of Public Works for Range Conservation* (January 1942), 1–105, prepared by representatives of the Department of the Interior and Agriculture for the Land Committee of the National Resources Planning Board, mimeographed, National Archives; *Evaluation of Public Works for Land Protection and Development* (January 1941), mimeographed, National Archives.

[46]*National Resources Committee, 1939, Progress Report*, (National Resources Committee, 1939), 2.

[47]*National Resources Committee, 1938, Progress Report*, 26, 44; *National Resources Committee, 1939, Progress Report*, 1–173.

[48]*National Resources Committee, 1939, Progress Report*, 45.

[49]Ibid.; *National Resources Committee, 1939, Progress Report*, 14–15.

[50]*National Resources Committee, 1938, Progress Report*, 1–51; *Regional Planning, Part I; Pacific Northwest* (May 1936), 1–192, prepared by the Pacific Northwest Regional Planning Commission; U.S. National Resources Committee Advisory Committee on Water Pollution, Third Report on Water Pollution in the U.S., Washington, 1939, 1–165; *Forest Resources of the Pacific Northwest* (March 1938), 1–86, prepared by the Pacific Northwest Regional Planning Commission; An excellent guide to the report of the National Planning Board and its successors is the *Subject Index of Reports* (Washington, 1940), 1–70, pamphlet, a National Resources Committee Publication issued by the National Resources Planning Board.

[51]F.D.R. Papers, Group 13, OF 1, Agriculture, 1933, Arthur C. Ringland to E. H. Clapp; *Monthly Labor Review*, 37:836–39 (October 1933).

[52]F.D.R. Papers, Group 13, PPF 104, April 24, 1933, Cornelius Vanderbilt to F.D.R.; OF 79, September 19, 1933, Wallace to F.D.R.

[53]Ibid., PPF 38, August 20, 1937, Nelson Brown to F.D.R.; October 15, 1937, Brown to F.D.R.

[54]Ibid., OF 149, May 3, 1935, F.D.R. to Chief Forester Silcox; OF 1-C, June 18, 1935, Silcox to F.D.R.

[55]Ibid., Presidential Secretarial File, 1938, C General, April 15, 1938, Cooke to F.D.R.; April 19, 1938, Cooke to F.D.R.; OF 114, Box 2, April 19, 1938, F.D.R. to Hopkins.

[56]Edgar B. Nixon, *Franklin D. Roosevelt and Conservation 1911–1945*, Vol. 2, Franklin D. Roosevelt Library, Hyde Park, New York, 1957, Item 1142.

[57]Ibid., Item 1153.

[58]Ibid., Item 1164.

[59]Ibid., Item 1165.

✌ 8 ✌
An Evaluation of
the Criticisms of
the F.D.R. Conservation
Policy

Conservation under the Franklin D. Roosevelt administration was not
to go unchallenged. Like the rest of the New Deal program, it was
subjected to both adverse criticism and favorable comment. One must
approach a critical judgment of the Roosevelt conservation policy by
throwing into relief the major issues. These are the partisan issue, the
economic issues, special legislative issues, and government interdepartmental issues, and they are discussed in this order. In each case both
sides of the arguments are presented for greater clarity.

PARTISAN ISSUES

The overwhelming victory of the Democratic party in 1933 left little
opening for strong partisan criticism or opposition in the early days of
the New Deal. Also, the dire conditions within the nation made cooperation of the parties imperative. Partisan politics were second to saving
the nation. Under these conditions, greatly expanded conservation activity became a part of the Democratic program. Like the rest of the
New Deal, it at first suffered little or no partisan attack. Seldom did
charges of "politics" appear, although occasionally within the projects
underway and among office holders a political question would come up.
For example, Chief Forester R. Y. Stuart protested to Henry Wallace,
May 23, 1933, against a purported plan

... to inject political consideration into the employment of men used in forest field supervisory positions in the Emergency Conservation Work. To follow this course would, in my judgment, so threaten the success of the project and public confidence in it as a non-partisan service that I believe every step should be taken to prevent it.[1]

In fact, it was not until the 1936 election drew near that specific comments on partisan aspects became at all frequent. By that date, the honeymoon had ended; the New Deal had been severely tested and sentenced by Supreme Court decisions, a critical spirit had developed, the Republican party had resumed a challenging attitude, and in Congress a conservative tone grew more frequent and more insistent. But even then, the conservation policy was not a main target. Congress members Dennis Chavez and A. Willis Robertson in 1936–37 asserted their faith in conservation and the feasibility of a continuing nonpartisan attitude.[2] Representative Robertson declared, "One thing that has always interested me in conservation is that it is a nonpolitical activity in which we can unite."[3] Senator Harry B. Howes reflected this attitude in a radio address in 1938 by stating that fortunately the great movement of conservation had been kept out of partisan politics.[4] Democrats and Republicans alike had witnessed the tragic calamities of nature—floods and dust storms. Floods did not favor the Republican party by carefully avoiding Republican states in order to lay waste the territory of Democrats. Dust storms respected no political party, economic class, age, or religion. The impersonal destruction of these natural forces thereby became a unifying factor. The principle of conservation was not partisan. There were, of course, causes for disagreement on the priority and size of different proposals. Endless questions of detail arose, about which bickering was only too possible. But even so, the support of politicians, normally critical, was more important than their occasional dissent.[5] By the end of the 1930s, warning cries arose that conservation was a word the politicians loved.[6]

ECONOMIC ISSUES

Economic issues formed a more evident basis for criticism. The Shelterbelt Project provides what is perhaps the most clear-cut example. Immediately after adoption on July 17, 1934, the Shelterbelt Project was subjected to critical attacks on economic ground. With political prescience, President Roosevelt had conferred with his office holders to determine the feasibility of spending money on a shelterbelt. The idea was one in which the president was particularly interested.[7] With the issuance of a presidential executive order, the newly erected shelterbelt project did receive favorable publicity.[8] At the same time, critical questions were raised. Jonathan Mitchell writing for the *New Republic* approved the shelterbelt idea but warned that it was suffering from over-publicity. He pointed out that too many ridiculous claims were being made for it. One of the president's own administrators, John R. McCarl, showed financial opposition to the chief executive's project by refusing to grant money for this purpose from funds set aside for drought relief. This was only the beginning of critical comment and action on the project that caught popular imagination. It was both condemned and praised in newspapers and periodicals alike.[10] Opposition to the project reached such proportion that Congress refused to appropriate funds to continue it in 1936.

Wallace's Advice on the Shelterbelt Opposition

Henry Wallace fully appreciated the growing antagonism to the shelterbelt and recommended to President Roosevelt that he bring the idea within broad legislation covering the development of farm forestry for the entire country. The value of this flank attack upon the opposition, as Wallace conceived it, was that those who stood against such a measure would appear to be against the national development of farm forestry, which would be a decidedly unpopular stand to take in Congress. Supported by such advice as Wallace's and by his own astuteness, Roosevelt had the Shelterbelt Project made a part of the long-range drought relief program.[11]

F.D.R.'s Request for Shelterbelt Publicity and Support

Thus the project continued, but as late as May 1939, the president deemed it wise to have more publicity on the project in Congress and throughout the country. He asked Secretary of Agriculture Wallace for a special drive to get this publicity.[12] The soundness of the project obviously had not been evident enough to make it easy to obtain funds as late as 1940, when various suggestions concerning its financing were considered. Should some of the general W.P.A. funds be taken? Should provision be made in the 1941 Emergency Relief Appropriation Act? And as to future support—should it stem from the S.C.S. and Forestry Act?[13] The president was insistent that the idea was a good one and, given time, would prove itself to be economic. Opposing opinion was equally insistent that the project was not financially sound. It was still open to conjecture whether the proposed belt of trees would prove an effective answer to the soil erosion problem or even influence climatic conditions. Indeed, many held that barring the originality of the idea, most of the claims associated with the project were grossly exaggerated. Adverse criticism of the project made necessary a frequent search for the money to carry it on and a continuous campaign of favorable publicity.[14]

Reclamation Judgments

In the field of reclamation, also, an economic issue appeared. The work of the Bureau of Reclamation, an agency established as early as 1902, was under criticism in the early 1930s. The high value of the reclamation projects was asserted by a number of people who were well placed to know the fact. Secretary Harold Ickes selected John W. Haw, director of the Agricultural Development Department of the Northern Pacific Railroad Company, St. Paul, Minnesota, and F. E. Schmitt, editor of *Engineering News Record,* New York City, to make an independent study of typical federal projects to ascertain their true conditions. The summary of their report stated:

> Reclamation by irrigation of land in the arid and semi-arid Western half of the United States is shown by its results to be a sound and desirable national undertaking. It represents a constructive policy of social development.[15]

Hearings before the Committee on Irrigation and Reclamation in June 1935, revealed a belief that conservation of the water supply and the use of unappropriated waters for irrigation was essential to the national prosperity.[16]

Revamping of Agricultural Adjustment Act Goals

When the oft-attacked Agricultural Adjustment Act, popularly known as the A.A.A., was nullified by the decision of the Supreme Court of January 6, 1936, the idea of adjusted production became part of the conservation story, for by enacting the Soil Conservation and Domestic Allotment Act on February 29, 1936, Congress shifted the basis of the operation of the former crop reduction of the A.A.A. to conservation. This obvious legislative makeshift met with cries of "Politics!" Was conservation to be a political football? Had the term itself acquired such a sweetness as to disguise the bitterest administrative pill, which might be economic poison? There were individual criticisms by farmers as well as printed charges.[17] For example, on April 21, 1937, Henry C. Turner returned a check to President Roosevelt for plowing under 9.7 acres of a clover crop in a Florida citrus grove on the ground that he had done nothing to earn the money.[18] The president's reply to Turner's disapproval of the practice of paying farmers to observe good conservation practices expressed the essence of his point of view: "The Government grants are intended to help the farmer avoid the cash sacrifices he would otherwise have to make in order to carry out good conservation practices." Thus, agricultural adjustment was carried on, and in 1938 the administration strengthened the link between regulation of production and induced conservation practices by passage of the new A.A.A. on February 16, 1938.[20]

Federal Government in Business

An important economic issue to arise from conservation undertakings was the criticism of the federal government activity in business, arising from the sponsorship of water power development. The New Deal power policy was indicated at an early date by the executive order of August 12, 1933, which designated the Federal Power Commission as an agency of the P.W.A. to aid in the development of water power and the transmission of electrical energy.[21] This plus the impetus given to public ownership in the power field caused private companies and financial control groups to complain of unfairness and to make other adverse criticisms.[22] The T.V.A. came to symbolize the trend toward public power activities, but it by no means comprised the whole power project in the nation. Vast enterprises such as the Bonneville and Grand Coulee Dams in the Columbia River, the Fort Peck Dam in the Missouri, and the Passamaquoddy Maine project indicate the rapid spread of public hydroelectric development.[23]

Objectives of Public Ownership

Supporting this tremendous extension of public ownership was a combination of motives. Complete socialization of the entire power industry was not the objective. But the New Deal policy did reflect dissatisfaction with the high rates, low use, and inadequate extension of power lines under the existing system. In general, the idea was that future water power projects should be preserved for public exploitation. The claim was that new developments necessarily would be of such a scale that public control was essential—that the existence, or threat, of public competition would aid greatly in removing existing defects in the power position. There was also the aim of linking new power developments with developments in other fields, like flood control and irrigation, and this needed overall coordination. Finally, there was the motive of providing work for the unemployed through developmental projects, among which power was considered to deserve high priority.[24]

Power Production of the Tennessee Valley Authority and Its Struggle with Private Companies

Power production was merely a part of the T.V.A.—a multipurpose project. The T.V.A. is, however, an excellent example for a detailed discussion of the opposition encountered by the administration to its power policy. At the time the T.V.A. went into effect, the Tennessee Valley was almost entirely served by privately owned utilities, among which companies belonging to the Commonwealth and Southern system formed a predominant part. Problems arose promptly upon the erection of new federal dams and the generation of additional power. How was the power to be distributed? Naturally, the private companies preferred to buy it in bulk for retailing at their usual high rates, but the T.V.A. Act specifically gave preference to municipalities and farmers' cooperatives. Thereby the T.V.A. power had a choice of purchasing the existing systems of private companies or constructing competing systems and creating a major economic issue.[25]

Negotiations with the Commonwealth and Southern Corporation were undertaken, and a contract was signed on January 4, 1934. However, the intention of the T.V.A., as a follow-up to the contract to acquire Alabama and Tennessee properties, failed, and negotiation by municipalities for the Alabama Power Company (a subsidiary of the Commonwealth and Southern) was also unsuccessful. It was the beginning of the struggle between the private companies and the federal government. The attempts to negotiate met with charges by the private companies that they had no protection against municipal competition. Further conferences ended when Commonwealth and Southern and its associated companies joined in an application for a temporary injunction in the case of *Tennessee Electric Power et al.* v. *T.V.A.* (the so-called 18 Power Companies Case). On December 22, 1936, the granting of a sweeping injunction virtually suspended T.V.A. power activities. The contract with Commonwealth and Southern then was allowed to lapse, and the T.V.A. pursued more aggressive marketing policies elsewhere. It entered into new industrial contracts and also effected a contract with the Arkansas Power and Light Company. But seeds for a harvest of publicity antagonistic to the T.V.A. had been sown. The private utility interests and coal producers, who also feared the effects of the power development on their markets, joined forces in opposing the T.V.A. They had the support of a majority of Republicans on general grounds of policy.

The struggle over the issue of unfair competition between government and private business was a long and severe one.[26] The private companies insisted upon this seemingly unanswerable argument, but their attacks were weakened when early in 1938 the Supreme Court in *Alabama Power Company* v. *Ickes*[27] affirmed the validity of P.W.A. loans and grants and ruled in effect that private companies were not immune from lawful competition. That same year a three-judge district court also rendered a decision for T.V.A. in the 18 Power Companies case.[28] The backbone of opposition cracked. In 1939 the court decision in the 18 Power Companies case[29] held that power companies operating in T.V.A. territory had no standing in court to question the validity of the T.V.A.'s power program or the constitutionality of the T.V.A. Act. This served to reopen negotiations with Commonwealth and Southern, and eventually the T.V.A. approached the end of its program of acquisition of power facilities. After bitter struggles, terms were finally reached between the private companies and the T.V.A. One of the most controversial aspects of the federal power program had become history.

Yardstick Function of the Tennessee Valley Authority

No aspect of the T.V.A. experiment aroused greater controversy than its significance as a regulatory device—its "yardstick" function. The term yardstick is misleading, because it implies a clear, simple, fixed instrument for measuring. But the T.V.A. as a public ownership project exists under special cost conditions. If the effectiveness of government ownership and operation in producing and selling power is to be compared with private ownership and operations, a common measure had to be devised. With this in mind, the Engineering Staff of the Joint Congressional Committee investigating the T.V.A. declared that T.V.A. rates may constitute a "legitimate honest yardstick of the accomplishment of a public agency under the operating conditions confronting the T.V.A.," but that they should not be viewed as "an absolute comparative yardstick to be applied any time, any place, and under any conditions to private industry."[30]

It is not surprising that the idea that retail rates of T.V.A. distributors could be met at a profit by privately owned companies has been vigorously assailed by spokesmen of the power industry. They assert that T.V.A. distributors receive a subsidy in the form of low wholesale rates, a further subsidy in the form of free promotional services provided by the T.V.A. that enable them to increase rates within cost, and that the internal bookkeeping of these local agencies does not reflect the true costs of their operations nor does it show the costs that could be borne by private companies. These charges are countered by T.V.A. spokesmen who point out that T.V.A. wholesale rates cover costs, and that some private companies are selling large blocks of firm power at less than the T.V.A.'s wholesale rates. On the charge of free promotional services acting as subsidy, T.V.A. spokesmen reply by pointing out the services provided to local agencies are computed as costs covered by the T.V.A.'s wholesale rates. To the charge of incomplete bookkeeping, the reply is that both municipalities and cooperatives keep their accounts in accordance with the accounting system prescribed by the Federal Power Commission, which is also applicable to private companies.

Obviously the retail rates of T.V.A. distributors cannot be used as an exact measuring stick by which to judge the equitableness of private power rates, because costs of services do vary in different sections of the nation. Conditions must be qualified. Because of its implications, the metaphor of the yardstick was unfortunate. There is no doubt that, in practice, the threat of government competition has operated as a discipline, compelling private companies to stress efficiency and lower costs, to engage in aggressive sales campaigns, and to stress low rates and high utilization. This has not resulted in a loss of the private power companies' profit margins. In fact, the experience of Commonwealth and Southern subsidiaries in T.V.A. territory indicated that profit margins may even increase under the stimulus of low-rate, high utilization policy.[31] But this is not all. The real significance of the T.V.A. policy is to be seen in its low-rate policy with the view of developing its markets rapidly. In contrast,

> . . . the traditional marketing approach of private industry has been to establish rates which will cover as far as possible the costs of service immediately, and gradually reduce rates over the long period required to develop the market under such rate policies; in other words, to make the rate-payer earn his rate reduction in advance.[32]

SPECIAL LEGISLATIVE MEASURES

Taylor Grazing Bill

The third group of issues around which were centered criticism and opposition to the Roosevelt conservation policy was special legislative measures. One such was the Taylor Grazing Bill, which became law on June 28, 1934, but which encountered considerable challenge before its enactment. The bill underwent extensive hearings and discussion focused on the questions: Should the administration of the public domain be under the supervision of the two departments, Agriculture and Interior? And, was it or was it not a federal or state problem?[33]

Opposition to the bill was expressed in the views of Senator Henry F. Ashurst of Arizona, J. B. Wilson, secretary of the Wyoming Wool Growers' Association, and A. Johns, president of the Arizona Wool Growers' Association. Senator Ashurst argued that the bill would end homesteading. Mr. Wilson opposed the bill on the grounds that some livestock producers favored public domain control by the states rather than by the nation. He said that a small minority of livestock producers in Wyoming believed there should be some measure of federal control on the public domain but opposed the Taylor Bill in the form in which it was written. Mr. Wilson cited information designed to prove that overgrazing was not a problem. Mr. Johns, in opposing the Taylor Bill, stated that he recognized a need for federal control, but felt that it should be worked out in cooperation with the states.[34]

The legislation, however, also had strong advocates. Approval of the bill was expressed by Augustus S. Houghton, who represented the Camp Fire Club of America, New York City. He believed that the bill was valuable because it provided for the control basic to the conservation of grazing lands. Senator King from Utah also saw a need for the control of grazing lands. F. A. Silcox, chief of the Forest Service, as well as Robert Butler, secretary of the American Forestry Association, favored the bill. Oliver Lee, representing the New Mexico Cattle Raisers' Association, joined in approval of it; according to him 80 percent of the livestock raisers of New Mexico favored the general principles in the bill. Others who favored the bill itself were Henry I. Harriman, president of the United States Chamber of Commerce, and Edward T. Taylor, representative from Colorado. Mr. Harriman, speaking simply for himself, expressed the opinion that the bill was well drawn. Mr. Taylor stated that the bill as framed was the result of efforts begun years ago. He emphasized the point that it attempted to save 173 million acres from destruction. The opposition to the bill, he felt, came largely from people who did not want any control over the public domain. Testimony revealed that the people likely to be the most benefited were the local taxpayers, the little farmers, and the small stockmen.[35]

President Roosevelt sent a letter to Robert F. Wagner, chairman of the Committee of Public Lands, during the hearings of the Taylor Bill, expressing his hearty approval. Harold Ickes, when appearing before the Committee on Public Lands, stated that the 173 million acres of public domain usually called range needed to have a forage crop restored on what was now a badly damaged grazing land. He challenged the contentions that grazing districts would abrogate homestead laws; that the administration could not meet the problems of the livestock industry; and that land should be ceded to the states.[36]

After the Taylor Bill had become law, it received both adverse and favorable publicity.[37] President Roosevelt offered congratulations on the occasion of the Salt Lake City Grazing Conference and declared that "the grazing program on the public domain under the Taylor Grazing Act is a new conservation movement that promises historic significance."[38]

Flood Legislation

The flood legislation of the 1930s also involved many contentious issues. Hearings held in 1935 reflected the desire to have federal flood control work. Floods in 1936 spurred action. Newspapers carried accounts of individual criticism of the administration for its failures to act on a flood control program, individual demands for action, and congressional attempts to formulate new flood legislation.[39] Yet the support given to federal action ofttimes was with reservation in relation to questions of procedures. For example, the U.S. Chamber of Commerce declared that only when flood control projects were on major streams and affected a number of states should primary responsibility rest with the federal government.[40] Howard A. Meyerhoff, a geologist writing in *Science*, warned of the dangers of a too enthusiastic attitude toward flood control. He emphasized the need to see the whole problem.[41]

On the other hand, the urgency for action also led to unqualified support of flood control by some writers, government officials, and societies, as well as favorable discussion in periodicals, and newspapers.[41] Even after the flood control bill of 1936 became law on June 22, 1936, there still was a demand for more positive action, often on a critical basis. Letters demanding action were received by officials in responsible positions. R. Balter of the Balter Paper Company of Pittsburgh, Pennsylvania, wrote to Secretary Ickes on July 8, 1936, urging flood control and substantial appropriations, declaring that the last flood had caused considerable business loss.[43] That same month Tom Hulton of the Binghamton *Press*, New York, wrote to the acting director of the Division State Planning in Albany, New York, demanding a start in the current season of emergency flood control projects. He expressed irritation at the news that although the president made available $128 million, he had talked of delaying work because Congress had not made specific appropriations. Mr. Hulton clearly stated his impatience:

> There isn't any need in my pointing out that the people of these and other areas, who have been led to believe that in cases like ours

where the Army Engineers' plans are completed and approved emergency priority would be given to the work, are completely out of patience with the most recent development.[44]

Throughout the 1930s flood control obviously was widely discussed in the public press. Articles were frequent on both sides of each proposed way to effect control.[45] Items recurred demanding action instead of talk. Critics assailed the construction of flood curb dams as "slipshod." Questions were raised on the true meaning of conservation and its relation to flood control.[46] Roosevelt himself and the personnel within top administrative posts were publicly accused of being to blame for the suffering in Hartford caused by the hurricane. Legislation had provided for reservoirs to control the floods, but where were the reservoirs?[47] Roosevelt pointed out that it was impossible to complete any reservoirs begun in the summer. The administration was not to blame for what it could not do, what nobody could do; those who blamed it spoke unjustly and from partisan bias: "The mentality of those guilty of such complications is not very different from the words of those in international affairs who seek in very similar ways, to play with human lives."[48]

State's Rights

The foregoing issues never reached major proportions. It was the states' rights drama that captured the limelight. Here the struggle revolved about proposed projects and legislation, one so touching a live nerve in the body politic as to excite wide and continuing publicity. It had its beginning in the fall of 1937 when Governor George D. Aiken of Vermont publicly assailed the president's policies on the proposed Connecticut River interstate compact.[49] Aiken declared that the federal government wanted to broaden its activities in a way that threatened the very existence of the states. Any natural resource might be commandeered by the federal government if the present trend continued. Vermont, he concluded, opposed the loss of states' rights.[50] This was only the beginning of the controversy. Vermont needed flood control, as did her sister states New Hampshire, Massachusetts, and Connecticut, but they did not want to surrender power production. The resulting impasse held up dam building on the Connecticut and Merrimack Rivers. During the summer the four states had ratified an interstate compact under which federal funds were to be used to build dams and reservoirs, and state funds were to pay for land purchases and incidental expenses. The compact reserved to the states benefits and advantages of water conservation, power storage, and development. To President Roosevelt this reservation seemed in conflict with the Flood Act of 1936. Hence, a controversy arose over: the possible loss of tax revenue to states when the federal government got the property; the question of how much leeway would be given to private enterprises in the development of water power; and sentimental unwillingness on the part of the people of the states to alienate even a small part of territory.[51] The need for compromise was evident.

On September 21, 1937, the New England governors held a conference to plan cooperation between the New England states and the federal government on the question of flood control.[52] But, far from dying down, the cry of danger to state sovereignty continued during 1938. State governors of Vermont, Washington, and North Carolina sent a telegram to the Senate stating they were not ready to give the federal government complete control over resources and water rights as the Senate amendment provided in the flood control bill.[53]

The following year the nation's newspapers took opposing views of the states' rights issue. An article in the *New York Tribune* on January 15, 1939, "Not by a Dam Site, defended the stand of the states as rightfully challenging the federal government. The Vermont case was viewed as a test case, and the paper stated, "Here is an attack on the type of local autonomy which is the very essence of the American democracy."[54] The *Washington Post* on January 16, 1939, stressed the individualistic character of the Vermonters and supported their belief in self-government.[55] On the other hand, an editorial in the *Springfield Daily News* supported Congressman J. Casey's assertion that the problem of flood control was essentially a federal project rather than one of individual states.[56] Congress members also expressed similarly divergent views.[57]

The contending states did not let the issue die. On January 14, 1939, a message sent to Senator F. T. Maloney signed by the governors of Vermont, New Hampshire, Connecticut, Massachusetts, Maine, and Rhode Island urged the federal government to cooperate with the states to accomplish flood control without demanding the complete surrender to the federal government of basic rights belonging to the people in the states. They concluded:

> We believe that the natural resources of all the States belong to the people therein and that they should not be taken away without the consent of the States, acting through the duly chosen representative of the people.[58]

Governor Aiken continued to be a main spokesman and sent a telegram to Senator Maloney, on the same date, to say that he had been informed of the president's statement that if Vermont did not want dams it did not have to have them. Aiken told the senator he hoped the president was not trying to becloud the real issue. It was not flood control dams that were opposed, but the surrender of state sovereignty and resources to the federal government. Senator Maloney replied that he did not believe the president was beclouding the issue and the compact would not get approval. Maloney was anxious to preserve states' rights but he was not blind, he said, to the fact that changing conditions and a changing public desire necessarily bring about a change in governmental policy. The objective was to protect people from floods, and a time had come for action in which the national government had to take the lead.[59]

The resolution of the controversy was indicated by W. Whittington in his address before the National River and Harbors Congress on March 23, 1939. He explained the need for the national approach to flood control and the abuse of the states' right argument. He thrust a harpoon into the flank of the opposition by pointing out that state compacts were no longer necessary under terms of the act of 1938. Time proved the validity of his statement because without a doubt, the flood control policy of the country was a national one and transcended state jurisdiction.[60]

GOVERNMENTAL INTERDEPARTMENTAL ISSUES

Interdepartmental issues touched various phases of conservation, ranging from conflicting views and proposed projects to administrative changes. The proposed Colorado Big Thompson Transmountain Diversion Project encountered opposition. William P. Wharton, president of the National Parks Association, wrote President Roosevelt on July 1, 1937, that the Senate bill proposing the project menaced the entire National Parks System. He said that it did this by permitting economic use of natural resources within the Rocky Mountain National Park, thereby setting a precedent that might easily break down the barriers against similar projects in other parks. Wharton declared: "If the National Park System is to be maintained as a unique American institution, it is clear that economic development within every Park must be prevented."[61] Other individual opposition was made known to President Roosevelt, including that of J. C. Gregory, national director of the Izaak Walton League of America. President Roosevelt acknowledged the charges and declared he would do nothing to jeopardize the national park policy as declared in 1916. At the same time, individual support was given to the bill that was adequate to enable the adoption of the Colorado Big Thompson project in spite of opposition and apprehension.[62]

Mount Olympic National Park Project

The Mount Olympic National Park project received more stormy opposition.[63] The state of Washington and some people in the United States

Forestry Service strove to prevent the inclusion of Bogachiel River Valley in the Olympic National Park as a representative rain forest area. The state of Washington also opposed the proposed addition of 50,000 acres to the park.[64] On December 21, 1939, President Roosevelt wrote to Governor Clarence D. Martin of Washington that he had decided to include the tracts in the Olympic National Park and that he hoped the federal and state governments would act together to preserve the timberlands for the people.[65] In discussing his decision during a press conference, the president said that the question of adding a certain two areas hinged on two matters—"Some of the people out there thought . . . we might jeopardize what they call the sustained yield of pulpwood to supply paper . . ." and "the other question was the question of what is a rain forest?"[66] But by no means did the criticism or bitter feelings end with the decision. As late as June 15, 1940, publicity was still given to the issue. After all, the action had caused countrywide demonstrations, division among conservationists, debate in Congress, and bitter conflict between the Departments of the Interior and Agriculture.[67]

Proposed Transfer of the Forest Service

The conflict between the Departments of the Interior and Agriculture actually had started at a much earlier date during the Roosevelt administration. The proposed transfer of the Forest Service from the Department of Agriculture to the Department of the Interior incurred opposition from Gifford Pinchot as early as April 18, 1933. He asserted that the Department of Agriculture "is organized from the point of view of growth, and the main business of the Forest Service is to grow trees."[68] Pinchot's opposition to the proposed transfer was supported by individuals in such positions as the executive secretary of the Conservation Association of Los Angeles County and the head of the Forestry Department of Connecticut State College.[69]

Proposal to Change the Name of the Department of the Interior

Into this seething cauldron of ill-suppressed, conflicting beliefs, policies, and intentions fell the explosive measure S. 2665, proposing to change the name of the Department of the Interior. Then the pot boiled over. The bill came under sharp discussion in hearings held in the spring of 1935. Secretary of Agriculture Wallace said that the change would be likely to arouse suspicion.[70] During additional hearings held in the summer of 1935, Secretary Ickes expressed the opinion that sooner or later there ought to be in the government a Department of Conservation. He contended that conservation should be under one department for two reasons: (1) Under one department, conservation can be administered more economically and effectively than if scattered among various departments of the government. (2) We are not going to get very far in building up a real conservation policy for the government unless all conservation activities are in one department, under the scrutiny of people who are interested in conservation and can directly relate all conservation problems to each other. Plainly, this was a hot issue, as the statements by other people at the hearings demonstrated, for some were as outspoken in favor of a Conservation Department as others were bitterly against it.[71]

It was only the beginning of opposition to changing the name of the Department of the Interior. Dean W. W. Burr of the College of Agriculture, University of Nebraska, voiced objection.[72] Acting Secretary of Agriculture Tugwell, on August 3, 1935, sent to President Roosevelt typical letters of opposition to the proposal.[73] Ickes, ardently desiring the new department, began to fight the opposition. He wrote to his chief on May 21, 1936, that he would rather head a Department of Conservation than anything else.

> Now it appears that leaders of the House are reluctant to bring in a rule of their belief that the White House does not favor the passage of this bill.
>
> Accordingly, we find ourselves in this situation: Here is a bill which I never would have introduced except with your consent. In flagrant violation of your orders, the Department of Agriculture has opposed it by hook and crook from the beginning. The Forest Service particularly stirs up opposition and then Henry Wallace tells you that there exists the opposition which he and assistants have stirred up. It is represented that a great political issue has been raised.
>
> I do not know whether I know any more politics than my colleague in the Cabinet, but I take issue with that statement. I do not believe that the farmers of the country care one tinker's damn whether this Department is called the Department of the Interior or the Department of Conservation. The newspapers of the country do not indicate that the prairies are on fire about it. Even if the farmers have a mild interest in the matter, that interest would not carry beyond the accomplishment of the act . . . the lobby of the Department of Agriculture is the best organized and the most vocal of any lobby interested in Federal legislation.
>
> I feel this whole matter very keenly. I am willing to take my licking in a fair fight, but this has not been a fair fight. Is the Department of Agriculture to have its way in all matters? Isn't it time that we really did something real about conservation, the subject that

we have been talking about for a couple of generations? It seems to me that the politics of the situation is in favor of creating a department of conservation. Here would be something concrete; something to which this Administration would have a right to point with justifiable pride. . . .

I have had the situation in the House carefully canvassed. Chairman O'Connor is perfectly willing to support a rule just as he is willing to support this bill. The Speaker will follow what he believes to be your wishes. . . .

It is my honest opinion that the passage of this bill at this session would not lose the Democrat ticket in a single farmer vote next November.

. . . I cannot deny that this matter is of intense personal interest to me. . . . I would rather head a department of conservation than anything else I can think of.[74]

This was a battle cry. He was determined to have the support of the president. On May 24, 1936, he wrote to Roosevelt that the proposal to change the name of the Department of the Interior was attracting little attention, none of it adverse.[75] But the views of the opposition had been coming to the president. The Western Slope Wool Growers Association, Montrose, Colorado, telegraphed him against placing the Forest Service under the Department of the Interior. H. P. Chapman, president of the Society of American Foresters, wrote to resist any transfer of the Forest Service to a proposed Conservation Department.[76] Secretary Wallace sent an Interior Department release to President Roosevelt that indicated that the president did favor changing the name of the Department of the Interior. Wallace believed it important to clarify the situation and wrote:

Seriously, it seems to me that you can render the cause of reorganization a very great service by passing word out quietly in the right quarters that you do not want to see the name of the Department of Interior changed.[77]

Gifford Pinchot made public announcements attacking the Brownlow recommendations for reorganization of government departments. He assailed President Roosevelt and Secretary Ickes vehemently as "ambitious power seekers" and accused the president of trying to abolish Congress. The responsibility for the proposed departmental changes and bureau transfer he laid squarely to the ambitions of one man—Harold Ickes.[78]

Ickes and his supporters continued to fight for his cause. For example, the County Sportsmen League at Welch, West Virginia, adopted a resolution favoring a single Conservation Department.[80] Arthur Golding of the Izaak Walton League sent a petition to President Roosevelt supporting the creation of a Department of Conservation.[81] On April 20, 1939, Ickes, in corresponding with President Roosevelt, stated that he would make no further suggestions about powers given to the president under the Reorganization Act of 1939, acknowledging that although he had been working for the transfer of Forestry to the Interior, the plan did not seem to commend itself to the president. He had learned, he said, that the president did not propose to transfer the national forests. A week later, however, he showed his cooperative spirit, in answering Roosevelt's questions relating to the latter's authority under the Reorganization Act of 1939 to transfer certain functions presently administered in other agencies to the Department of the Interior. He enumerated a number of functions of the Department of Agriculture that he felt overlapped and conflicted with those of the Department of the Interior. These included the functions of the S.C.S. and the Bureau of Agricultural Engineering—in its activities relating to the control and utilization of water resources in arid and semiarid regions—and the function of administration of all grazing lands within national forests.[82]

Renewal of Forest Service Transference

By 1940 discussion again began to center on the transference of the Forest Service. At first, it looked as though the battle was a losing one for the secretary of the interior. Gifford Pinchot wrote to the president on January 1, 1940: "Your assurance, in our talk of October a year ago, that neither the Forest Service nor any of its functions would be transferred out of the Department of Agriculture was deeply appreciated. . . ."[83] To help the president, he secured opinions of faculty members of American Forest Schools by distributing a form letter to be signed and returned, the collection of them to go to Roosevelt. Then suddenly it seemed as though Ickes' growing defeat had changed to victory.

On January 6, 1940, Roosevelt's preliminary draft of a message to Congress, transmitting the Reorganization Plan to Congress, gave justification for the transfer of the Forest Service to the Interior.[84] At the same time, President Roosevelt showed a lack of confidence in the form letters Gifford Pinchot had circulated because the approach was too reminiscent of the organized drives, on him and on Congress, by individuals like Coughlin and groups like the U.S. Chamber of Commerce or the Ku Klux Klan itself. In his critical reply to Pinchot, Roosevelt discussed the two schools of thought with regard to the two departments concerned. One of these views was that everything that grows should be in the Department of Agriculture and only inanimate things like minerals should be in the Interior Department. Roosevelt pointed out that if this were done, the Department of Agriculture would be bigger than all the other departments of the government put together. He declared, "One of the essentials of Government is to prevent any one Department from becoming a tail that runs the Federal dog."[85] The president favored the school of thought that logical division went back to the origin of both departments, and concluded ". . . incidentally, the days have passed when any human being can say that the Department of Agriculture is wholly pure and honest and the Department of the Interior is utterly black and crooked."[86] Pinchot acknowledged the president's letter, giving reasons why Forestry should not be transferred to the Interior Department and concluded:

> It strikes me as particularly unfortunate that conservation should become a controversial issue just at this time when I believe it can be made the foundation of enduring peace between nations. This is what I wanted to see you about. . . .[87]

Roosevelt sent this message of Pinchot's to Ickes, who wrote the president that he would not answer Pinchot's arguments; the case was in Roosevelt's hands.[88]

Secretary of Interior Ickes' Position on the Forest Service Issue

Pinchot was not without support in the recent developments. George W. Norris wrote to President Roosevelt expressing his disappointment over the president's change of mind in his decision to transfer the Forest Service to the Interior. Norris suggested that the president make Ickes secretary of war, where "he would have a wonderful opportunity to do a real service in carrying out your ideas of conservation." Roosevelt forwarded this message to Ickes: "To read for your amusement and return for my files."[89] Ickes conferred with Norris on the matter and reported to President Roosevelt that Norris had no objection to the transfer on principle. He merely felt that action at the present time might be adverse to reelection. In fact, Ickes himself came round to Norris' view as stated in the latter's terms. He decided that while the transfer might have been possible to effect in the last session, he could not, under the now-existing circumstances, ask the president to press the matter through. This was a big decision for him to make, for the issue was to his mind absolutely fundamental. It had become so much a symbol to him that in sacrificing his point of view he lost heart, and desired to be relieved of his post as secretary of the interior:

I have had one consistent ambition since I have been Secretary of the Interior, and that has been to be the head of the Department of Conservation, of which, necessarily, Forestry would be the keystone. I have not wanted merely to be a Secretary of the Interior; I have wanted to leave office with the satisfaction that I had accomplished something real and fundamental. I have told you frankly that, as this Department is now set up, it does not interest me.

So I have come to the reluctant conclusion, that, as matters now stand, I cannot be true to myself nor measure up to the high standards that you have a right to expect of a man whom you have honored by making him a member of your Cabinet. Accordingly, I am resigning as Secretary of the Interior. . . .

You have highly honored me by naming and retaining me as a member of your Cabinet for practically seven years. Until last July 1, I thoroughly enjoyed my work. Although I now feel that I cannot go on, I want you to know how much I appreciate the many expressions of regard and confidence that I have had from you and what an inspiration it has been to work in such close cooperation with the man whom I regard as the outstanding statesman of this generation.[90]

As has been noted in Chapter 3, Roosevelt simply waved aside Ickes' resignation. "I continue to need you," he wrote. Ickes' reply expressed his admiration and love. In reiterating his devotion and loyalty, he added:

However, in all sincerity, I believe that the flank attack on Forestry . . . is the proper approach at this time. You cannot afford to be beaten on this issue. . . . Least of all would I want to be even indirectly responsible for your defeat.[91]

Thus the issue was closed, and thus too was demonstrated a tie of loyalty that even strong interdepartmental differences could not break. (See Appendix C for further documentation of Ickes' loyalty to and admiration of F.D.R. as a leader.)

Proposal to Transfer the Soil Conservation Service

In the spring of 1940, it was proposed to transfer certain functions of the S.C.S. from the Department of Agriculture to that of the Interior. These were such soil and moisture-conserving operations as were conducted on lands under the jurisdiction of the latter.[92] Secretary Ickes wrote to Roosevelt complaining that this proposal did not give Interior reclamation powers. He did not intend to argue about it in view of the "hopelessness of trying to get even powers that logically belong to Interior when Agriculture is involved, unless Henry Wallace is willing that they should come here." Ickes stated that he was bitterly disappointed because when he had lost Forestry, he had presented an alternative plan with which he would have been content, although it failed to meet his legitimate expectations. "Now even this is being whittled down to a point that leaves me without present or further interest."[93] In a more sarcastic vein, on July 21, 1940, he answered a letter in which President Roosevelt dealt with the financing of the section of the S.C.S. that Reorganization Plan IV scheduled for transfer to Interior. Ickes said that he did not want this "little starveling," which the Department of Agriculture had neglected because Henry Wallace had not favored a just and fair amount of soil conservation work on the public lands.[94]

Death of the Forest Service Issue

The larger issue of the Forest Service transfer died hard. As late as September 12, 1940, James Byrnes informed President Roosevelt that he had heard that there still was the possibility of transferring the Forest Service under the Reorganization Act and that an effort would be made to have the president issue such an order and submit it to the next Congress. Byrnes was anxious to learn if the president had changed his views on the subject and contemplated such a move. He believed Roosevelt should deny such intention, and pointed out that Wilkie planned to accuse him of it in his western speeches.[95] So the forest Service transfer question became entangled in politics. Departmental office holders had writhed in the controversy, but uppermost now in the minds of all was the importance of the coming election.

VALUE JUDGMENT

Although it is particularly revealing to examine the criticism of Roosevelt conservation policy according to the issues involved, there was a more general criticism, in the sense of an implied judgment of value, in the extent of publicity that conservation, as such, was accorded in the public press. These accounts presented conservation issues as they appeared as major news in which the public had a spontaneous interest. One must, of course, sift out other publicity that was only special pleading appearing under the guise of disinterested reporting.

During the First Hundred Days, conservation measures were welcomed by the American people alongside other emergency measures. At the very outset, conservation received favorable press.[96] As time went on, newspapers, scientific journals, and popular periodicals expressed faith in the new leader, Roosevelt, as one who had preserved not only lives but natural resources through a sound program of benefit to all. Publicity stressed an intelligent and constructive procedure in the administration's handling of the natural resources.[97] Indeed, Roosevelt conservation never did lose favorable publicity. Throughout the years 1933–42, there were always articles appearing that commended the national resource policy. Some articles reported projects under construction, others presented statistics of what conservation had accomplished, others expressed approval of new legislation in the field, others, again, stressed the value of conservation achievement to human happiness, and others strongly supported a national policy of conservation.[98] No facet of the rapidly growing conservation movement was overlooked in U.S. publications. The newspaper and periodical accounts did vary in their coverage, style, and dramatic quality, but the supremely important fact is that all types of publications found some space for material on conservation. These included the scientific journals, such as the *Science ns* publication, academic publications like the *Annals of American Academy*, and such periodicals of a more popular nature as *Business Week, Survey Graphic, Saturday Evening Post, Colliers,* and the *Reader's Digest.*

Evidence proves without a doubt a wide support and approval of the Roosevelt administration's natural resource policy. However, it would be misleading to indicate that the public press never questioned the developing conservation policy; articles of such a nature did appear. For example, in 1936 the administrative organization carrying on conservation activity was challenged for working at cross-purposes and duplicating effort.[99] Scientists criticized a lack of practical application in the conservation efforts and urged that it be elevated from the ranks of the political system.[100] An article appearing in the *Rotarian* (May 1941) urged that we give Mother Nature a chance to work things her way.[101] Of a more serious nature was the attack based on the claim that the word "conservation" was being misused. Jay N. Darling, one-time chief of the Biological Survey, flung the accusation on the printed page that the word conservation had been used indiscriminately.[102] This danger was voiced elsewhere. Albert W. Atwood, writer for the *Saturday Evening Post,* reminded Americans of the potency in the word conservation, pointing out that it could be a real boon to the politicians because the public always approved of conservation, not knowing what it means, and that it was the chosen synonym for practically everything the New Deal was doing. A cry was raised that conservation might be pushed too suddenly and violently, thereby creating new problems.[103] The foregoing type of publication was, however, minor compared with the overwhelmingly favorable publications.

Diligent searching reveals some examples of unfavorable publicity for the Roosevelt national resource policy. However, it is true to say that, more generally, the policy captured the attention, the imagination, and the support of the citizens of the country. An even more valid test than publicity offers proof of the popularity of the conservation of natural resources; this is, that the Roosevelt policy survived the critical test of the day: partisan issues, economic issues, special legislative issues, and interdepartmental issues—all had been met. True, all problems had not, perhaps, been completely solved, but the national conservation policy had met challenges and charges with victory rather than defeat. This victory meant the establishment of a permanent conservation policy rather than an emergency or partisan program. And those many elements of existing national conservation policy that can be traced back to the influence and ideas of the Roosevelt administration stand out in Paul Bunyan-like relief before the record of criticisms.

NOTES

¹F.D.R. Papers, Group 13, OF 1-C, May 23, 1933, Chief Forester R. Y. Stuart to Henry Wallace.

²*Congressional Record,* 74 Congress, 2 session (1936), 6779–80, radio address by Chavez.

³Ibid., 75 Congress, 1 session (1937), 593–600.

⁴Ibid., 3 session (1938), 183–84.

⁵*New York Times,* January 16, 18, 24, 1939; also see Chapter 3.

⁶Paul B. Sears, "Science and the New Landscape," *Harper's Magazine,* 179:207–16 (July 1939).

⁷F.D.R. Papers, Group 13, OF 1-C, Agriculture, August 8, 1933, R. Y. Stuart, forester, to F.D.R.; August 14, 1933, F.D.R. to Stuart; September 13, 1933, F.D.R. to Wallace; July 17, 1934, executive orders; July 26, 1934, F. A. Silcox, chief forester, to secretary of agriculture; July 31, 1934, Tugwell memo on shelterbelt; September 18, 1934, memo from F.D.R. to director of budget; PPF 1P, Box 204, September 21, 1934, President Conference, Number 144, 4–5.

⁸"The Establishment of a Forest Shelter Belt," *Science,* 80:91 (July 27, 1934); "President Approves Plan for Record Reforestation," *Literary Digest,* 118:39 (July 28, 1934); "Planting a Shelterbelt through Middle of America," *Literary Digest,* 118:15 (August 11, 1934).

⁹Jonathan Mitchell, "Shelter Belt Realities," *New Republic,* 80:69–71 (August 29, 1934); *Newsweek,* 4:11 (September 29, 1934).

¹⁰Raphael Zon, "Shelter Belts—Futile Dreams or Workable Plans?" *Science ns,* 81:391–94 (April 26, 1935); Wilson Compton, "Government Versus Desert," *Forum,* 93:237–39 (April 1935); *New York Times,* February 25, July 9, 11, August 1, 4, 1936, June 19, 1939.

¹¹F.D.R. Papers, Group 13, OF 1-C, May 27, 1936, Wallace to F.D.R.; *New York Times,* August 1, 4, 1936.

¹²*New York Times,* August 1, 1937, June 19, 1939, F.D.R. Papers, OF 1-C, May 15, 1939, F.D.R. to Wallace.

¹³F.D.R. Papers, Group 13, OF 1-C, March 28, 1940, Wallace to F.D.R.; OF 79, May 3, 1940, Harold D. Smith, director of budget, to F.D.R.; OF 1-C, May 6, 1940, F.D.R. to Wallace.

¹⁴Ibid., OF 149, October 1, 1940, John Moses, governor of North Dakota, to F.D.R.;

November 4, 1940, Wickard, secretary of agriculture, to F.D.R.; OF 79, November 6, 1941, Harold Smith to F.D.R.; OF 149, February 15, 1945, Cooke to F.D.R.; February 26, 1945, F.D.R. to Cooke; April 6, 1945, Cooke to F.D.R.; April 9, 1945, F.D.R. to Cooke; *New York Times,* February 25, July 11, August 4, 1936, August 1, 1937; Compton, "Government Versus Desert," *Forum,* 93:237–39 (April 1935); Mitchell, "Shelter Belt Realities," *New Republic,* 80:69–71 (August 29, 1934).

¹⁵*Annual Report of the Secretary of the Interior, 1935,* (Washington, 1935), 44.

¹⁶U.S. Congress, House of Representatives, Committee on Irrigation and Reclamation, *Hearings before the Committee on Irrigation and Reclamation,* 74 Congress, 1 session, on H.R. 5533, "To Provide for the Impounding, Conserving and Making Use of the Unappropriated Waters of the Eastern Slope of the Rocky Mountains, and for Other Purposes," June 12, 13, 1935 (Washington, 1935), 1–186.

¹⁷"A.A.A. Conservation Instead of Crop Control May Save the Day," *Newsweek,* 7:16–17 (January 25, 1936); *Business Week* (March 28, 1936), 24; "Save the Soil," *Review of Reviews,* 93:28–30 (April 30, 1936); Jonathan Mitchell, "Mr. Wallace Tries Again," *New Republic,* 87:41–43 (May 20, 1936); also see Chapter 4.

¹⁸F.D.R. Papers, Group 13, OF 1-R, April 21, 1937, Henry C. Turner to F.D.R.

¹⁹Ibid., May 8, 1937, F.D.R. to Turner.

²⁰*U.S. Statutes at Large,* 52, Chapter 30, p. 31, 75 Congress, 3 session, Act 430.

²¹*Public Papers and Addresses of Franklin D. Roosevelt; 1935* (New York, 1938), 325–28.

²²*Congressional Record,* 75 Congress, 2 session (1937), 187–89; 5–6; 3 session (1938), Appendix 730–31; *New York Times,* August 6, 1934, November 7, 26, 1937; James Lawrence Fly, "National Approach to Water Conservation," *Congressional Digest,* 17:19–21 (January 1938).

²³"The 'New Deal,' Program for Electric Utilities," *Congressional Digest,* 15:230–31 (October 1936).

²⁴*Congressional Record,* 76 Congress, 3 session (1940), 11,524–25, address by the president at opening of Chickamauga Dam; 75 Congress, 2 session (1937), 187–89; John Scott, "Water Power Development," *Public Utilities Fortnightly,* (January 30, 1941), appears in *Congressional Record,* 77 Congress (1941), Appendix 394–97; "Water Planning Committee," *The American City,* 50:9 (May 1935).

²⁵F.D.R. Papers, Group 13, PPF 5850, May 17, 1933, F.D.R. to the editor of *Knoxville* (Tennessee) *Journal;* Merle Fainsod and Lincoln Gordon, *Government and the American Economy* (New York, 1948), 346–51.

²⁶"Electric Power and Government Policy," *Twentieth Century Fund* (New York, 1948), 601–16.

²⁷J. C. Swidler, R. H. Marquis, and C. H. Pritchett, "T.V.A. in Court," *Iowa Law Review,* 32:296–338 (January 1947).

²⁸"Electric Power and Government Policy," *Twentieth Century Fund* (New York, 1948), 607; *Tennessee Electric Power Company* v. *T.V.A.* 21, F Supp. 947 (1938), 360 U.S. 118 (1939).

²⁹Swidler, Marquis, and Pritchett, "T.V.A. in Court," *Iowa Law Review,* 32:296–338 (January 1947); Fainsod and Gordon, *Government and the American Economy* (New York, 1948), 355; James D. Bennett, "Roosevelt, Wilkie, and the TVA," *Tennessee Historical Quarterly,* 28:388–96 (Winter 1969).

³⁰Investigation of the T.V.A., *Senate Document 56,* Pt. 3, 76 Congress, 1 session (10308), 202, Washington, 1939.

³¹Investigation of the T.V.A., *Hearings before the Joint Committee,* 75 Congress, 3 session, Pt. 1, 158–59, Washington, 1939.

³²Investigation of the T.V.A., *Senate Document 56,* Pt. 1, 76 Congress, 1 session (10307), 190–98, Washington, 1939; Pt. 3, 76 Congress, 1 session (10308), 200–3, Washington, 1939; Fainsod and Gordon, *Government and the American Economy* (New York, 1948), 357–60.

[33]*United States Statutes at Large*, 48, Chapter 865, 1269–75; *Miscellaneous Senate and House Hearings*, 73 Congress, 1 session, on H.R. 6462, "An Act to Stop Injury to the Public Grazing Lands by Preventing Overgrazing and Soil Deterioration, To Provide for Their Orderly Use, Improvement and Development, To Stabilize the Livestock Industry Dependent upon the Public Range and for Other Purposes," *Hearings before the Committee on Public Lands and Surveys*, U.S. Senate, April 20–May 2, 1934 (Washington, 1934), 1–128.

[34]*Miscellaneous Senate and House Hearings, 1933–34*, U.S. Congress, Senate, Committee on Public Lands and Surveys, "An Act to Stop Injury to the Public Grazing Lands," *Hearings before the Committee on Public Lands and Surveys*, 73 Congress, 1 session (Washington, 1934), 1–128.

[35]Ibid., U.S. Congress, House of Representatives, Committee on Public Lands, "A Bill to Stop Injury to the Public Grazing Lands by Preventing Overgrazing and Soil Deterioration; to Provide for Their Orderly Use, Improvement and Development and Stabilize the Livestock Industry Dependent upon the Public Range," *Hearings before the Committee on the Public Lands*, 73 Congress, 1 session, on H.R. 2835, and 73 Congress, 2 session, on H.R. 6462, June 7–9, 1933, February 19–21, 23, 30, March 1–3, 1934 (Washington, 1934), 10–210.

[36]*Miscellaneous Senate and House Hearings, 1933–34*, U.S. Congress, Senate, Committee on Public Lands and Surveys, "An Act to Stop Injury to the Public Grazing Lands," *Hearings before the Committee on Public Lands and Surveys*, 73 Congress, 1 session (Washington, 1934), 1–128.

[37]C. S. Shea, "The Conservation of Public Lands," *Science ns*, 83:204 (February 28, 1936); "Hamilton Desert Maker," *Nation*, 148:229 (August 29, 1936); F.D.R. Papers, Group 13, OF 378, January 28, 1935, F.D.R. to Ickes and Wallace.

[38]F.D.R. Papers, Group 13, OF 633, January 3, 1936, F.D.R. to Ickes.

[39]U.S. Congress, House of Representatives, Committee on Flood Control, "A Bill to Authorize Funds for the Prosecution of Works for Flood Control and Protection against Flood Disasters," *Hearings before the Committee on Flood Control*, 74 Congress, 1 session, on H.R. 6803, March 22, 23, April 2, 1935 (Washington, 1935), 1–38; *New York Times*, March 22, 23, 30, April 1, 16, 1936; also see Chapter 3.

[40]*New York Times*, May 1, 1936.

[41]Howard A. Meyerhoff, *Science ns*, 83:622 (January 26, 1936).

[42]*New York Times*, March 22, May 24, June 19, 20, 1936; Arthur E. Morgan, "Downstream," *Survey Graphic*, 25:301 (May 1936); Morris L. Cooke, "Upstream," *Survey Graphic*, 25:300 (May 1936); Paul B. Sears, *Science ns*, 83:Supplement 9 (March 27, 1936); National Archives, Flood Control, Box 551.431–552.4 (1) series of clippings on flood control, (2) folder—news release, clip sheets, clippings.

[43]National Archives, Flood Control, 11 Boxes, Group No. 551, correspondence.

[44]Ibid.

[45]*Congressional Record*, 75 Congress, 1 session (Washington, 1937), 81; 2 session (Washington, 1937), 268; F.D.R. Papers, Group 13, OF 83, Box 4, September 26, 1938, Herman P. Kopplemann, M. C. Connecticut, to F.D.R.; September 29, 1938, F.D.R. to Senator F. H. Brown, also folder of correspondence and telegrams on floods; September 30, 1938, F.D.R. to Herman P. Koppleman; *New York Times*, January 12, March 19, 22, 24, 25, 30, 31, April 1–3, 10, 15, 19, 22, 26, 28, 29, May 16, 17, 19, June 20, July 12, 14, 19, August 2–4, 7, September 24, 1936; *New York Times*, January 4–6, 24–27, September 16, 18, 20, 21, December 11, 1937; *New York Times*, March 8, July 9, September 24, November 18, 1938; *New York Times*, January 13, 16, 18, April 30, May 6, 28, August 4, 6, 7, 1939; *New York Times*, January 15, 16, April 7, 1940; *New York Times*, August 18, 20, October 27, 1941.

[46]*Washington Herald*, January 27, 1937 (*Congressional Record*, 75 Congress, 1 session, 1937, 81); *New York Times*, September 24, 1936, December 11, 1937.

[47]F.D.R. Papers, Group 13, OF 83, Box 4, September 26, 1938, Herman P. Kopplemann, M. C. Connecticut, to F.D.R., editorials from *Hartford Courant* and *Times* enclosed.

[48]Ibid., September 29, 1938, F.D.R. to Senator Fred H. Brown, folder of correspondence and telegrams on floods; September 30, 1938, F.D.R. to Herman P. Kopplemann.

[49]*New York Times*, September 16, 18, 20, 21, 1937.

[50]Ibid., September 16, 1937.

[51]Ibid., September 18, 1937.

[52]Ibid., September 21, 1937.

[53]*Congressional Record*, 75 Congress, 3 session (1938), 9220; Appendix, a number of articles on flood control in New England and relationship or effect of national flood control to New England; *New York Times*, October 6, 1938, Governor Aiken said Vermont would cooperate if it did not need to surrender ownership of natural resources.

[54]*New York Tribune*, January 15, 1939 (*Congressional Record*, 76 Congress, 1 session [1939], Appendix 150).

[55]D. Thompson, "Green Mountain Holiday," *Washington Post* (January 16, 1939); *Congressional Record*, 76 Congress, 1 session (1939), Appendix 146.

[56]*Congressional Record*, 76 Congress, 1 session (1939), Appendix 414.

[57]Ibid., 1144–46, 846–48, 452–59, Appendix 1428–30, 1719, 323–24.

[58]Ibid., 470.

[59]Ibid.; *New York Times*, November 18, 1938.

[60]*Congressional Record*, 76 Congress, 1 session (1939), 1136–38; see Chapter 3; *New York Times*, March 8, 11, July 9, 1938; May 28, 1939, April 7, 1940, August 18, 20, 1941.

[61]F.D.R. Papers, Group 13, OF 402, July 1, 1937, W. P. Wharton to F.D.R.

[62]Ibid., July 8, 1937, Albert Z. Gray to F.D.R.; July 9, 1937, J. C. Gregory to F.D.R.; July 9, 1937, Alva B. Adann to McIntyre; December 20, 1937, Ickes to F.D.R.; August 4, 1937, F.D.R. to Albert Z. Gray (note on adoption).

[63]Ibid., May–July, 1938, 23 items relating to the establishment of Olympic National Park and others; Group 13, OF 6-P, March 21, 1938, F.D.R. to Cammer and Silcox.

[64]Ibid., Group 13, OF 6-P, December 11, 1939, Irving Brant to F.D.R.; December 11, 1939, E. K. Burlow, acting secretary of interior, to F.D.R.

[65]Ibid., OF 6, Box 36, December 21, 1939, F.D.R. to C. D. Martin, governor of Washington.

[66]Ibid., PPF 1-P, January 2, 1940, press conference, Number 161, 1–3.

[67]"How Much Conservation?" *Saturday Evening Post*, 212:12–13 (June 15, 1940).

[68]F.D.R. Papers, Group 13, PPF 289, April 18, 1933, Pinchot to F.D.R.

[69]Ibid., OF 1-C, Agriculture, October 30, 1934, George H. Cecil, ex-secretary, Conservation Association of L.A. County, to F.D.R.; November 1, 1934, A. E. Moss, head of Forestry Department, Connecticut State College, to F.D.R.

[70]U.S. Congress, Senate, Committee on Expenditures, "To Change the Name of the Department of the Interior and to Coordinate Certain Governmental Functions," *Hearing before the Committee on Expenditures in the Executive Departments*, 74 Congress, 1 session, on S. 2665, "A Bill to Change the Name of the Department of the Interior," May 16, 1935, 1–23; *Senate Reports on Public Bills, III* 925–1461, 74 Congress, 1 session, Report No. 1150, "Change the Name of the Department of the Interior," 1–7.

[71]U.S. Congress, Senate, Committee on Public Lands and Surveys, "Change the Name of the Interior Department," *Hearings before the Committee on Public Lands and Surveys*, 74 Congress, 1 session, on S.2665, "A Bill to Change the Name of the Department of the Interior and to Coordinate Certain Governmental Functions," July 11, 16, 1935, 1–55, *Miscellaneous Senate and House Hearings 1835–36*.

[72]F.D.R. Papers, Group 13, OF 1-C, Agriculture, June 19, 1935, Burr to J. Hamilton

Lewis, chairman of Committee on Expenditures, U.S. Senate; Gifford Pinchot, "A Forest Appeal," *Literary Digest,* 120:30 (July 1935).

[73]F.D.R. Papers, Group 13, OF 1-C, Agriculture, August 3, 1935, Acting Secretary of Agriculture Tugwell to F.D.R., letters opposing S. 2665 and H.R. 7712 to change name of the Department of Interior enclosed: (1) W. W. Burr, dean, College of Agriculture, University of Nebraska, to J. Lewis; (2) W. L. Wilson to Senator Duncan A. Fletcher, July 18, 1935; (3) Chris L. Christensen, University of Wisconsin, to Senator R. M. LaFollette, June 11, 1935; and (4) Carl E. Ladd, Cornell University, to Secretary Wallace, July 9, 1935.

[74]Ibid., Presidential Secretarial File, 1936, Interior Department—Ickes, Box 14, May 21, 1936, Ickes to F.D.R.

[75]Ibid., May 24, 1936, Ickes to F.D.R.

[76]Ibid., OF 6, Box 15, May 27, 1936, Western Slope Wool Growers Association to F.D.R.; OF 1-C, February 23, 1937, Chapman to F.D.R.

[77]Ibid., Presidential Secretarial File, 1937, Agriculture, Box 22, 1937, Wallace to F.D.R.

[78]Ibid., April 30, 1937, speech of Gifford Pinchot before Izaak Walton League, Chicago, April 30, 1937; *New York Times,* May 1, 1937.

[79]Harold Ickes, "A Department of Conservation," *Vital Speeches,* 3:693–95 (September 1, 1937), broadcast; Eugene Trani, "Conflict or Compromise: Harold L. Ickes and Franklin D. Roosevelt," *North Dakota Quarterly,* 36:20–29 (Winter 1968).

[80]*Congressional Record,* 75 Congress, 3 session (1938), 2488.

[81]F.D.R. Papers, Group 13, OF 177A, Arthur Golding, Izaak Walton League of America, Washington, D.C., to F.D.R.

[82]Ibid., OF 79, April 27, 1939, Ickes to F.D.R.

[83]Ibid., Presidential Secretarial File, 1940, Interior—Ickes, January 1, 1940, Gifford Pinchot to F.D.R.

[84]Ibid., OF 79, January 6, 1940, draft of the message transmitting Reorganization Plan to Congress and additional text apparently prepared by the budget in accordance with Roosevelt's memo to H. D. Smith, January 3, 1940; Richard Polenberg, "The Great Conservation Contest," *Forest History,* 10:13–23 (January 1967).

[85]F.D.R. Papers, Group 13, Presidential Secretarial File, 1940, Interior—Ickes, Box 58, January 15, 1940, F.D.R. to Pinchot.

[86]Ibid.

[87]Ibid., January 17, 1940, Pinchot to F.D.R.

[88]Ibid., January 23, 1940, Ickes to F.D.R.

[89]Ibid., January 25, 1940, Norris to F.D.R.; F.D.R. to Norris.

[90]Ibid., February 7, 1940, Ickes to F.D.R.

[91]Ibid., February 8, 1940, F.D.R. to Ickes; Ickes to F.D.R.

[92]Ibid., OF 79, April 5, 1940, Reorganization Plan Number IV, presidential draft.

[93]Ibid., Presidential Secretarial Files, 1940, Interior—Ickes, April 10, 1940, Ickes to F.D.R.

[94]Ibid., OF 79, July 23, 1940, Ickes to F.D.R.

[95]Ibid., Presidential Secretarial Files, 1940, Interior—Ickes, Box 58, September 12, 1940, James Byrnes to F.D.R.

[96]See Chapters 3 and 5; *New York Times,* March 11, 1933, *New York Times,* April 9, May 24, August 6, 1934; "What New Land Policy Will Do," *Saturday Evening Post,* (December 23, 1933); "Soil Erosion," *Science ns,* 78:Supplement 9 (August 4, 1933); "Energy Turned Into Mass for First Time in History," *Science ns,* 77:Supplement 9 (April 7, 1933).

[97]"Roosevelt and Conservation," *Nature Magazine,* 21:269 (June 1933); Harold L. Ickes, "Saving the Good Earth," *Survey Graphic,* 23:52–59 (February 1934); Richard Lieber, "Our Inherited Wealth," *Review of Reviews,* 89:44–45 (May 1934); "The National Domain and

the New Deal," *Saturday Evening Post,* 206:10–11 (December 23, 1933); *New York Times,* February 27, 1934.

[98]*New York Times,* February 27, 1934, April 17, 1936, November 27, 1939; Marquis James, "The National Domain and the New Deal," *Saturday Evening Post,* 206:10–11 (December 23, 1933), interview with Harold Ickes; *Nature Magazine,* (April 1935), editorial; Dr. Isaiah Bowman, "Our Better Ordering and Preservation," *Science ns,* 93:191–97 (February 28, 1941); *Congressional Record,* 76 Congress, 3 session (1940), Appendix 91–92; F.D.R. Papers, Group 13, PPF 1-P, Box 210, April 8, 1938, press conference, Number 449-A, 3–4.

[99]Arthur N. Pack, "Let's Get Together," *Nature Magazine,* 27:46–47 (January 1936).

[100]Dr. Harley J. Van Cleave, "Man Muddles with Nature," *The Scientific Monthly,* 40:339–48 (April 1935); *New York Times,* May 21, 1938 (M. L. Fernald of Harvard).

[101]Hendrick William Van Loon, "Give Mother Nature a Chance," *Rotarian,* 58:10–12 (May 1941).

[102]Jay N. Darling, "Conservation, a Typographical Error," *Review of Reviews,* 94:35–37 (November 1936).

[103]Albert W. Atwood, "Is This Conservation?" *Saturday Evening Post,* 209:23 (September 26, 1936); *New York Times,* October 11, 1936.

✑ 9 ✑
Conclusions

The period between the Great Depression of the early 1930s and the World War of the early 1940s was one of great significance in the history of the United States. During these years the economy underwent tremendous changes in the process of recovery from depression and a concurrent and rapid movement toward leadership amongst the nations. On this stage of history, Franklin Delano Roosevelt was, beyond dispute, a central figure. In internal affairs the so-called "New Deal" became associated with his name, for it involved changes effected under his administration. One aspect of this New Deal was a reevaluation and considerable extension of policy directed at the conservation of natural resources.

In this book the nature and achievements of conservation policy during this period have been examined. On the basis of the information presented, the following conclusions may be drawn.

The principle of conservation was no invention of the Roosevelt administration. With respect to many resources, conservation activities had been introduced by earlier governments, both federal and state. Notable examples are the withdrawal of land for national forests and the National Conservation Conference of Governors called by Theodore Roosevelt. But never before did conservation acquire such a comprehensive character. During the 1930s no resource escaped consideration for conservation. More significant still is the fact that although the approach was comprehensive, the record of achievement in the conservation of any single resource surpassed that of any previous administration.

Conservation was taken to be an immediate task by the new Roosevelt administration of 1933. There was also the important problem of bringing the nation out of depression. The fact that the two problems could be attacked jointly was recognized. This was one of the more important contributions of the administration. The idea of "pump priming" through government expenditure during depression was, itself, in its infancy. But, in addition, political economy owes much to the Roosevelt administration for the idea that this expenditure could be concentrated on conservation activities, of permanent benefit to the nation with a minimum of interference in the private sector of the economy.

Conservation activities, however, were not halted with an improvement in general economic conditions. It was obvious that the Roosevelt administration had conceived of long-term conservation programs, irrespective of economic conditions, early in its life. This is to say that it believed that the United States had not previously paid sufficient attention to the conservation of natural resources in order to guarantee long-term economic security. This mistake would have to be corrected even if it meant an extended social cost. In seeking support for this belief, the Roosevelt administration was greatly aided by the increasing severity of dust storms, water erosion, floods, and resulting widespread distress. In the years that followed, there was to be incorporated within the workings of the United States democracy what might rightly be termed a permanent conservation policy. This had its basis in the new concepts and procedures whereby effective activities associated with this objective comprised elements of a long-term character.

Important among the new concepts was that of the essential role of the federal government in effective conservation. It came to be recognized that the states as separate entities were no longer capable of coping with the problems alone. They needed financial assistance and leadership from the federal government. In addition, it was recognized that many then-existing conservation problems and projects transcended state boundaries. In response to these conditions, a dynamic federal conservation policy emerged during the 1930s, based on organization, supervision, and financial contribution.

Another important concept was that of coordinated planning. There was growing appreciation of the fact that the conservation of particular resources could not be set apart from that of other resources. The means available were scarce in relation to the possible conservation projects. There was a question of choosing what resource should receive attention over another, and of determining the scale of conservation activity with respect to a chosen resource. Fortunately, it was possible to achieve several purposes at the same time, but only through careful planning. It is here that the Roosevelt administration made another important contribution, for it was largely responsible for the practical development of the multipurpose approach to resource development and conservation. The idea of the Tennessee Valley Authority, involving the planned development of a whole river basin, and the subsequent experience obtained in the practical implementation of this scheme were critical steps toward the acceptance of multipurpose development as a characteristic feature of the American system.

There is another side to this question of coordination, involving coordination of the activities of the various government agencies concerned with resource work. The conservation activities of the 1930s inevitably resulted in a great expansion of the work of many federal agencies. There did develop a very real danger of an overlap of the functions of these agencies and even wasteful competition among them. The problem of effective coordination of these agencies, and of these with the various state governments, also attained increasing proportion. Although it might well be claimed that much was left to be done in this direction, there are notable examples in the record of the Roosevelt administration of attempts to achieve better coordination among various forms and levels of governmental activity.

Further, governmental action in a democracy has to be coordinated with both the interests and the activities of the citizen. Here the Roosevelt administration made important contributions. As the recovery program had within it a deep respect for the American tradition of free individual enterprise in economic activities, so in conservation and developmental work there was real appreciation of the tradition of self-determination and respect for the individual. Indeed, in the development of the concept of planning, there was involved the idea that this, far from impinging on the freedom of the individual, should provide both greater individual opportunity and greater individual participation in self-improvement. Overall plans were considered essential, but not the need to impose schemes against the will of the people. The concept of "grass roots" administration appears throughout the conservation work of the 1930s.

One of the most interesting observations that can be made on the basis of a survey of conservation during the Roosevelt administration related to criticisms of this policy. Whether we consider the opinions of the average person, of the press, or of opposing political groups, the record is one of widespread agreement with Roosevelt's overall policy of conservation. Instances of critical debate revolved around specific proposals rather than general principles. In addition, although Roosevelt did not receive a "blank check" for his conservation policy, and at times was disappointed with the extent of appropriations, criticisms of his proposals were more often constructive than destructive. It has been noted that in the later years of the administration, there was a growing antagonism toward the idea of national planning, which resulted eventually in the termination of the existence of the National Planning Board. The evidence shows, however, that this opposition to planning was not directed specifically at conservation.

The question as to whether the conservation policy of the Roosevelt administration was conducted along sound economic lines cannot be given a simple answer. The idea was implied, and generally accepted, that conservation expenditure was warranted even at an immediate economic cost. That is, the profit and loss account of conservation, correctly viewed, should extend beyond the period of this book. The least that can be said is that, so far, history has not offered proof for a social loss from the conservation policy of the Roosevelt administration. Rather it would seem that the policy has received social approval. Evidence has been presented to indicate that certain specific measures, such as the Shelterbelt Project and public power development, were closely questioned on economic grounds during the life of the administration. More generally, however, if questions of social costs and returns are excluded, there remains a creditable record of immediate returns in relation to the costs involved in particular projects.

Finally, the central personality in the record of conservation activity during the 1930s was none other than Franklin Delano Roosevelt. It is true that conditions were ripe for his leadership. It is also true that he had able supporters. Harold Ickes in particular, but also Henry Wallace, Senator Norris, H. H. Bennett, and others, in their own right, made substantial contributions to the developing conservation policy. Further, Roosevelt's task was made easier by a cooperative Congress and the sympathy and support of the scientist, the press, and the average American citizen. However, this does not minimize the importance of Roosevelt as practical conservationist, a man of vision, and a great leader. Examination shows his personal interest in conservation and how he applied this interest to the care of natural resources long before he became president of the United States. In public office as senator, as assistant secretary of the navy, and as governor, F.D.R. was active in promoting conservation. His conservation record as governor of New York was merely repeated on a larger scale as president of the nation. In New York, he had used conservation as a relief measure, and had urged legislation to protect and utilize resources fully. He had opposed groups bent upon exploitation. During his presidential campaign, Roosevelt promised to conserve the country's resources and indicated the procedure he would follow. Promptly after his election, he instigated legislation to that end. Throughout his presidential years he maintained a careful check and an alert supervision. He slighted no phase, no resource, no project, no detail. And while he carried out his determination to develop an all-encompassing conservation policy with diplomatic tact, he did not hesitate to use strong persuasion or pressure to achieve his ends. For he had utmost faith in the objective he sought—an objective that few understood or could express as clearly as himself.

> We seek to use our natural resources not as a thing apart but as something that is interwoven with industry, labor, finance, taxation, agriculture, homes, recreation, good citizenship. The results of this interweaving will have a greater influence on the future American standard of living than the rest of our economics put together.[1]

Conservation under Franklin Delano Roosevelt demonstrates the function of mature leadership in a democracy such as the United States, when a multiplicity both of competing interests and of possible techniques requires some courageously far-sighted individual, imbued with public spirit, to synthesize and channel the creative forces that must replace those of destruction.

NOTES

[1]*Congressional Record,* 74 Congress, 1 session (1935), 865, message from the president of the United States to Congress.

Bibliography

FRANKLIN D. ROOSEVELT LIBRARY
THE NATIONAL ARCHIVES
HYDE PARK, NEW YORK

Papers of Franklin D. Roosevelt: Manuscripts

Papers of Franklin D. Roosevelt as New York State Senator, 1910–13 (Group 8). Classified by file numbers and box numbers.
Papers of Franklin D. Roosevelt as Assistant Secretary of the Navy, 1913–20 (Group 9). Classified by box numbers.
Papers of Franklin D. Roosevelt Relating to Political Activities, 1913–20 (Group 10).
Papers of Franklin D. Roosevelt Relating to Political Activities, 1920–28 (Group 11).
Papers of Franklin D. Roosevelt as Governor of New York, 1929–32 (Group 12). Classified by correspondence, group records—Albany papers, and box numbers.
Papers of Franklin D. Roosevelt as President, 1933–45 (Group 13).

OF White House Official File.
PPF President's Personal File.
PSF President's Secretary's File.
  OF 1-C Agriculture Department, Forestry Service.
  OF 1-K Agriculture Department, Agricultural Adjustment Agency.
  OF 1-F Agriculture Department, Bureau of Biological Survey.
  OF 1-R Agriculture Department, Soil Erosion Service.
  OF 6 Interior Department.
  OF 6-P Interior Department, National Park Service.
  OF 42 Tennessee Valley Authority.
  OF 79 Budget Bureau.
  OF 83 Disasters.
  OF 108 Fishing.
  OF 114 Inland Waterways.
  OF 132 Floods.
  OF 149 Forests.
  OF 177 Conservation Matters.

OF 200   Trip File (by date)
           200 EE: Four boxes of material on the Drought trips.
           OF 285:   Great Plains
OF 235   Federal Power Commission.
OF 268   Civilian Conservation Corps.
OF 296   Indians.
OF 378   Wildlife.
OF 402   Irrigation Reclamation Projects.
OF 633   Public Domain.
OF 732   Soil Erosion.
OF 1092   National Resources Planning Board.
PPF 1-P   President's Press Conferences.
PPF 38   Brown, Nelson C.
PPF 191   Park, Charles L., American Tree Association.
PPF 267   Fishing.
PPF 771   Osborne, Lethgou.
PPF 1112 Society of American Foresters.
PPF 1742 Johnson, Robert Underwood.
PPF 1820 Speech Material and Suggestions.
PPF 2265 Civilian Conservation Corps.
PPF 2570 Washington Street Sportmen's Council.
PPF 5850 Knoxville Tennessee *Journal.*
PSF   President's Secretary's File by folder and boxes by years and numbers.
Papers of Franklin D. Roosevelt Pertaining to Family, Business, and Other Personal Affairs, 1882–1945 (Group 14). Classified by subject files, Hyde Park and box numbers.

Subject Files, Hyde Park: Farming on the Roosevelt Estate, 1911–33.
Subject Files, Hyde Park: Forestry.
Subject Files, Hyde Park: General.

Miscellaneous Papers of Franklin D. Roosevelt

F.D.R. Papers, Franklin D. Roosevelt Journal 1911–17, Farm activities at Hyde Park. Notes in longhand.
F.D.R. Papers, *Demonstration at Roosevelt's Farm,* Hyde Park, New York. Mimeographed.
F.D.R. Papers, *Announcement: Cooperative Extension Work,* Poughkeepsie, New York, October 15, 1934. Mimeographed.
F.D.R. Papers, *Program: Joint Meeting New York and New England Sections.*

NATIONAL ARCHIVES
WASHINGTON, D.C.

Materials of the following were examined in the Natural Resources Record Division, Department of Interior Records, and Department of Agriculture Records. Emphasis is on the following classified sections:

Records of the National Resources Planning Board and its predecessor agencies;
Correspondence of the commissioners of Agriculture and secretary of Agriculture, 1879–1939;
Coordinator of Land Use Utilization, 1937;
Emergency Work Relief Records, 1933–43;
Records of the Bureau of Biological Survey, 1902–41;
Records of the Soil Conservation Service, General, 1933–43;
National Park Service;
Forest Service;
Soil Conservation.

Materials were of a miscellaneous nature: letters, telegrams, addresses, newspaper clippings, press releases, articles, minutes of meetings, and reports. Frequently, material was not paged or dated.

Appleby, Paul H., Letter, General Correspondence of Secretary of Agriculture, 1936. Folder.

Confidential Progress Report. National Resources Committee. Information on public relations.

"Conservation Program of the U.S. Government." May 1939. Box 631–636.2, Folder 635.1. Excellent material on the history of conservation.

"Conservation, Secretary of Agriculture." *General Correspondence, Record Number 16, Group, 1933 folder*. Letters and telegrams.

———. Record, Number 16, Folder 1933, 1934, 1935, 1935, 1937.

Draft Report of the Subcommittee on National Water Supply. October 8, 1940. Informative study.

Economic Effects of the Federal Public Works Experience, 1933–1938. A discussion of public works and its tie-up with full employment.

Eliot, C. W. "National Planning." Address before Graduate School of City Planning, Harvard University, January 11, 1935. A discussion of planning.

Evaluation and Long Time National Public Works Program for Wildlife Conservation.

Evaluation of Public Works for Land Protection and Development.

"Flood Control." *Box 551.431–552.4*. A series of newspaper clippings on flood control, correspondence, and minutes of the Flood Control Committee.

Flood Control, Correspondence, Group 551, 11 boxes.

"Flood Damage." *Boxes 553*. Three boxes of correspondence, reports on flood damages, and miscellaneous reports.

Land Committee Minutes, 106.6. Material on national land policy.

Land Use Planning Committee 106.4. 1932–34 press releases, reports, and addresses.

A National Program of Public Works for Range Conservation. January 1942, 1–105, mimeographed. Good information.

A National Program of Public Works for Forest Conservation. February 1942, 1–198, mimeographed. Material on the shelterbelt.

A National Program of Public Works for Recreational Land. January 1942. Indicates social values.

National Resources Committee Interior Building Progress Report and Report Digests. June 30, 1937. Material on minerals.

National Water Policy 578. Box and 1/4. Correspondence, minutes of the Water Resources Committee.

Natural Resource Record Division, Washington, D.C., Box 631–636.2, Folder 635.1.

"Security Work and Relief Policies." *Comparison of National Resources Planning Boards.* Comparison with Beveridge Report.

Shelterbelt Project. Mimeographed. Factual information.

"Soil Conservation Service." *General Files 1933–1935,* 100–100.9. Material on the Soil Erosion Service.

Soil Conservation. Box 631, Folder on Soil Conservation Education and letters.

Statements, Resolutions, and Editorials Supporting National Planning Legislation. January 1936, 1–26, mimeographed. Very useful information.

Summary History of the National Planning Board. Factual information.

Summary Outline on National Land Policy. 1940. Factual information.

"Transfer Forest Service." *Reorganization, 1934.* Two folders of summary.

Water Committee Minutes. January 1940–October, 1940, 106–31. Technical information.

Water Resources Committee: Committee on National Water Policy. October 15, 1939, mimeographed. Contains recommendations.

Western Water Problems, 572. Box. Correspondence, press clippings, and articles.

"Western Water Problems," Box 572, Folder—Drought Conditions, General Correspondence of Secretary of Agriculture.

Wolman, Abel. *Highlights of the National Water Resources Study.* Mimeographed. A study of water use and control in U.S.

Works Progress Administration, 1935–1938. 223. Six folders. Correspondence.

INTERVIEWS

Draiss, Frank. June 1950. Hyde Park, New York.

Mr. Draiss recounted incidents that gave great insight into F.D.R. as a man and into his concern for his fellow citizens. Accounts of human interest. (Assistant Gardener at Hyde Park)

Ickes, Harold. March 1949. Washington, D.C.

An unusually fine, lengthy interview. Valuable information that was nowhere available in printed or written records was obtained. Meaningful insight was gained on the relationship between President Roosevelt and Ickes as well as Ickes' personal opinion of F.D.R. At the time of the interview, Ickes was writing a syndicated newspaper column. (Former Secretary of the Interior under President Franklin D. Roosevelt)

Kahn, Herman. June 1950. Hyde Park, New York.

Invaluable information of useful factual content and Kahn's personal observations and insights proved to be valuable guidelines in certain instances. The director believed no subject was of greater significance than conservation during President Roosevelt's time; hence the first major undertaking of the staff at the Franklin D. Roosevelt Library, Hyde Park, New York, was work on conservation.

Director Kahn believed the leading conservationist in the country in the 1950s was Harlean James, president of the American Science and Planning Preservation Society, and that the man who sold the country on conservation for recreational purposes was Horace Albright, first director of the National Park Service. Kahn felt that the most significant development in conservation under President Roosevelt was the tremendous energy with which conservation was pushed. (Director of Franklin D. Roosevelt Library, Hyde Park, New York)

Plog, William. June 1950. Hyde Park, New York.

A very informative and valuable interview. Attempts had been made to have Mr. Plog recount his experience, impressions, etc., of F.D.R., particularly of F.D.R. as a boy, for recording on tape, but with no success. Mr. Plog was an elderly gentleman at the time, and his relationship with F.D.R. was a very personal one, which was evident in long conversations with him wherein he referred to the president as "young Franklin." I was fortunate in being able to gain his confidence and while gardening with him learned much about F.D.R. I was particularly impressed with Mr. Plog's loyalty to F.D.R. and his affection for him; however, of great interest was learning in detail the forestry conservation work undertaken by Mr. Plog and F.D.R. at Hyde Park. Indeed, it was a close working relationship. (Superintendent of Grounds)

Roosevelt, Eleanor. 1953. Madison, Wisconsin.

An interesting, stimulating, and valuable interview. Mrs. Roosevelt was gracious, warm, and very approachable. I saw her alone without any other person present. She gave me useful information and stressed in our conversation the personal commitment F.D.R. had to conservation.

Suckley, Margaret. June 1950. Hyde Park, New York.

A useful and informative interview. Miss Suckley stated that President Roosevelt often spoke of the C.C.C. and wanted it to be permanent. She also spoke of F.D.R.'s love for trees, his wit, and sense of humor. She stated that no picture did justice to his expressive face, which was constantly changing. Of particular interest was her account of the reason why F.D.R. was interested in old age pensions. (Archivist at Franklin D. Roosevelt Library, Hyde Park, New York)

GOVERNMENT DOCUMENTS*

Activities of the Civilian Conservation Corps: July 1, 1938–June 30, 1939. Washington, 1940.

Agricultural Conservation: A National Farm Policy. Washington, December 30, 1936. Publication of the U.S. Department of Agriculture. Material on the acceptance of soil conservation.

Agriculture Conservation in 1938—Why? Washington, October, 1937. General information series issued by the U.S. Department of Agriculture. Discussion of advantages of conservation.

---

*Washington, D.C., publications are cited as Washington.

Annual Report of the Bonneville Power Administration, 1940. Washington, 1940. A good discussion of the federal government's long-range program.

Annual Report of the Director of the Civilian Conservation Corps: Fiscal Year Ending June 30, 1939. Washington, 1939. Perhaps the best report of the organization, work, and changes in the C.C.C. The report reviews the operation of the C.C.C. from 1933 to 1939.

Annual Report of the Director of the Civilian Conservation Corps: Fiscal Year Ending June 30, 1940. Material on the training of C.C.C. enrollees and their work.

Annual Report of the Director of the Civilian Conservation Corps: Fiscal Year Ending June 30, 1941. Excellent material on the work and training of C.C.C. enrollees.

Annual Report of the Director of Emergency Conservation Work: Fiscal Year Ending June 30, 1936. Washington, 1936. Contains information on the activities and organization of the C.C.C.

Annual Report of the Director of the Fish and Wildlife Service. Washington, 1942. Good material on conservation education.

Annual Report of the Director of the Fish and Wildlife Service to the Secretary of the Interior. Washington, 1941. Excellent tables on the number of refuges and a good discussion of federal aid in wildlife restoration.

Annual Report of the Secretary of the Interior, 1933. Washington, 1933. Material on new agencies in the department.

————. 1934. Washington, 1934. An excellent section on the Soil Erosion Service.

————. 1935. Washington, 1935. A statement of the objectives of the Taylor Grazing Act, work of the Bureau of Reclamation, and useful statistical data.

————. 1936. Washington, 1936. Useful material on the development of water resources and mineral resources.

————. 1937. Washington, 1937. A good summary of activity from 1933 to 1937.

————. 1938. Washington, 1938. Information from Harold Ickes to the President and factual information on the year's accomplishments.

————. 1939. Washington, 1939. Material on conservation objectives, accomplishments, and the future.

————. 1940. Washington, 1940. A discussion of the relationship of conservation to social welfare and an account of the work accomplished.

————. 1941. Washington, 1941. An excellent extensive report on all aspects of conservation.

Annual Report of the T.V.A., 1948. Washington, 1948. Useful information.

————. 1950. Washington, 1950. Material on the progress of the T.V.A., the physical plant and its use, the job of the valley institutions and people, and its management.

Bennett, H. H. *Erosion.* Bennett, director of Soil Erosion Service, submitted papers on erosion control activities in foreign countries and a paper on a proposed National Program of Erosion Control.

Blaisdell, Donald C. *Government and Agriculture: The Growth of Federal Farm Aid.* Washington, 1940. Good material on soil conservation and agriculture adjustment.

"Bonneville to Market Grand Coulee Power." *The Reclamation Era,* 30:322. November 1940. A good article discussing the president's executive order.

Brown, Nelson C. *The Civilian Conservation Corps Program in the United States.*

Washington, 1934. A bulletin that is a copy of a paper given at the annual meeting of the Woodlands section Canadian pulp and paper association, January 25, 1933, by Professor Nelson C. Brown, New York State College of Forestry.

The C.C.C. at Work: A Story of 2,500,000 Young Men. Washington, 1941. Written in a simplified style and containing illustrative material of factual value.

The C.C.C. and Wildlife. Washington, 1939. History of wildlife conservation practices in United States and the wildlife work of the C.C.C. enrollees.

C.C.C. Workers Spent 1,801,907 Man-Days in the Control of Forest Fires: The Civilian Conservation Corps Program during the First Two Years. Washington, 1936. Contains material on the purposes of the C.C.C., the organization of the C.C.C., and camps at work. A very useful folder.

The C.C.C.: A Youth Program Washington, 1938. A folder designated primarily for use by prospective C.C.C. enrollees.

The Civilian Conservation Corps. Washington, 1941. A bulletin reprinted from *American Conservation* by Ovid Butler, 1941. States the growth and activities of the C.C.C.

The Civilian Conservation Corps: Contributing to the Defense of the Nation. Washington, 1941. Contains a very good account of C.C.C. defense work.

The Civilian Conservation Corps and Public Recreation. Washington, 1941. Recreational work completed by the enrollees is described on a regional basis.

The Civilian Conservation Corps: What It Is and What It Does. Washington, January 1941. Valuable information stated in question and answer form. Material on the organization of the C.C.C., and C.C.C. regulations, selections, training, and life in the camps.

Civilian Conservation Corps: Work Completed, All Services, April 1933–June 30, 1941. Washington, 1941. A processed bulletin containing a statistical chart of the work completed by the Corps. The material has excellent detail.

The Columbia River Basin Project. Washington, 1949. Factual information on the Columbia Basin.

Congressional Record, 73 Congress, special session (March 1933), 5. President Roosevelt's inaugural address.

———. 73 Congress, 2 session (1934), 4035–36. Discussion of three wildlife conservation bills that were passed.

———. 73 Congress, 2 session (1934), 4748–52. Remarks on the case of soil erosion and an insert by H. H. Bennett.

———. 73 Congress, 2 session (1934), 6709–11. Discussion of conservation progress.

———. 73 Congress, 2 session (1934), 6777–78. Address by Hon. Henry T. Rainey, Speaker of the House, over N.B.C. on April 8, 1934, on "Conservation and Citizenship."

———. 73 Congress, 2 session (1934), 10,311–12. Discussion of the drought situation in the middlewest.

———. 73 Congress, 2 session (1934), 10,399. Message from the president of the U.S. to Congress on improvement and development of the water resources.

———. 74 Congress, 1 session (1935), 94–97. Annual message of the president of the U.S.

―――. 74 Congress, 1 session (1935), 865–66. Message from the president of the U.S. to Congress.

―――. 74 Congress, 1 session (1935), 1263–64. Remarks on soil erosion.

―――. 74 Congress, 1 session (1935), 2573–74. Discussion of the use of water power.

―――. 74 Congress, 1 session (1935), 3550–53. The urging of a permanent Department of Soil Erosion.

―――. 74 Congress, 1 session (1935), 4127–28. A radio address by Mr. Nichols of Oklahoma on dust storms.

―――. 74 Congress, 1 session (1935), 4770–71. Proposed legislation to control erosion.

―――. 74 Congress, 1 session (1935), 4803–10. Discussion of soil erosion bill.

―――. 74 Congress, 1 session (1935), 6012–14. Soil erosion control discussed.

―――. 74 Congress, 1 session (1935), 8905–6. Erosion control discussed.

―――. 74 Congress, 1 session (1935), 9376–78. Discussion of forest conservation.

―――. 74 Congress, 1 session (1935), 12,002. Letter by F.D.R. on the Bonneville Dam.

―――. 74 Congress, 1 session (1935), 12,871–72. Discussion of flood control.

―――. 74 Congress, 1 session (1935), 13,505–7. Discussion of the need of erosion control.

―――. 74 Congress, 1 session (1935), 14,686–87. The need of conservation is discussed.

―――. 74 Congress, 1 session (1935), 14,764–65. Material on floods.

―――. 74 Congress, 2 session (1936), 683–85. Article, "Rise of Grass," written by Chester C. Davis.

―――. 74 Congress, 2 session (1936), 830–32. Discussion on flood control legislation.

―――. 74 Congress, 2 session (1936), 1026–29. Address by Dr. Walter C. Lowermilk at Third International Congress of Soil Science in London, England, on August 7, 1935.

―――. 74 Congress, 2 session (1936), 1084–85. Address on floods delivered at annual meeting of Mississippi Valley Association in St. Louis, November 25, 1935.

―――. 74 Congress, 2 session (1936), 1150–52. Radio address by Representative A. Willis Robertson, January 24, 1936.

―――. 74 Congress, 2 session (1936), 1584–85. Statement by President Roosevelt on "A Permanent National Soil Program."

―――. 74 Congress, 2 session (1936), 2941–45. Critical comments on the shelterbelt.

―――. 74 Congress, 2 session (1936), 2946–51. Material on forests.

―――. 74 Congress, 2 session (1936), 3098. Statement by President Roosevelt on the significance of the Soil Conservation and Domestic Allotment Act.

―――. 74 Congress, 2 session (1936), 4197–98. Article by Senator Robert F. Wagner on flood control.

―――. 74 Congress, 2 session (1936), 4238. Radio speech by Hon. Edith N. Rogers on flood relief.

―――. 74 Congress, 2 session (1936), 4420–22. Material on flood control.

————. 74 Congress, 2 session (1936), 4511–12. Radio speech by H. F. Kopplemann, "The Flood in Connecticut."

————. 74 Congress, 2 session (1936), 4643–44. Address by Senator Guffey, "Averting the Flood Peril."

————. 74 Congress, 2 session (1936), 4947. Statement of soil conservation objectives.

————. 74 Congress, 2 session (1936), 6245–49. Address by Wm. M. Whittington, delivered at Annual Convention of National Rivers and Harbors Congress.

————. 74 Congress, 2 session (1936), 6315–16. Radio broadcast on flood control by Mr. Wallgen.

————. 74 Congress, 2 session (1936), 6318. Address by Wilson of Louisiana before the Rivers and Harbors Congress on flood control.

————. 74 Congress, 2 session (1936), 6547. Remarks by Maverick on conservation.

————. 74 Congress, 2 session (1936), 6779–80. Radio speech by Senator Chavez, "Soil Conservation in the Southwest."

————. 74 Congress, 2 session (1936), 6790–92. Address by Harry G. Vavra on "Conservation and Citizenship."

————. 75 Congress, 1 session (1937), 74–75. *Washington Post* editorial on floods.

————. 75 Congress, 1 session (1937), 80–81. *New York Times* editorial on floods.

————. 75 Congress, 1 session (1937), *Washington Herald* editorial on floods.

————. 75 Congress, 1 session (1937), 106–7. *Hartford Times* editorial on floods.

————. 75 Congress, 1 session (1937), Radio address by T. G. Bilbo on "Flood Control."

————. 75 Congress, 1 session (1937), 173–74. *Washington Post* article on floods.

————. 75 Congress, 1 session (1937), 184–86. Radio address by Hon. B. C. Clark, February 8, 1937, on floods.

————. 75 Congress, 1 session (1937), 200–1. Radio address by J. F. Rankin, February 11, 1937, "Permanent Flood Control—Additional T.V.A.'s."

————. 75 Congress, 1 session (1937), 473–75. Speech by Harold Ickes, February 23, 1937, before the New York Rod and Gun Editors Association on conservation work.

————. 75 Congress, 1 session (1937), 547–52. Address by W. M. Whittington at St. Louis, Missouri, March 12, 1937, at Flood Control Conference of Mississippi Valley Association.

————. 75 Congress, 1 session (1937), 567–69. Address by Representative Orville Zimmerman at St. Louis, Missouri, March 12, 1937, at Flood Control Conference of Mississippi Valley Association.

————. 75 Congress, 1 session (1937), 593–600. Remarks on wildlife conservation.

————. 75 Congress, 1 session (1937), 596–97. Address by Maj. Gen. E. M. Markham, chief engineer, U.S. Army, on flood control.

————. 75 Congress, 1 session (1937), 705–7. Article by Morris L. Cooke on soil conservation.

————. 75 Congress, 1 session (1937), 950–53. Address by W. M. Whittington before the National Rivers and Harbors Congress, April 26, 1937, on planning.

————. 75 Congress, 1 session (1937), 1077. Address by Senator J. N. Overton before the National Rivers and Harbors Congress, April 27, 1937, on flood control.

————. 75 Congress, 1 session (1937), 1127. *St. Louis Star Times* editorial, "The Floods and Congress."

————. 75 Congress, 1 session (1937), 1169–72. Address by Sam Rayburn, April 24, 1937, on flood control.

————. 75 Congress, 1 session (1937), 1173–74. Radio address by N. G. Vavra on conservation and education.

————. 75 Congress, 1 session (1937), 1179–81. Address by Senator R. S. Copeland before the U.S. Chamber of Commerce, April 27, 1937, on flood control.

————. 75 Congress, 1 session (1937), 1227–30. Radio address by Hon. Clyde L. Herring, May 17, 1937, on soil conservation.

————. 75 Congress, 1 session (1937), 1301–2.Radio address by B. C. Clark, May 27, 1937, on flood control.

————. 75 Congress, 1 session (1937), 1314–16. Radio address by Senator Lewis B. Schwellenbach, "Conservation of Natural Resources," August 21, 1937.

————. 75 Congress, 1 session (1937), 1336–40. Address by W. M. Whittington before the American Forestry Association, May 31, 1937, on national policy.

————. 75 Congress, 1 session (1937), 2437–39. Remarks on water conservation.

————. 75 Congress, 1 session (1937), 2465. Address by Hon. J. Buell Snyder before Western Pennsylvania Flood Control Committee in Pittsburgh, August 10, 1937.

————. 75 Congress, 1 session (1937), 4172–80. Remarks on water power.

————. 75 Congress, 1 session (1937), 4479. Resolution adopted by City Council of McKeesport, Pennsylvania, on flood control.

————. 75 Congress, 1 session (1937), 5280–81. Message to the Senate from President Roosevelt.

————. 75 Congress, 1 session (1937), 5734–35. Remarks on flood control.

————. 75 Congress, 1 session (1937), 5754–57. Remarks on water power.

————. 75 Congress, 1 session (1937), 7822–88. Remarks on water power.

————. 75 Congress, 1 session (1937), 9442–44. Discussion of floods as a national problem.

————. 75 Congress, 1 session (1937), 9567. Remarks on Flood Control Act, June 22, 1936.

————. 75 Congress, 2 session (1937), 5–7. Radio address by H. P. Koppelmann on water power.

————. 75 Congress, 2 session (1937), 175–79. Address by W. M. Whittington at St. Louis, Missouri, November 22, 1937, on national policy.

————. 75 Congress, 2 session (1937), 187–89. Article by Harold Ickes on "Conservation Phases of Government's Power Program."

————. 75 Congress, 2 session (1937), 268. *Boston Transcript* article, "Flood Control."

————. 75 Congress, 2 session (1937), 597–602. Discussion on regionalization of natural resources.

————. 75 Congress, 3 session (1938), Appendix 114–15. Article by Hon. William M. Citron on New England Flood Control.

———. 75 Congress, 3 session (1938), Appendix 183–84. Radio address by Senator Harry B. Howes, "Conservation Progress."

———. 75 Congress, 3 session (1938), Appendix 293–94. Address by Hon. John L. McCellan, "Floods, Their Prevention and Control."

———. 75 Congress, 3 session (1938), Appendix 306–8. Address by W. M. Whittington at Second Annual Meeting of the Mississippi Valley Flood Control Association, January 19, 1938.

———. 75 Congress, 3 session (1938), Appendix 314–18. Address by W. M. Whittington before the National Rivers and Harbors Congress, January 20, 1938, on flood control.

———. 75 Congress, 3 session (1938), Appendix 347. Radio address by Peter J. De Muth, "Flood Control Delay."

———. 75 Congress, 3 session (1938), Appendix 730–31. Address by Hon. Phil Ferguson before Rivers and Harbors Congress, January 21, 1938, on power.

———. 75 Congress, 3 session (1938), Appendix 1043–46. Remarks on flood protection.

———. 75 Congress, 3 session (1938), 1774–75. *Shenandoah Herald* editorial, "Conserve the Resources."

———. 75 Congress, 3 session (1938), 1842. Address by James Carew on soil.

———. 75 Congress, 3 session (1938), Appendix 2275–76. Remarks on flood control.

———. 75 Congress, 3 session (1938), 2488. Resolution adopted by McDowell County Sportsmen League at Welch, West Virginia, on separate Conservation Department.

———. 75 Congress, 3 session (1938), 2696–720. Discussion of reclamation.

———. 75 Congress, 3 session (1938), 3149. Message of the president of United States.

———. 75 Congress, 3 session (1938), Appendix 3159–60. Radio address by Peter J. De Muth, "New Flood Control Act," June 25, 1938.

———. 75 Congress, 3 session (1938), 5501. Memorial laid before Senate for federal aid.

———. 75 Congress, 3 session (1938), 7216–17. Message from President Roosevelt on soil.

———. 75 Congress, 3 session (1938), 8270–71. Statement of Buena Vista Farmers' Union on soil conservation program.

———. 75 Congress, 3 session (1938), Telegrams from governors stating opposition to proposed Senate amendments to flood control bill.

———. 76 Congress, 1 session (1939), Appendix 146. *Washington Post* article on flood control program in Vermont.

———. 76 Congress, 1 session (1939), Appendix 150. *New York Times* editorial on states rights.

———. 76 Congress, 1 session (1939), Appendix 325. Remarks on nationwide forest survey.

———. 76 Congress, 1 session (1939), Appendix 323–24. Address by W. M. Whittington before Ohio Conservation and Flood Control Congress, January 27, 1939, "Task Ahead in National Flood Control."

————. 76 Congress, 1 session (1939), Appendix 414. *Springfield Daily News* editorial on flood control.

————. 76 Congress, 1 session (1939), 452–59. Remarks on flood control.

————. 76 Congress, 1 session (1939), 470. Statement by governors to Senator F. T. Maloney on "Flood Control in States."

————. 76 Congress, 1 session (1939), Appendix 782. Table of natural resources of democratic and nondemocratic forces.

————. 76 Congress, 1 session (1939), 846–48. Remarks on states rights.

————. 76 Congress, 1 session (1939), 889. Memorial from Arkansas.

————. 76 Congress, 1 session (1939), 955. Remarks on wildlife conservation.

————. 76 Congress, 1 session (1939), Appendix 1136–38. Address by W. M. Whittington before National Rivers and Harbors Congress, March 23, 1939, "Flood Control and States Rights."

————. 76 Congress, 1 session (1939), Appendix 1144–46. Address by Charles Plumley on flood control and states rights.

————. 76 Congress, 1 session (1939), Appendix 1201–2. Address by J. Randolph on tributary stream control.

————. 76 Congress, 1 session (1939), Appendix 1428–30. Address by W. M. Whittington before Ohio Valley Improvement Association, April 11, 1939, "Program in Flood Control."

————. 76 Congress, 1 session (1939), 1484–85. Message from President Roosevelt on the nation's energy resources.

————. 76 Congress, 1 session (1939), Appendix 1719. Address by Clyde T. Ellis before National Rivers and Harbors Congress, March 23, 1939, "An American Plan for Flood Control."

————. 76 Congress, 1 session (1939), Appendix 1800–1. Radio address by John Coffee, April 29, 1939, "Our National Resources."

————. 76 Congress, 1 session (1939), Appendix 1913–14. Remarks on appropriations.

————. 76 Congress, 1 session (1939), Appendix 1965–66. Remarks on appropriations.

————. 76 Congress, 1 session (1939), 5376, 5381, 5835. Remarks on appropriations.

————. 76 Congress, 1 session (1939), 5393–96. Amendments in House to increase appropriations.

————. 76 Congress, 3 session (1940), Appendix 86–87. Address by Clare E. Hoffman on the meaning of conservation.

————. 76 Congress, 3 session (1940), Appendix 91–92. Remarks on reforestation.

————. 76 Congress, 3 session (1940), Appendix 250–51. Letter by Lyle H. Born to members of Congress on planning and appropriations.

————. 76 Congress, 3 session (1940), 269–70. Message from President Roosevelt.

————. 76 Congress, 3 session (1940), Appendix 312. *Gazette* editorial on floods.

————. 76 Congress, 3 session (1940), Appendix 532–33. Remarks on Forest Service transfer.

———. 76 Congress, 3 session (1940), Appendix 671. Remarks on soil conservation.

———. 76 Congress, 3 session (1940), Appendix 837–38. Remarks on water conservation.

———. 76 Congress, 3 session (1940), Appendix 1433–35. Address by W. M. Whittington before Mississippi Valley Flood Control Association, March 13, 1940, on rivers.

———. 76 Congress, 3 session (1940), Appendix 1444–45. Address by Maj. Gen. Julian L. Schley, March 13, 1940, on conservation background.

———. 76 Congress, 3 session (1940), Appendix 1450–52. Address by W. M. Whittington, March 14, 1940, discussing flood control legislation.

———. 76 Congress, 3 session (1940), Appendix 1517. Remarks on planning.

———. 76 Congress, 3 session (1940), Appendix 1572–73. Radio adddress by Hon. G. Pinchot, February 17, 1940, "Farmers and Forest Services."

———. 76 Congress, 3 session (1940), Appendix 1622. Speech by O. Brooks before Rivers and Harbors Congress, March 15, 1940, "Flood Control in Mississippi Valley."

———. 76 Congress, 3 session (1940), Appendix 1913–14. Remarks on forestry.

———. 76 Congress, 3 session (1940), Appendix 2056–58. Pollution information.

———. 76 Congress, 3 session (1940), 2182. Presidential message on water pollution.

———. 76 Congress, 3 session (1940), Appendix 2231–32. Remarks on forestry in the North Pacific.

———. 76 Congress, 3 session (1940), Appendix 2410–14. Statement by C. T. Ellis before House Flood Control Committee.

———. 76 Congress, 3 session (1940), Appendix 2481–82. Remarks on forests.

———. 76 Congress, 3 session (1940), Appendix 2550. Remarks on flood control.

———. 76 Congress, 3 session (1940), Appendix 2570–71. Remarks on forests.

———. 76 Congress, 3 session (1940), Appendix 2761–62. Radio address by John Coffee "Public Ownership, Unemployment and Natural Resources."

———. 76 Congress, 3 session (1940), Appendix 2857. Table of city appropriations on flood control.

———. 76 Congress, 3 session (1940), Appendix 3142. Resolutions and letters on flood control.

———. 76 Congress, 3 session (1940), Appendix 3170–72. Remarks on flood control.

———. 76 Congress, 3 session (1940), Appendix 3367. Remarks on flood control protection as part of national defense.

———. 76 Congress, 3 session (1940), Appendix 3505–7. Remarks on soil conservation and flood control.

———. 76 Congress, 3 session (1940), Appendix 3531–35. Address by James P. Pope, director of T.V.A., before New School for Social Research, N.Y.C., May 16, 1940.

———. 76 Congress, 3 session (1940), Appendix 4002–3. Address by Gifford Pinchot at 8th American Scientific Congress, "Conservation as a Foundation of Permanent Peace."

————. 76 Congress, 3 session (1940), 4802. Remarks on flood control.

————. 76 Congress, 3 session (1940), Appendix 4944. Article on forest problems in Oregon.

————. 76 Congress, 3 session (1940), Appendix 5187–88. Remarks on road building and its relation to resources.

————. 76 Congress, 3 session (1940), Appendix 5566. Remarks by Cart T. Curtis, "Flood Control Program Should Move Forward."

————. 76 Congress, 3 session (1940), Appendix 6833–34. Address by Frederic C. Walcott before Maryland State Game and Fish Protective Association, "America Must be Kept Worth Defending."

————. 76 Congress, 3 session (1940), 11,524–26. Address by the president on opening of Great Smoky Mountain National Park.

————. 77 Congress, 1 session (1941), 4543. Designation of conservation week.

————. 77 Congress, 1 session (1941), 8502. Flood control.

————. 77 Congress, (1941), Appendix 394–97. John Scott article, "Water Power Development and the New River Case."

————. 77 Congress, (1941), Appendix 1136. Pro article on T.V.A., *Associated Press* Knoxville, Tennessee.

————. 77 Congress, (1941), Appendix 1248–49. Charles Leavy, "Reason Why Federal Reclamation and Water Conservation Program Should be Carried Forward."

————. 77 Congress, (1941), Appendix 1351–52. Editorial, *Divide County Farmers Press*, Crosby, North Dakota, on shelterbelt.

————. 77 Congress, (1941), Appendix 1396. John Rankin, "Nationwide Water Power Development."

————. 77 Congress, (1941), Appendix 1521–22. Address by R. R. Gardner on wildlife conservation.

————. 77 Congress, (1941), Appendix 1745–46. Statement of Frank Carlson before Subcommittee on Appropriations.

————. 77 Congress, (1941), Appendix 1880. Statement of Usher L. Burdick on Department of Interior Appropriations.

————. 77 Congress, (1941), Appendix 2390–97. Louisiana flood control problems.

————. 77 Congress, (1941), Appendix 2591. Flood control needs in Fall River, South Dakota.

————. 77 Congress, (1941), Appendix 3061. Editorial pro flood control, *Southwest American*, Fort Smith, Arkansas.

————. 77 Congress, (1941), Appendix 5117. Address W. M. Whittington before special session of National Rivers and Harbors Congress, November 13, 1941, "Question of Flood Control and National Defense."

Conservation: Program of the U.S. Government. Washington, June 1939. Mimeographed material on the history of conservation.

Conservation: The Resources We Guard. Washington, 1940. An extremely useful bulletin citing landmarks in conservation.

Department of Interior Bulletins. Numerous bulletins in small magazine form on subjects such as the Boulder Dam, plants in wildlife, national parks, transplanting trees, attracting birds, etc.

Development of Resources and of Economic Opportunity in the Pacific Northwest. Washington, 1942. National Resources Planning Board publication. Good regional information.

Development of Resources and Stabilization of Employment in the United States. Washington, 1941. National Resources Planing Board publication. Of economic evaluation use.

Drainage Basin Problems and Programs, 1937. Washington, 1938. National Resources Committee publication. Material on attempts to formulate a national water plan.

The Economic Effects of the Federal Public Works Expenditures, 1933–1938. Washington, 1940. National Resources Planning Board publication. Informative report.

Electricity Comes to Rural America. Washington, n.d. Written in propaganda style. Contains informative material.

"Energy Resources and National Policy." *Monthly Labor Review,* 49:1082–85. November 1939. A discussion of the nation's energy resources in relation to a national policy.

Energy Resources and National Policy, 1939. Washington, 1939. National Resources Committee publication. The report contains recommendations for the utilization and conservation of energy resources of the nation in relation to each other and to the national economic structure and includes supporting papers by specialists. Useful information and particularly good historical material.

Executive Order, Number 6101, April 5, 1933, "Relief Unemployment through the Performance of Useful Public Work." Numbers 6071–299, Washington, 1933. State the appointment of Fechner as director of the C.C.C., the role of the government departments, and the funds for C.C.C. use. Number 6135, May 20, 1933. Purchase of national forest land.

———. Number 6148, May 31,1933. "Relief of Unemployment through the Performance of Useful Public Work."

———. Number 6162, June 7, 1933. "Board of Directors of T.V.A. Directed to Make Such Surveys, Plans, Experiments, and Demonstrations as May Be Suitable to Aid the Proper Use, Conservation, and Development of Natural Resources of Tennessee River Drainage Basin."

———. Number 6793, July 11, 1934. "Allocating Funds from the Appropriation to Meet the Emergency and Necessity for Relief in Striken Areas."

———. A continuous array of Executive Orders are found annually relating to conservation.

Facts and Background about the Reclamation Program: 1849—A Century of Conservation—1949. Mimeographed publication by the Department of the Interior containing factual information.

Federal Aid to Local Planning. Washington, 1940. National Resources Planning Board publication. Information aids to local planning with particular reference to the Department of Interior.

Federal Power Commission Report on Review of Allocation of Costs at the Multiple Purpose Water Control System in the Tennessee River Basin. Washington, 1949. Useful information.

A Forest Conservation Program. Washington, 1943. Leaflet published by the U.S.

Department of Agriculture Forest Service containing factual information on timber land, volume of timber, forest ownership, private forest lands, and a program proposed by the Forest Service.

Forest Improvements by the C.C.C. Washington, 1939. Very good information on the forestry improvement work of the enrollees in forestry administration, recreation, water conservation, and protection. A contribution of the Forestry Division.

Forests and People: Report of the Chief of the Forest Service, 1941. Washington, 1942. An excellent discussion on the social implications of forests, public cooperation, and work of the Forest Service.

Forests Protected by the C.C.C. Washington, 1938. Contains information on the fire-fighting activity of the C.C.C. and insect control work. A contribution of the Forestry Division.

"Forests to Farmers." *Land Policy Review,* 1:3, 8–11. 1938–1940. Discussion of combined forest and farm enterprises.

Forestry in Wartime: Report of the Chief of the Forest Service, 1942. Washington, 1942. Discussion of forestry.

Future Value of Civilian Conservation Corps Accomplishments Over Past Eight Years Exceeds $1,500,000,000. Washington, 1941. A processed copy of a letter written by Director McEntee to Malcolm C. Traver, chairman of the Subcommittee of Labor Federal Security Appropriations Committee. The letter evaluates the work of the C.C.C.

Frank, Bernard, and Botts, Clifford A. *Water and Our Forests.* Washington, 1946. An excellent explanatory study of the relationship of water and forests.

Gray, L. C. "Our Land Policy Today." *Land Policy Review,* 1:3, 3–8. June 1938.

Green, C. J. *Analysis of the Real Cost of T.V.A. Power.* Washington, 1948. Chamber of Commerce, U.S. Natural Resources Department. Valuable factual information.

Hands to Save the Soil. Washington, 1938. Good simple explanations of soil erosion work practices completed by enrollees. Materials prepared by the C.C.C. and Soil Conservation Service.

Hanson, Alvin H., and Perloff, Harvey S. *Regional Resource Development.* Washington, 1942. No. 16 planning pamphlet issued by the National Planning Association. It contains information on resource development and economic expansion, regional problems, and the T.V.A.

Hearings

Hearings before a Subcommittee of the Commmittee on Agriculture and Forestry, United States Senate. 74 Congress, 1 session. "Protection of Land Resources Against Soil Erosion." Washington, April 2, 3, 1935.

Hearings before a Subcommittee of the Commmittee on Agriculture and Forestry, House of Representatives. 74 Congress, 1 session. "Program of Forest Land Management." Washington, April 12, 1935.

Hearings before a Subcommittee of the Commmittee on Agriculture and Forestry, United States Senate. 74 Congress, 2 session. "A Bill to Provide for the Control of

Flood Waters in the Mississippi Valley to Improve Navigation on the Mississippi River and Its Tributaries, to Provide for the Irrigation of Arid and Semiarid Lands and for Other Purposes." Washington, March 24–April 15,1936.

Hearings before a Subcommittee of the Commmittee on Agriculture and Forestry, United States Senate. 74 Congress, 2 session. "To Amend the Soil Conservation and Domestic Allotment Act." Washington, June 3, 1936.

Hearings before a Subcommittee of the Commmittee on Agriculture and Forestry, United States Senate. 75 Congress, 1 session. "A Bill to Provide for the Creation of Conservation Authorities and for Other Purposes." Washington, June 21–July 7, 1937.

Hearings before a Subcommittee of the Commmittee on Appropriations, House of Representatives. 76 Congress, 3 session. "On the Interior Department Appropriation Bill for 1941." Washington, 1941.

Hearings before the Select Committee on Conservation of Wildlife Resources, House of Representatives. 75 Congress, 1 session. "On Migratory Waterfowl Conservation and Restoration." Washington, June 16, 1939.

Hearings before the Select Committee on Conservation of Wildlife Resources, House of Representatives. 75 Congress, 3 session. "A Resolution to Continue the Select Committee on Wildlife Authorized by House Resolution 237 of the 73 Congress and Continued under Authority of House Resolution 44 of the 74 Congress to Investigate All Matters Pertaining to the Replacement and Conservation of Wild Animal Life with a View to Determining the Most Appropriate Method of Carrying Out Such Purposes." Washington, 1938.

Hearings before the Select Committee on Conservation of Wildlife Resources, House of Representatives. 76 Congress, 1 session. "A Resolution to Authorize the Select Committee in Wildlife of the 76 Congress to Investigate All Matters Pertaining to the Replacement and Conservation of Wild Animal Life." Washington, 1939.

Hearings before the Committee on Expenditures in the Executive Departments, United States Senate. 74 Congress, 1 session. "To Change the Name of the Department of the Interior and to Coordinate Certain Governmental Functions." Washington, May 16, 1935.

Hearings before the Committee on Flood Control, House of Representatives. 73 Congress, 1 session. "Progress and Present Status of Flood Control on the Mississippi River and Its Tributaries." Washington, March 30, May 12, 1933.

Hearings before the Committee on Flood Control, House of Representatives. 74 Congress, 1 session. "A Bill to Authorize Funds for the Prosecution of Works for Flood Control and Protection Against Flood Disasters." Washington, March 22, 23, April 2, 1935.

Hearings before the Committee on Flood Control, House of Representatives. 74 Congress, 1 session. "A Plan to Modify and Extend the Project for Flood Control and Improvement of the Mississippi River Authorized by the Flood Control Act of 1928." Washington, April 1–13, 1935.

Hearings before the Committee on Flood Control, House of Representatives. 74 Congress, 2 session. "To Provide for a Permanent System of Flood Control and for Other Purposes." Washington, May 21, 1936.

Hearings before the Committee on Flood Control, House of Representatives. 75 Congress,

1 session. "A Bill to Amend an Act Entitled, 'An Act Authorized the Construction of Certain Public Works on Rivers and Harbors for Flood Control and for Other Purposes Approved June 22, 1932.'" Washington, June 7–11, 15–18, 1937.

Hearings before the Committee on Flood Control, House of Representatives. 75 Congress, 3 session. "Comprehensive Flood Control Plans." Washington, March 30–April 19, 1938.

Hearings before the Committee on Flood Control, House of Representatives. 76 Congress, 3 session. "A Bill Authorizing the Construction of Certain Public Works on Rivers and Harbors for Flood Control and for Other Purposes." Washington, March 18–April 9, 1940.

Hearings before the Committee on Flood Control, House of Representatives. 77 Congress, 1 session. "A Bill Authorizing the Construction of Certain Public Works on Rivers and Harbors for Flood Control and for Other Purposes." Washington, April 21–May 14, 1941.

Hearings before the Committee on Irrigation and Reclamation, United States Senate. 74 Congress, 2 session. "Federal Reclamation of Arid Lands." Washington, February 1, 1936.

Hearings before the Committee on Irrigation and Reclamation, House of Representatives. 75 Congress, 1 session. "A Bill to Prevent Speculation in Lands in the Columbia Basin"; "A Bill to Authorize an Appropriation for the Construction of Small Reservoirs under the Reclamation Laws"; "A Bill to Authorize an Appropriation for Investigations under the Federal Reclamation Laws." Washington, 1937.

Hearings before the Committee on Public Lands, House of Representatives. 73 Congress, 1 session. "A Bill to Stop Injury to the Public Grazing Lands by Preventing Overgrazing and Soil Deterioration." Washington, June 7–9, 1933, February 19–20, 21, 23, 28, March 1–3, 1934.

Hearings before the Committee on Public Lands, House of Representatives. 74 Congress, 2 session. "Establishment of a National Resource Board." Washington, February 20, 21, 26, 28, March 3, 1936.

Hearings before the Committee on Public Lands and Surveys, United States Senate. 73 Congress, 2 session. "To Provide for the Orderly Use, Improvement and Development of the Public Range." Washington, April 20–May 2, 1934.

Hearings before the Committee on Public Lands and Surveys, United States Senate. 74 Congress, 1 session. "A Bill to Change the Name of the Department of the Interior and to Coordinate Certain Governmental Functions." Washington, July 11–16, 1935.

Hearings before the Committee on Rivers and Harbors, House of Representatives. 75 Congress, 1 session. "A Bill to Authorize Completion, Maintenance and Operation for Bonneville Project for Navigation and for Other Purposes." Washington, March, April, May, June 1937.

Hearings before the Committee on Rivers and Harbors, House of Representatives. 75 Congress, 1 session. "Bills to provide for the Regional Conservation and Development of the National Resources and for Other Purposes." Washington, July, August, 1937.

Hearings before a Special Committee on Survey of Land and Water Policies of the United

States, United States Senate. 74 Congress, 2 session. "A Resolution Authorizing a Survey of All Land and Water Policies and Projects of the Various Executive Agencies and Establishments of the Government." Washington, August 21, 1935.

Highlights in the History of Forest Conservation. Washington, January 1948. An extremely useful factual guide by date.

Hoover Dam. Washington, n.d. Leaflet issued by the U.S. Department of the Interior, which contains historical information of value.

House Documents. Number 140. 75 Congress, 1 session. "Public Works Planning Message from the President of the U.S., Transmitting a Proposed Plan of a 6 Year Program Submitted by the National Resources Committee Based on Selection and Priority of Public Works Projects."

House Miscellaneous Documents. Number 539. 75 Congress, 2, 3 session. "Immediate Study of the National Forest Problem"

————. Number 261. 75 Congress, 1 session. "Creation of National Planning Board to Provide for Conservation and Development of National—Message from the President of U.S. Transmitting the Proposed Creation of Regional Authorities or Agencies to be Known as the National Planning Board to Provide for the Regional Conservation and Development of National Resources."

House Reports. Number 2030. 75 Congress, 3 session. "National Planning for Regional Conservation and Development of the National Resources."

House Reports on Public Bills II. Number 830. 74 Congress, 1 session. "Program of Forest Land Management."

Ickes, Harold L. *Not Guilty: An Official Inquiry Into the Charges Made by Glavis and Pinchot Against Richard A. Ballinger, Secretary of the Interior, 1909–1911.* Washington, 1940. Publication of the U.S. Department of the Interior. A well-written and informative study of the controversy.

Industrial Location and National Resources. Washington, 1942. National Resources Planning Board publication. Material on natural resources and location.

Inventory of the Water Resources of the Mississippi River Drainage Area. Washington, 1935. National Resources Board publication. Specialized report.

Kieley, James F. *C.C.C.* Washington, 1938. A very valuable booklet on the organization of the C.C.C. and the types of C.C.C. work. A great amount of the basic material in the booklet was supplied by the director of the C.C.C. and the various departments cooperating in the work of the Corps.

Kylie, H. R., Hieronymus, G. H., and Hall, A. G. *C.C.C. Forestry.* Washington, 1937. Book published by the Department of Agriculture containing material on forestry practices.

Land Classification. Washington, 1941. National Resources Planning Board publication. Useful information on soil conservation.

Laurent, Francis W. *Tennessee Valley Authority.* Washington, March 15, 1938. A compilation of the more important congressional acts, treaties, presidential messages, judicial decisions, and official reports and documents having to do with the control, conservation, and utilization of water resources.

Mahoney, J. R. *Natural Resources Activity of the Government.* Washington, May 1950. Public Affairs Bulletin Number 76. An excellent historical, descriptive, and analytical study.

McEntee, James J. *The C.C.C. and National Defense.* Washington, 1940. An evaluation of the work and cost of the C.C.C. Bulletin reprinted from *American Forests*, July 1940.

The Mineral Reserves of the U.S. and Its Capacity For Production. Washington, 1936. National Resources Committee publication. Technical information.

National Planning Board, Federal Emergency Administration of Public Works, Final Report 1933–1934. Washington, 1935. National Resources Board Publication. An excellent comprehensive report.

National Resources Committee Progress Report, 1938. Washington, 1938. National Resource Committee publication. Excellent information.

National Resources Committee Progress Report, 1939. Washington, 1939. National Resources Committee publication. A summary of the work of the board.

National Resources Development: Part I Post-War Plan and Program. Washington, January 1943. A National Resources Planning Board publication containing useful material on valley development, energy resource development, and wartime planning for resource use.

Objectives and Results of the C.C.C. Program. Washington, 1936. A mimeographed bulletin containing a great deal of information on the organization and work of the C.C.C.

Our American Land: The Story of Its Abuse and Its Conservation. Washington, 1948. Bulletin issued by the Soil Conservation Service on soil problems.

Our Forests: What They Are and What They Mean to Us. Washington, 1944. U.S. Department of Agriculture publication on the history of the U.S. forest background, and scientific information on forest care.

Pack, C. L. "Auditing the C.C.C. Ledger." *Review of Reviews*, 89:28–29. January 1934. Material on the C.C.C.

Page, John C. "Water Conservation and Control." *The Reclamation Era*, 27:253–55. November 1937. A discussion of national reaction to the drought.

————. "Water Conservation and Control." *The Reclamation Era*, 27:46–49. March 1937. Material on the droughts and floods.

Pamphlets Relating to National Forests. A series of pamphlets on national forests.

Planning Our Resources. Washington, March 1938. Publication of the National Resources Committee that contains valuable information on the meaning of planning, planning at different levels, and a guide to planning publications.

"President Roosevelt Dedicates Boulder Dam, September 30, 1935." *The Reclamation Era*, 25:193–94. October 1935. Text of Dedicatory Address.

Public Land. Washington, 1940. National Resources Board publication. Useful information.

Public Works Planning. Washington, 1936. National Resources Committee publication. A report recommending a proposed policy for planning, programming, timing, and division of cost of public works.

Recreational Developments by the C.C.C. in National and State Forests. Washington, 1936. Material prepared by the Forest Service on the types of work by the enrollees.

Reforestation by the C.C.C. Washington, 1941. Contains material on planting trees, timber stand improvement, nursery work, and timber surveys.

Regional Factors in National Planning and Development. Washington, 1935. National

Resources Board publication. Deals with important problems of planning and development that overlap state lines or with federal and state or local interests and jurisdictions.

A Report of the Activities Carried on by the Agricultural Adjustment Administration. Washington, 1939. Factual.

Report of the Chief of the Forest Service. Washington, 1934. The place of forestry in planned development.

———. Washington, 1935. Material on emergency relief.

———. Washington, 1936. Discussion on ownership and legislation.

———. Washington, 1937. Discussion of conservation with human welfare as a fundamental objective.

———. Washington, 1938. Discussion of the need of national forests, the primary purpose a social one.

———. Washington, 1939. Discussion of problems of private owners.

Report of the Chief of the Soil Conservation Service. Washington, 1938. Discussion on soil conservation districts, cooperative relations, and planning.

———. Washington, 1940. Excellent material on erosion and conservation milestones.

———. Washington, 1941. A discussion of the year's progress and planning completed.

———. Washington, 1947. A good discussion of the 14 years of progress of the Service.

———. Washington, 1949. Useful information on progress in soil and water conservation and conservation needs.

Report of the Forester, 1934. Washington, 1934. Material on the drought of 1934.

———. Washington, 1935. Material on the shelterbelt.

A Report of National Planning and Public Works in Relation to Natural Resources and Including Land Use and Water Resources with Findings and Recommendations, December 1, 1934. National Planning Board publication. A report on national planning and public works in relation to natural resources and including land use, and water and mineral resources with findings and recommendations. Very useful material.

Report of the Secretary of Agriculture, 1933. Washington, 1933. Excellent discussion of social objectives of forestry.

———. Washington, 1934. Good material on land utilization problems and wildlife conservation.

———. Washington, 1935. Material on the relation of forestry to agriculture and soil conservation.

———. Washington, 1936. A good discussion of land policy.

———. Washington, 1937. An excellent presentation of forest and human conservation, as well as material on a national conservation program, land treatment for flood control, and forestry.

———. Washington, 1938. A discussion of economic planning, democracy in soil conservation districts, and social objective forestry.

———. Washington, 1939. An excellent discussion of soil conservation and land use planning.

————. Washington, 1940. Material on land use, flood control, and the relation of conservation to defense.

————. Washington, 1941. Useful material on planning and forests.

Report on Water Pollution. Washington, 1935. National Resources Committee publication. Specialized information.

Review of Educational Legislation 1935–1936. Washington, 1937. Publication by the U.S. Office of Education.

Roberts, A. B. *Certain Aspects of Power Irrigation and Flood Control Projects.* Washington, 1949. A report prepared for the Commission on Organization of the executive branch of the government. Excellent historical material.

Security, Work, and Relief Policies. Washington, 1942. National Research Planning Board publication. Report on long-range work and relief policies.

Senate Miscellaneous Documents, Number 95. 75 Congress, 1 session. "Comprehensive National Plan for Prevention and Control of Floods—Veto Message from President of U.S."

Soil Conservation. August, 1935—January 1942. Official organ of the Soil Conservation Service, largely technical in nature.

Soil Conservation Service. A series of pamphlets on dust storms, erosion control, dams, farming practices, and miscellaneous information.

Standards of Eligibility for Junior Enrollees. Washington, 1941. C.C.C. information.

Subject Index of Reports. Washington, 1940. Useful guide issued by the National Resources Planning Board on principal subjects dealt with in publications by the National Resources Committee and its predecessors.

Summary Report of the Director of Emergency Conservation Work; For the Period Extending from April 1933 to June 30, 1935. Washington, 1935. Excellent summary of the work and purposes of the C.C.C., the organization of the C.C.C., and growth of the Corps.

Swenson, Bennett. "Monthly Weather Review," *U.S. Weather Bureau,* 65:71–86. February 1937. Information on floods.

T.V.A. Washington, 1938. A pamphlet on floods, planning, and electricity.

T.V.A. Washington, 1941. An excellent pamphlet discussing the work of the T.V.A. It also contains useful charts.

United States Government Manual, 1948. Washington, 1948. Information on the Works Progress Administration and the Public Works Administration.

Vote Cast in Presidential and Congressional Elections, 1928–1944. Washington, 1946. Publication by the U.S. Department of Commerce, Bureau of the Census.

United States Statutes at Large

United States Statutes at Large, 48:22–23. An act, "For the Relief of Unemployment through the Performance of Useful Public Work, and Other Purposes." March 31, 1933.

————. 48:58–72. An act, "To Improve the Navigability and to Provide for the Flood Control of the Tennessee River; to Provide for Reforestation and the Proper Use of Marginal Lands in the Tennessee Valley; to Provide for the Agricultural and Industrial Development of Said Valley; to Provide for the

National Defense by the Creation of a Corporation for Operation of Government Proprieties at and near Muscle Shoals in Alabama, and for Other Purposes." May 18, 1933.

———. 48:200–10. An act, "To Encourage National Industrial Recovery, to Foster Fair Competition, and to provide for the Construction of Certain Useful Public Works, and for Other Purposes." June 16, 1933.

———. 48:400. An act, "To Establish Fish and Game Sanctuaries in the National Forests." March 10, 1934.

———. 48:401. An act, "To Promote the Conservation of Wild Life, Fish and Game and for Other Purposes." March 10, 1934.

———. 48:1269–75. An act, "To Stop Injury to the Public Grazing Lands by Preventing Overgrazing and Soil Deterioration, to Provide for Their Orderly Use, Improvement, and Development to Stabilize the Livestock Industry Dependent upon the Public Range, and for Other Purposes." June 28, 1934.

———. 49:30–33. An act, "To Regulate Interstate and Foreign Commerce in Petroleum and Its Products by Prohibiting the Shipment in Such Commerce of Petroleum and Its Products Produced in Violation of State Law." February 22, 1935.

———. 49:163. An act, "To Provide for Protection of Land Resources against Soil Erosion." March 25, 1935.

———. 49:163–64. An act, "To Provide for the Protection of Land Resources against Soil Erosion and for Other Purposes." April 27, 1935.

———. 49:991–1011. An act, "To Stabilize Bituminous Coal Mining Industry and Promote Its Interstate Commerce . . . to Conserve the Bituminous Coal Resources of United States." August 30, 1935.

———. 49:1148. An act, "To Promote the Conservation and Profitable Use of Agricultural Land Resources by Temporary Aid to Farmers and by Providing for a Permanent Policy of Federal Aid to State for Such Purposes." February 29, 1936.

———. 49:1148–52. An act, "To Promote Conservation and Profitable Use of Agricultural Land Resources by Temporary Federal Aid to Farmers and by Providing for a Permanent Policy of Federal Aid to State for Such Purposes." February 29, 1936.

———. 49:1570–97. An act, "Authorizing the Construction of Certain Public Works on Rivers and Harbors for Flood Control and Other Purposes." June 22, 1936.

———. 50:429. An act, "To Extend the Period during which the Purposes Specified in Section 7a of Soil Construction and Domestic Allotment Acts May Be Carried Out by Payments by Secretary of Agriculture to Producers." June 28, 1937.

———. 50:429. An act, "To Provide for Protection of Land Resources against Soil Erosion and for Other Purposes." June 29, 1937.

———. 50:517–18. An act, "To Modify Appropriation." July 19, 1937.

———. 50:869. An act, "To Promote Conservation in the Arid and Semiarid Areas of the United States by Aiding in Diversion of Facilities for Water Storage and Utilization and for Other Purposes." August 28, 1937.

———. 52:1248. An act, "To Proclaim the Week of May 31, 1938, National Flood Prevention Week." June 29, 1938.

———. 54:1119. An act, "Authorizing Construction of Water Construction and Utilization Projects in Great Plains and Arid and Semiarid Regions of United States." October 14, 1940.

———. 57:169. An act, "Making Appropriations for Executive Office and Sundry Independent Bureaus and Commission and Office for Present Year Ending January 30, 1944, and Other Purposes." June 26, 1943.

Wickard, Claude R. "Conservation, a Lasting Emergency." *Land Policy Review*, 4, 5. April 1941. The future of conservation is discussed.

Wildlife and the Land: A Story of Regeneration. Washington, 1937. Printed for use of the Special Committee on Conservation of Wildlife Resources.

Woodmanship for the Civilian Conservation Corps. Washington, 1941. Booklet devoted largely to Forestry instructions to by used by C.C.C. enrollees.

The Work of the C.C.C. in Water Conservation. Washington, 1936. Engineering and erosion control work of C.C.C. enrollees.

Work Experience Counts. Washington, 1941. Excellent material on the work, training, and life of C.C.C. enrollees.

The Work of the U.S. Forest Service. Washington, January 1945. Excellent information on the forest conservation movement.

Yearbook of Agriculture 1935. Washington, 1935. Material on land planning.

———. Washington, 1937. Information on the recognition of a rational land policy.

Yearbook of Agriculture 1938: Soils and Men. Washington, 1938. Entire publication is devoted to soil.

Yearbook of Agriculture 1940: Farmers in a Changing World. Washington, 1940. An excellent study for historical information and conservation work underway.

PERIODICALS

"A.A.A: Conservation Instead of Crop Control May Save the Day." *Newsweek*, 7:16–17. January 25, 1936. Discussion of the soil conservation idea as a hope to save the A.A.A.

"All Aboard for $470,000,000." *Business Week*, 24. March 28, 1936. Discussion of the Soil Conservation Domestic Allotment Act.

Allen, B. W. "Is Planning Compatible with Democracy." *American Journal of Sociology*, 42:510–20. January 1937. A critical article discussing planning and conservation accomplishments.

"Agriculture Policy and National Welfare." *Fortune*, 22:68–69. July 1940. An informative article.

Arrington, Leonard J., and Dittmer, Lowell. "Reclamation in Three Layers: The Ogden River Project, 1934–1965," *Pacific Historical Review*, XXV. February 1966. Importance of the Ogden River project to industrial development.

Ashby, L. W., and Dawson, H. C. "Harrison-Black-Fletcher Bill." *National Education Association Journal*, 26:49–56. February 1937. Educational material.

Atwood, Albert W. "Is This Conservation?" *Saturday Evening Post*, 209:23. September 26, 1936. Discussion of the meaning of conservation.

Baldridge, Kenneth W. "Reclamation Work of the Civilian Conservation Corps, 1932–1942." *Utah Historical Quarterly*, 39:265–85. Summer 1971. Discusses C.C.C. project work in Utah.

Barde, Robert E. "Arthur E. Morgan, First Chairman of TVA." *Tennessee Historical Quarterly*, 30:299–314. Fall 1971. An evaluation of Arthur Morgan and an analysis of his work.

Bathurst, E. G. "Progress of Teaching Conservation." *School Life*, 23:41–42, October 1937. Educational material.

Bennett, H. H. "Emergency and Permanent Control of Wind Erosion in the Great Plains." *Scientific Monthly*, 47:381-99. November 1938. Discusses the objectives of conservation.

———. "Facing the Erosion Problem." *Science ns*, 81:321–26. April 5, 1935. Discusses the need of a soil conservation program.

———. "Soil Erosion—A National Menace." *The Scientific Monthly*, 39:385–404. November 1934. Discusses control of erosion.

———. "This Is Your Land." *Vital Speeches*, 6:51–54. November 1939. A discussion of accomplishments in soil erosion control.

Bennett, James D. "Roosevelt, Wilkie, and the TVA." *Tennessee Historical Quarterly*, 28:388–96. Winter, 1969. Discusses the views and arguments, pro and con of Roosevelt and Wilkie on the T.V.A.'s threat to private enterprise.

Bliven, Bruce. "Human Welfare in the T.V.A." *New Republic*, 113:340–42. September 17, 1945. Social values of the T.V.A. are discussed.

Bowman, Isaiah. "Our Better Ordering and Preservation." *Science ns*, 93:191–97. February 28, 1941. Discusses the need for conservation education.

"But the Dust Bowl Is Still There." *Saturday Evening Post*, 210:22. July 24, 1937. A critical article of the dust bowl condition and recommendation for conservation practices.

Chase, Stuart. "Slaves of the Flood." *American Magazine*, 123:16–17. May 1937. Warns of flood danger and pro governmental projects to control floods.

———. "When the Crop Lands Go." *Harper's Magazine*, 173:225–33. August 1936. Discussion of the dangers of erosion and mining the soil.

———. "Disaster Rides the Plains." *American Magazine*, 124:46–47. September 1937. A discussion of accomplishments.

———. "Working with Nature." *Survey Graphic*, 26:624–28. December 1937. An article on regional planning.

Chew, Arthur P. "Save America First." *Atlantic Monthly*, 159:194–203. February 1937. A pro conservation approach.

Christie, Jean. "The Mississippi Valley Committee: Conservation and Planning in the Early New Deal." *The Historian*, 32:449–69. May 1970. Analysis of Morris Cooke's report on planning.

Collier, C. W. "At Last—A Soil Erosion Program." *New Republic*, 83:68–70. May 29, 1935. Discussion of erosion and floods.

Compton, Karl T. "Engineering in an American Program for Social Progress." *Science ns*, 83:301–02. March 26, 1937. A discussion of planning.

Compton, W. "Government Versus Desert." *Forum*, 93:237-39. April 1935. Discusses the fallacy of the shelterbelt.

"Conservation." *Nature Magazine*. April 1935. A pro editorial.

"Conserving Our Country." *Business Week*, 40. August 10, 1935. A praising article of the Roosevelt administration conservation work.

"Conservation Thinking." *Nature Magazine*, 20:149. October 1932. An editorial.

Cooke, M. E. "Twenty Years of Grace." *Survey Graphic*, 24:276–82. June 1935. Material on planning.

Cooke, Morris L. "Upstream." *Survey Graphic*, 25:300. May 1936. Discussion of floods and need of flood control.

———. "New Steps to save the Land." *Survey Graphic*, 29:246. April 7, 1940. Critical discussion of accomplishments.

———. "Is the United States a Permanent Country?" *Forum*, 99:236-40. April 1938. Contains historical and soil conservation material and discusses objectives.

Coyle, David Cushman. "Balance What Budget?" *Harper's Magazine*, 175:449–59. October 1937. A warning to the nation in the danger of misusing resources.

———. "America National Planning Board." *Political Quarterly*, 16:246–52. July 1945. Discussion of planning.

Creel, G. "Plan or Perish." *Colliers*, 94:10–11. December 5, 1934. An excellent article on the need of planning.

Cross, P. G. "Our Soil or Our Life." *Country Life*, 75:40–42. November 1938. A pro conservation article.

Cross, Whitney R. "Ideas in Politics: The Conservation Policies of the Two Roosevelts." *The Journal of the History of Ideas*, 14:421–38. June 1953. Examines the policies of the Roosevelts.

Daniels, Jonathan. "A Native at large." *Nation*, 151:174. August 31, 1940. An article urging preparedness.

Darling, J. N. "Conservation, a Typographical Error." *Review of Reviews*, 94:35–37. November 1936. A scathing article on the misuse of the term conservation.

Davenport, W. "Land Where Our Children Die." *Colliers*, 100:12,13. September 18, 1937. A colorful article sketching life and death in the dust bowl.

Davis, Chester C. "Lost Acres." *American*, 121:63. February 1938. Discussion of the danger of erosion and dust storms.

"Democracy: Its Essentials—Its Problems." *Scholastic*, 35:185–205. December 11, 1939. A discussion of the relationship of conservation and the general welfare.

Domorowski, J. "Some Social Aspects of T.V.A." *American Scholar*, 14:479–84. October 1945. T.V.A. article.

"Do They Offer the Needed Clue to Solving Our Economic Crisis?" *Nature Magazine*, 20:101. September 1932. A comparison of the laws of nature and the laws of economics.

Drummond, W. I. "Dust Bowl." *Review of Reviews*, 93:37–40. June 1936. Technical discussion and brief material on control projects.

Duncan, Kunigunde. "New U.S. Life Liner." *Current History*, 52:22–23. February 13, 1941. A discussion of techniques used to save the soil.

———. "Restraining the Dust Bowl." *Nation*, 149:269–71. September 9, 1939. An article praising citizens for winning the fight against erosion.

"Dust and Flood: Man Made Disasters." *Literary Digest*, 121:32. April 4, 1936. Urges land reform.

"The Dust Bowl Can be Saved." *Saturday Evening Post,* 210:16–17. December 18, 1937. Praise of the Soil Conservation Service.

"Dust Bowl Into Grazing Land." *Literary Digest,* 121:9. March 7, 1936. A critical discussion of governmental activity.

"Earth Disease." *Survey Graphic,* 25:302. May 1936. Article discusses governmental work in controlling erosion.

"Energy Turned Into Mass for First Time in History." *Science,* 77:Supplement 9. April 7, 1933. Of little value.

"Establishment of a Forest Shelter Belt." *Science,* 80:91. July 27, 1934. Discusses the executive order.

"Federal Government and Water Power, 1788–1930." *Congressional Digest,* 15:227–29. October 1936. Traces historically governmental activity in water power.

Fergusson, Edna. "Tearing Down the West." *Yale Review,* 25:331–43. December 1935. Discussion of the erosion control program.

"First National Conference on Conservation Education," *School and Society,* 46:172–73, August 7, 1937. Educational material.

Fly, James Lawrence. "National Approach to Water Conservation." *Congressional Digest,* 17:19–21. January 1938. Excellent background material.

Forbes, Reginald D. "Ruling the River." *Scientific Monthly,* 38:524–33. June 1934. A discussion of the forests and relation to floods.

"Forestry." *Newsweek,* 4:11. September 29, 1934. Article on the shelterbelt.

Gabrielson, Ira N. "National Defense Uses of Natural Resources." *Science ns,* 93:Supplement 8. February 21, 1941. Discusses the meaning of defense to conservation.

"Geologist's Conservation Warning." *Literary Digest,* 120:19. July 13, 1935. Article traces history of forestry work.

Glover, Katherine. "Blue Ribbon Citizen." *Survey Graphic,* 29:180–81. March 1940. Article discusses state conservation activity.

"Grasslands." *Fortune,* 12:58–67. November 1935. Discussion of past use of grasslands and need of cooperation of government and citizen and science.

"Hamilton Desert Maker." *Nation,* 143:229. August 29, 1936. A critical editorial; discussion of grazing land policy.

"How Much Conservation." *Saturday Evening Post,* 212:12–13. June 15, 1940. A stimulating, questioning article.

Humphreys, Hubert. "In a Sense Experimental: The Civilian Conservation Corps in Louisiana." *Louisiana History,* 5:345–67, 27–52. Fall, Winter 1964. A detailed account of C.C.C. work in Louisiana and the C.C.C. educational program.

Ickes, Harold L. "Saving the Good Earth." *Survey Graphic,* 23:52–59. February 1934. A discussion of the Mississippi Valley Committee and its plan.

———. "Thought of the Morrow." *Colliers,* 94:21. December 8, 1934. Article on the need for planning.

———. "A Department of Conservation." *Vital Speeches,* 3:693–95. September 1, 1937. Ickes' definition of conservation and reasons why he desires a Department of Conservation.

James, M. L. "The National Domain and the New Deal." *Saturday Evening Post,* 206:10–11. December 23, 1933. An interview by M. James with Secretary Ickes.

Kennedy, Renwick C. "Land." *Christian Century*, 57:213–15. February 14, 1940. Written in a very dramatic style urging the saving of soil.

Kirschten, Ernest. "T.V.A. the First 15 Years." *Nation*, 166:656–59. June 12, 1948. Evaluation of T.V.A.

Knappen, Theodore M. "Operating on a Continent." *Reader's Digest*, 28:59–60. March 1936. A survey of conservation work.

Knight, Oliver. "Correcting Nature's Error: the Colorado-Big Thompson Project." *Agricultural History*, 30:157–69. October 1956. Discusses the first major attempt to provide water for an ongoing agricultural area.

Larisch, L. "States and Decentralized Administration of Federal Functions." *Journal of Politics*, 12:3–12. February 1950. Article on T.V.A.

"The Laws of Nature," *Nature Magazine*, 20:101. September 1932. A critical editorial.

Lawson, H. A. "New Federal Aid Bill—Harrison Thomas Fletcher Bill." *National Education Association Journal*, 27:130. May 1938. Educational material.

"Legislative Action." *School Life*, 24:146. February 1938. Educational material.

Leuchtenburg, William. "Roosevelt, Norris and the 'Seven Little TVAs.'" *The Journal of Politics*, 14:418–41. August 1952. Discusses Roosevelt's position on legislation for a regional T.V.A. system.

Lieber, R. "Our Inherited Wealth." *Review of Reviews*, 89:44–45. May 1934. Discusses need of conservation.

Lipman, Jacob G. "The Conservation of Our Land Resources." *Science ns*, 83:65–69. January 24, 1936. Traces history of what has happened to land; discusses plans and programs of land use, and the protection of our land and soil resources.

Lodge, J. E. "New Federal Service to End Destruction of Our Farms." *Popular Science Monthly*, 124:38–39. January 1934. A discussion of soil erosion control.

Lourie, Walter E. "Roosevelt and the Passamaquoddy Bay Tidal Project." *The Historian*, 31:64–89. November 1968. Discusses the opposition forcing F.D.R. to give up his project.

Lusk, Robert D. "Life and Death of 470 Acres." *Saturday Evening Post*, 211:5–6. August 13, 1938. An account of erosion written in story form.

Malone, A. W. "Desert Ahead." *New Outlook*, 164:14–17. August 1934. Discussion of dust storms and people beginning to be conscious of them.

Melcher, F. S. "Support the Education Bill, F. S. Fletcher." *Publisher's Weekly*, 133:1749. April 30, 1939.

Merriam, Charles E. "The National Resources Board," *The American Political Science Review*, 38:1075–89. December 1944. An excellent article on planning.

Meyerhoff, Howard A. "Floods and Dust Storms." *Science ns*, 83:622. June 26, 1936. Article cautions against too enthusiastic an attitude for flood control—must see whole problem.

Mitchell, Jonathan. "Mr. Wallace Tries Again." *New Republic*, 87:41–43. May 20, 1936. Discussion of soil conservation.

———. "Shelter Belt Realities." *New Republic*, 80:69–71. August 29, 1934. An article critical of the shelterbelt.

Morgan, Arthur E. "Downstream." *Survey Graphic*, 25:301. May 1936. Discussion of the need of flood control and that it is beyond the ability of local communities.

Morgan, H. A. "National Conservation." *Forum*, 99:Supplement 11. June 1938. Discusses the need of farmer aid.

Neuberger, Richard L. "Public Domain." *Survey Graphic*, 30:72–78. February 1941. Discussion of defense and its effect on conservation.

"New Deal program for Electric Utilities." *Congressional Digest*, 15:230–32. October 1936. A discussion of power accomplishments.

"New Farm Aid Slogan." *Literary Digest*, 121:4. January 25, 1936. Emphasis on soil conservation rather than crop control method.

Pack, Arthur N. "Let's Get Together." *Nature Magazine*, 27:46–47. January 1936. A critical article on organization.

Pearson, G. A. "Conservation and Use of Forests in the Southwest." *Scientific Monthly*, 45:150–57. August 1937. Forestry background material.

"Plains Penance: Governmental Committee Outlines Scourge; Aid for Dust States." *Literary Digest*, 123:8–9. February 26, 1936. Article stresses need of long-term program.

Pinchot, Gifford. "A Forest Appeal." *Literary Digest*, 120:30. July 20, 1935. Discussion of struggle between Departments of Interior and Agriculture over care of forests.

"Planting a Shelter Belt Through Middle of America." *Literary Digest*, 118:15. August 11, 1934. Discusses the scope of the plan.

Polenberg, Richard. "Conservation and Reorganization: The Forest Service Lobby, 1937–1938." *Agricultural History*, 39:230–39. October 1965. Examines the lobby's efforts to block the transfer of the Forest Service to the Department of Interior.

————. "The Great Conservation Contest." *Forest History*, 10:13–23. January 1967. Discusses Ickes' ambition to have a Department of Conservation.

"President Approves Plan for Record Reforestation." *Literary Digest*, 118:39. July 28, 1934. Article on the shelterbelt.

"Preventing Soil Blowing on the Great Plains." *Farmer's Bulletin*, 1771:1–28. 1937. Technical information.

"Protecting Southern Pines." *Business Week*, 24. January 7, 1939. Favorable discussion of forestry conservation.

Randall, Robert H. "Conservation of Natural Resources." *Annals of the American Academy*, 206:142–46. November 1936. Conservation background material and a discussion of planning.

Richardson, Elmo R. "Olympic National Park." *Forest History*, 12:6–15. April 1968. Legislative history of Olympic National Park.

"Roosevelt and Conservation." *Nature Magazine*, 21:269. June 1933. The president is looked to as a leader in saving natural resources.

"Roosevelt's Pet Project." *Newsweek*, 4:11. September 29, 1934. Discussion of the reception of the shelterbelt plan.

"Save Our Forests." *New Republic*, 83:321–22. July 31, 1935. An editorial discussing the relationship of governmental lumber regulations and effect on lumbering industry.

"Save the Soil: Ancient Truths Are Rediscovered." *Review of Reviews*, 83:28–30. April 1936. Critical article of farm relief program.

"Save Our Soil." *Colliers*, 97:86. March 14, 1936. An editorial discussing the absolute need to save soil and that no political controversy ever shall harm the principle of reclaiming land.

Sears, Paul B. "Death from the Soil." *American Mercury*, 42:440–47. December 1937. Pro soil conservation article.

———. "Floods and Dust Storms." *Science ns*, 83:Supplement 9. March 27, 1936. Pro flood control article.

——— "Science and the New Landscape." *Harper's Magazine*, 179:207–16. July 1939. Critical discussion of conservation and the dangers it holds.

Shear, C. L. "The Conservation of Public Lands." *Science ns*, 83:204. February 28, 1936. Discussion on grazing lands need control.

Silcox, F. A. "The Chief Forester Voices His Creed." *Nature Magazine*, 26:51. July 1935. Pro forestry article.

"Soil Conservation." *Congressional Digest*, 16:7. January 1937. Discussion of direct federal cash benefits.

"Soil Defense in the Northeast." *Farmer's Bulletin*, 1810:1–63. Technical information.

"Soil Erosion." *Science ns*, 78:Supplement 9. August 4, 1933. Pro erosion control by government.

"Soil and Water Conservation in the Pacific Northwest." *Farmer's Bulletin*, 1773:1–59. 1937. Discussion of conservation accomplishments.

"State Legislation Affecting Education." *School Life*, 23:107–8. December 1938. Educational material.

Stoney, George C. "A Valley to Hold to." *Survey Graphic*, 29:391–99. July 1940. Discussion of T.V.A. objectives.

Stout, Joe A. Jr. "Cattlemen, Conservationists and the Taylor Grazing Act." *New Mexico Historical Review*, 45:311–32. October 1970. Discussion of the Taylor Grazing Act and the reaction of stockers.

Swain, Donald C. "Harold Ickes, Horace Albright, and the Hundred Days: A Study in Conservation Administration." *Pacific Historical Review*, 34:455–65. November 1965. An analysis of Albright's influence on Ickes.

———. "The Bureau of Reclamation and the New Deal, 1933–1940." *The Pacific Northwest Quarterly*, 61:137–46. July 1970. Finances of the Bureau of Reclamation.

Taylor, A. "Celebrate Decade of T.V.A. Benefits." *Christian Century*, 66:1429. November 30, 1949. Evaluation of T.V.A.

Trani, Eugene. "Conflict or Compromise: Harold L. Ickes and Franklin D. Roosevelt." *North Dakota Quarterly*, 36:20–29. Winter 1968. Discusses Ickes' fight for a Department of Conservation.

Van Cleave, H. J. "Man Meddles with Nature." *The Scientific Monthly*, 40:339–48. April 1935. Critical article of conservation work that does not observe laws of nature.

Wallace, Henry A. "The War at Our Feet." *Survey Graphic*, 29:104–14. February 1940. Conservation background material.

"The War on Erosion." *Newsweek*, 13:54. March 20, 1939. Critical account of soil erosion.

"Washington Notes." *New Republic*, 91:128. June 9, 1937. Pro soil conservation.

"Water Planning Committee." *The American City*, 50:9. May 1935. Discusses the objectives of the water-planning committee.

Wengert, Norman. "TVA—Symbol and Reality." *The Journal of Politics*, 13:369–92. August 1951. Evaluates the T.V.A.

Wessel, Thomas R. "Roosevelt and the Great Plains Shelterbelt." *Great Plains Journal*, 8:57–74. Spring 1969. Discusses varied reactions to the shelterbelt.

Weybright, Victor. "The Valleys and the Plains." *Survey Graphic*, 26:145–59. March 1937. Discussion of water planning.

"What New Land Policy Will Do." *Saturday Evening Post*, December 23, 1933. Material on land use.

White, O. P. "Land of the Pilgrims' Pride." *Colliers*, 96:112–13. July 27, 1935. Discusses dust storms.

———. "Timber for the Future." *Colliers*, 95:12. June 22, 1935. Pro forest conservation article.

Wilcox, W. "Economic Aspects of Soil Conservation." *Journal of Political Economics*, 46:702–13. October 1938.

William, Hendrick. "Give Mother Nature a Chance." *Rotarian*, 58:10–12. May 1941. Entertaining article on conservation.

"Wisconsin Establishes Conservation Courses in Schools." *Bird Lore*, 38:39. January 1936. Educational material.

Zon, R. "Shelterbelts—Futile Dreams or Workable Plan." *Science ns*, 81:391–94. April 26, 1935. Weighs value of the shelterbelt.

NEWSPAPERS

New York Times. March 1933, to January 1942.
Poughkeepsie News Press. March 5, 1912.

DOCTORAL DISSERTATIONS

Engelbert, Ernest A. "American Policy for Natural Resources: A Historical Survey to 1862." Harvard University, April 1, 1960. An unpublished doctoral dissertation that contains an extensive discussion on early conservation efforts.

Rockwell, Landon C. "National Resources Planning." Princeton University, May 1942. An unpublished doctoral dissertation that traces the development of the National Planning Board.

Smallwood, Johnny B. "George W. Norris and the Concept of a Planned Region." University of North Carolina, 1963.

MISCELLANEOUS

Boeckel, Richard M., editor. *Editorial Research Reports*. 1933–41 inclusive. Contains useful varied material.

Campaign Book of the Democratic Party: Candidates and Issues. New York, 1932. Contains Franklin D. Roosevelt's "Issues Defined in the Speech of Acceptance," address accepting the presidential nomination.

The Era of Franklin D. Roosevelt: A Selected Bibliography of Periodical, Essay, and Dissertation Literature, 1945–1971, compiled and annotated by William J. Stewart with the assistance of Jeanne Schaube. Franklin D. Roosevelt Library, National Archives and Records Service. General Service Administration. Hyde Park, New York, January 30, 1974.

Forestry Practice on the Roosevelt Farm. New York State College of Forestry, August 1931. Personal copy belonging to William Plog given to me in June 1950. Leaflet folder containing useful information.

Franklin D. Roosevelt and Conservation, 1911–1945, compiled and edited by Edgar B. Nixon, former archivist of the Roosevelt Library, Vol. I and II, General Services Administration, National Centers and Records Service. Franklin D. Roosevelt Library, Hyde Park, New York, 1957. U.S. Government Printing Office, 1957.

"President Roosevelt Practices Selective Logging." *Southern Lumberman.* December 15, 1942. Useful leaflet.

BOOKS

The following is a selective listing of books applicable to subjects investigated and discussed and is in no way exhaustive.

Allen, F. L. *Only Yesterday.* New York, 1931. Of general value.

Arnold, Thurman. *The Folklore of Capitalism.* New Haven, 1937. Discusses New Deal thinking.

Atkinson, R. C. *Federal Role in Unemployment Compensation Administration.* Washington, 1941. Report prepared for Committee on Social Security. An excellent section on resources.

Beals, C. *Pan American.* Boston, 1940. Of little value on U.S. conservation.

Beard, C. A., and Smith, H. E. *The Old Deal and the New.* 1940. Discusses the New Deal and its effect on society.

Bellush, Benard. *Franklin D. Roosevelt as Governor of New York.* New York, 1955.

Bernstein, Irving. *The Lean Years.* Boston, 1960. An account of the depression.

Blum, John Morton. *From the Morgenthau Diaries.* Boston, 1959.

Brown, Nelson. *General Introduction to Forestry in U.S.* New York, 1935. Largely technical information.

Burns, E. M. *Toward Social Security.* Colorado University, 1936. Discussion of the Social Security Act.

Burns, James MacGregor. *Roosevelt: The Lion and the Fox.* New York, 1956. Study of F.D.R.

Butlin, J. A., ed. *Economics of Environmental and Natural Resource Policy.* Boulder, 1981.

Chase, Stuart. *Rich Land and Poor Land.* New York, 1936. Written in popular journalistic fashion and pro conservation in tone, however, containing factual information of value.

Chase, Stuart, and Tyler, Marian. *Men at Work.* New York, 1945. T.V.A. material.

Clark, J. M. *Economics of Planning Public Works.* Columbia University, 1935. Study made for National Planning Board of the Federal Emergency Administration of Public Works. Material on the types of public work projects, watershed authorities, and land utilization.

Commager, H. S., and Morison, S. E. *The Growth of American Republic.* New York, 1942. General information.

Conkin, Paul Keith. *FDR and the Origins of the Welfare State.* New York, 1967.

———. *The New Deal.* New York, 1975.

Cooper, W. S., Pearson, G. A., and Zon, R. *Conservation of Renewable Natural Resources.* Philadelphia, 1941. Technical information.

Cox, George W., ed. *Readings in Conservation Ecology.* New York, 1969.

Curti, Merle. *The Growth of American Thought.* New York, 1943. Very useful information.

Decker, D. G. *Relationship between Natural Resources and Activities of People in Colorado.* Colorado, 1943. A specific study of conservation relating it to society.

Dorfman, Joseph. *The Economic Mind,* Vol. 5. New York, 1959.

Dows, Olin. *Franklin Roosevelt at Hyde Park.* New York, 1949. Documented drawings and text.

Einandi, Mario. *The Roosevelt Revolution.* New York, 1959.

Ekirch, Arthur A. *Ideologies and Utopias: The Impact of the New Deal on American Thought.* Chicago, 1969.

Elliott, C. M. *Conservation of American Resources.* Atlanta, 1940. Text in conservation.

Fainsod, Merle, and Gordon, Lincoln. *Government and the American Economy.* New York, 1941. A stimulating and very informative study.

Freidel, Frank Burt. *Franklin D. Roosevelt, Vol. 3,* Boston, 1952.

———. *The New Deal in Historical Perspective.* Washington, 1965.

Freidel, Frank Burt, and Pollack, Norman, eds. *American Issues in the Twentieth Century.* Chicago, 1966.

Frisch, Morton J. *Franklin D. Roosevelt: Contributions of New Deal in American Political Thought.* New York, 1975.

Furnas, C. C. *Storehouse of Civilization.* New York, 1939. A technical discussion of natural resources.

Fusfield, Daniel Roland. *The Economic Thought of Franklin D. Roosevelt and the Origins of the New Deal.* New York, 1956. Important study of New Deal thought.

Galbraith, John Kenneth. *The Great Crash.* Boston, 1955.

Gaus, J., and Wolcott, L. C. *Public Administration and United States Department of Agriculture.* Chicago, 1940. An excellent study; some information on land use.

Gayer, A. D. *Public Works in Prosperity and Depression.* New York, 1935. Publication of the National Bureau of Economic Research. Information on the planning activity of the federal government.

Glover, Katherine. *America Begins Again.* New York, 1939. Typical "torch conservation" book persuasive of pro conservation; lacks critical insight into conservation movement.

Goldsmith, Edward, and others. *Blueprint for Survival.* Boston, 1972.

Graham, Frank. *Man's Dominion: The Story of Conservation in America.* Philadelphia, 1971.

———. *The Adirondack Park: A Political History.* New York, 1978.

Grant, M. *Old Age Security.* Washington, 1939. Information on the security of people.

Greer, Thomas. *What Roosevelt Thought.* East Lansing, 1958.

Gustafson, A. F. *Conservation in the U.S.* New York, 1944. Technical information.

Heifendahl, Orris Clemens. *Resource Economics: Selected Works.* Baltimore, 1974.

Held, R., and Clawson, Marion. *Soil Conservation in Perspective.* Baltimore, 1965.

Highsmith, Richard Morgan. *Conservation in the United States.* Chicago, 1969.

Hollingsworth, Harold M., and Holmes, William F., eds. *Essays on the New Deal.* Austin: University of Texas Press, 1969.

House, Peter William. *Planning and Conservation: The Emergence of the Frugal Society.* New York, 1977.

Hynning, C. J. *Trends in State Resources Planning.* Chicago, 1938. A study of state conservation programs.

Ickes, Harold L. *The Autobiography of a Curmudgeon.* New York, 1943. Illuminating material.

———. *Back to Work: The Story of the P.W.A.* New York, 1935. Useful information on the P.W.A.

———. *The Secret Diary of Harold Ickes.* 3 volumes. New York, 1954.

Leuchtenberg, William E. *Franklin D. Roosevelt and the New Deal 1932–1940.* New York, 1963. An excellent analysis of the 1930s.

———, ed. *Franklin D. Roosevelt: A Profile.* New York, 1967.

Lieber, Richard. *America's Natural Wealth.* Harpers, 1942. Aim is to set forth nature of our natural resources and their bearing on national security, prosperity, and politics.

Lilienthal, D. E. *The T.V.A.: Democracy on the March.* New York, 1944. T.V.A. material.

Magee, J. D., Atkins, Walland, and Stein, Emanuel. *The National Recovery Program* New York, 1933. Excellent—a collection of source materials.

Martin, Roscoe, ed. *T.V.A.: The First Twenty Years.* University of Alabama Press, University, 1956.

McHenry, Robert, ed. *A Documentary History of Conservation in America.* New York, 1972.

Meyers, William Starr. *The State Papers and Other Public Writings of Herbert Hoover.* New York, 1934. Contains material on Hoover's views on conservation.

Nash, Gerald D., ed. *Franklin Delano Roosevelt.* Englewood Cliffs, 1967.

Nash, Roderick. *The American Environment: Readings in the History of Conservation.* Reading, 1968.

Norris, George W. *Fighting Liberal.* New York, 1945. Excellent autobiography with T.V.A. background material.

Nourse, E. G., Davis, J. S., and Black, J. D. *Three Years of the Agricultural Adjustment Administration.* Washington, 1937. An excellent study.

Oliver, Alfred C., and Dudley, Harold M., eds. *This New America: The Spirit of the Civilian Conservation Corps.* New York, 1937. Much of the material for this book was taken from *Happy Days,* data on government files made available to the editors.

Osborn, Fairfield. *Our Plundered Planet.* Boston, 1948. Of little value.

Parkins, A. E., and Whitaker, J. R., eds. *Our Natural Resources and Their Conservation.* New York, 1939. Excellent material on the actual conservation of natural resources.

Perkins, Dexter. *The New Age of Franklin Roosevelt, 1932–45.* Chicago, 1957. General history.

Perkins, Francis. *The President I Knew.* New York, 1946. Excellent personal memoirs.

Person, H. S. *Little Waters.* Washington, 1936. A study of headwater streams and other little waters frequently referred to by Franklin D. Roosevelt.

Phillips, C. F. *Government Spending and Economic Recovery.* New York, 1938. Good factual plus theoretical material.

Pinchot, Gifford. *Breaking New Ground.* New York, 1947. Excellent historical material.

———. *The Fight for Conservation.* University of Washington Press, 1967.

Ransmeier, J. *Tennessee Valley Authority.* Nashville, 1942. T.V.A. material.

Rauch, Basil. *The History of the New Deal.* New York, 1944. Very fine account of the New Deal in analysis and factual content.

Ravage, M. E. *The Story of Teapot Dome.* New York, 1924. Useful study of a governmental scandal.

Robinson, Edgar Eugene. *The Presidential Vote 1896–1932.* Stanford, 1934. Election material.

———. *The Roosevelt Leadership, 1933–1945.* Philadelphia, 1955.

Roosevelt, Elliot, ed. *F.D.R., His Personal Letters 1928–1945.* 2 volumes. New York, 1950.

Roosevelt, Elliot, and Brough, James. *A Rendezvous with History.* New York, 1975.

Roosevelt, F. D. *Looking Forward.* New York, 1933. Useful material.

Roosevelt, James, and Shallet, Sidney. *Affectionately F.D.R.* New York, 1959.

Rosenman, Samuel, ed. *The Public Papers and Addresses of Franklin D. Roosevelt.* 13 volumes. New York, 1938–50.

Schlesinger, Arthur Meier. *The Age of Roosevelt.* 3 volumes. Boston, 1957–62.

Schortemeir, Frederick E., ed. *Harding, Warren O.: Our Common Country.* Indianapolis, 1921. Harding's views on conservation

Sears, Paul Bigelow. *Deserts on the March.* University of Oklahoma, 1935. General information.

Sherwood, Robert E. *Roosevelt and Hopkins: An Intimate History.* New York, 1948. One of the best books on Franklin Roosevelt.

Tugwell, Rexford. *The Democratic Roosevelt.* New York, 1957. Study of F.D.R.

———. *FDR, Architect of an Era.* New York, 1967.

———. *In Search of Roosevelt.* Cambridge, 1972.

———. *Roosevelt's Revolution.* New York, 1977.

Trull, E. *Resources and Debts.* New York, 1937. Of little value.

Tully, Grace. *FDR, My Boss.* New York, 1949.

Vogt, William. *Road to Survival.* New York, 1948. A stimulating discussion of humans and their relationship to the environment.

Wallace, S. C. *The New Deal in Action.* Columbia, 1934. Information of a general nature.

Wallace, H. *New Frontiers.* New York, 1934. Information on the A.A.A.

Wann, A. *The President as Chief Administrator.* Washington, 1968.

Wecter, Dixon. *The Age of the Great Depression 1929–1941.* New York, 1948. An excellent study of the period.

Wengert, Norman. *Valley of Tomorrow.* Knoxville, 1952. Study of the T.V.A.

Whitaker, Russell J., and Ackerman, Edward A. *American Resources: Their Management and Conservation.* New York, 1951. Excellent historical material.

Zinn, Howard, ed. *New Deal Thought.* New York, 1966. Excellent collection of source materials.

Appendix A
Soil Conservation Work

TABLE A-1. Farmer applications, acreages planned, and acreages treated in district, project, and camp areas [1]

Item	Fiscal years					
	1935	1936	1937	1938	1939	1940
Applications received for farm plans	1,300,000 [2]	6,500,000	12,000,000	18,000,000	26,500,000	38,000,000
Acreages planned	1,259,684	5,887,179	10,304,798	15,654,871	22,019,856	29,534,818
Treatment completed	341,293	1,891,164	3,066,134	5,359,021	9,333,350	13,297,343

[1] Cumulative acreages by fiscal years shown in this table represent only the work on privately owned or leased state and municipal farms.

[2] Acres.

Source: Report of the Chief of the Soil Conservation Service, 1940, 9.

TABLE A-2. Total plans prepared to date by Soil Conservation Service technicians in areas within which the Service was working or cooperating as of June 30, 1940

	Soil conservation districts [1]		Demonstration and watershed projects [2]		Land utilization projects [3]		Water facilities projects [4]	
	No.	Acres	No.	Acres	No.	Acres	No.	Acres
Region 1								
Total	543	78,731	2,751	332,779	14	231,936		
Region 2								
Total	11,901	2,026,783	10,646	1,035,677	20	1,215,420		
Region 3								
Total	473	39,637	1,900	195,229	13	267,239		
Region 4								
Total	12,344	1,925,523	5,375	728,181	12	278,350	601	396,443
Region 5								
Total	987	172,306	3,778	542,733	12	1,588,182		
Region 6								
Total	1,220	1,502,575	1,361	521,236	15	738,408	513	488,080
Region 7								
Total	1,494	553,189	1,007	292,652	18	4,614,806	234	553,176
Region 8								
Total	246	218,372	1,149	4,546,034	6	564,675	67	53,403
Region 9								
Total			616	154,742	5	672,513	125	53,878
Region 10								
Total	114	22,263	725	71,946			72	14,850
U.S. Total	29,322	6,539,379	29,308	8,421,209	115	10,171,529	1,612	1,559,830

[1] District plans were principally farm and range conservation plans. However, a few public land and roadside erosion control plans were included in these state totals.

[2] This list includes only the detailed farm and range conservation plans prepared within demonstration and watershed project areas.

[3] Land utilization plans were detailed plans prepared for the development of these areas.

[4] Water facilities project plans were farm and range conservation plans supplemented by plans for water facilities installations, funds for the installation of which were provided under the water facilities program. Approximately 15 percent of these plans was in conjunction with plans included under district, project, and camp totals.

[5] Farm forestry project plans were farm and range conservation plans supplemented by plans for farm forestry work in connection with the farm forestry program. A number of these plans were in the form of amendments to farm conservation plans in district, project, and camp areas.

[6] Soil Conservation Service–Civilian Conservation Corps (S.C.S–C.C.C.) camp plans were farm and range conservation plans prepared in areas outside of districts and projects. In addition to these farms and ranges, camps have worked on several thousand additional farms and ranches

| Farm forestry projects[5] | | Technical cooperation | | | | | | Total[9] | |
| | | S.C.S.–C.C.C.[6] | | Public land[7] | | Other[8] | | | |
No.	Acres	No.	Acres	No.	Acres	No.	Acres	No.	Acres
2	320	4,677	641,385	19	5,026	392	45,937	8,398	1,336,114
9	2,396	11,769	1,991,019	83	7,880	659	122,945	35,087	6,402,120
7	486	6,445	1,059,316	58	14,886	1,940	19,244	10,836	1,596,037
1	31	12,364	2,163,886	7	15,876	1,210	108,501	31,914	5,616,791
		9,483	1,554,943	22	2,641	4,181	185,676	18,463	4,046,481
		2,197	1,729,706	19	4,969	501	815,940	5,826	5,800,914
		2,055	510,417	16	2,353,377	869	455,828	5,693	9,333,445
		275	122,172	216	5,748,170	60	397,664	2,019	11,650,490
		1,105	644,232	111	1,687,087	232	251,584	2,194	3,464,036
10	1,619	728	109,174	26	476,723	164	79,979	1,839	776,554
29	4,852	51,098	10,526,250	577	10,316,635	10,208	2,483,298	122,269	50,022,982

located in district and project areas. S.C.S.–C.C.C. plans in connection with drainage districts were included under "Other" plans.

[7] Public land plans were detailed operations plans prepared on Indian reservations, Forest Service national parks, grazing districts, and other public lands. In addition to these acreages, approximately 12 million acres in the Navajo Indian Reservation were covered by one overall plan.

[8] Other plans include: 2,349 S.C.S.–Extension Service demonstration farm plans, covering 1,710,927 acres; 3,859 drainage district plans; 772 roadside erosion-control project plans; 396 Farm Security Administration tenant purchase and reorganization farm plans, covering 512,249 acres; and 2,832 plans in cooperation with state institutions, municipalities, drought relief programs, and others, covering 260,122 acres.

[9] The total number and acreage covered by all plans include a duplication of approximately 250 plans covering 250,000 acres where water facilities and farm forestry plans were developed in conjunction with district, project, and camp plans.

[10] Wind erosion districts.

TABLE A-3. Land uses before and after planning for all farms and ranches for which detailed land use plans had been developed by Soil Conservation Service technicians, to June 30, 1940[1]

		Land uses[2] on farms and ranches	
		After planning	
Land uses[2]	Before planning (Acres)	Cultivated (Acres)	Permanent hay (Acres)
Cultivated	10,099,080	(8,489,676)	498,815
Permanent hay	391,557	26,888	(338,764)
Orchard and vineyard	125,600	3,602	1,283
Pasture and range	21,967,145	83,596	32,229
Forest range and wooded pasture	1,926,026	6,064	1,566
Woodland	2,956,424	34,119	6,020
Wildlife	27,452	87	12
Idle	450,598	106,243	67,480
Miscellaneous	879,637	29,929	13,527
Total acreages	38,823,519	8,780,204	959,696
Net changes		−1,318,876	+568,139

236

Land uses [2] on farms and ranches after planning

	Orchard and vineyard (Acres)	Pasture and range (Acres)	Forest range (Acres)	Woodland (Acres)	Wildlife (Acres)	Miscellaneous (Acres)
Cultivated	12,691	939,634	405	142,725	4,627	10,507
Permanent hay	247	23,022	89	1,817	115	615
Orchard and vineyard	(114,759)	4,943	24	717	36	236
Pasture and range	7,634	(21,599,558)	3,632	198,543	23,558	18,395
Forest range and wooded pasture	62	179,586	(1,504,479)	231,843	2,174	252
Woodland	1,850	184,187	10,392	(2,713,318)	4,174	2,364
Wildlife	18	191		86	(27,032)	26
Idle	2,021	182,584	773	65,770	11,305	14,422
Miscellaneous	1,293	52,491	192	67,358	5,879	(708,968)
Total acreage	140,575	23,166,196	1,519,986	3,422,177	78,900	755,785
Net changes	+14,975	+1,199,051	−406,040	+465,753	+51,448	−123,852

[1] Does not include acreages in land utilization projects and in some public land areas.

[2] In each of the first nine lines is shown the land use acreage before planning and the uses to be made of the acreage after the planning. The acreage figures shown in parentheses represent the amount of before-planning acreage to remain in its original use. Total acreage values are the total acreages in all land uses and the total to be in each land use after planning. Net changes values represent the difference plus or minus between before-planning and after-planning acreage for each land use.

Source: Report of the Chief of the Soil Conservation Service, 1940, 14.

Appendix B
**Summary of Expenditures of
Federal Public Works and
of Expenditures for
Federal Grants for
Public Construction, and
Summary of Federal Expenditures,
Corporation Outlays, Grants,
Loans, and Guarantees for
New Construction**

TABLE B-1. Summary of expenditures for construction of federal public works classified according to function, fiscal years 1933–41, inclusive[1] (all figures in thousands)

Function	1933	1934	1935	1936	1937	1938	1939	1940	1941
Water use and control									
Flood control	$35,118	$41,862	$34,403	$41,474	$50,280	$64,979	$76,444	$105,749	$114,281
Tennessee Valley Authority	—	8,020	31,179	41,565	35,545	36,538	31,543	39,136	60,000
Reclamation and irrigation	24,067	25,170	42,548	50,947	51,648	66,982	82,099	98,690	84,351
Transmission and electric plant	14	1,444	1,389	6,640	4,600	7,169	11,650	13,380	23,000
Total	59,199	76,496	109,519	140,626	142,073	175,668	201,736	256,955	281,632
Public land development									
Parks	6,537	8,675	13,826	14,538	23,190	18,023	21,158	16,072	17,723
Forests	12,799	25,048	22,784	20,900	22,913	18,462	18,703	12,911	10,658
Wildlife	158	568	843	1,995	1,987	1,490	2,747	1,098	755
Soil erosion control	2	—	10,334	24,080	300	215	2,819	1,824	767
Total	19,496	34,291	47,787	61,513	48,390	38,190	45,427	31,905	29,903
Transportation									
Roads	5,617	3,754	4,096	2,741	2,026	1,941	1,917	2,129	1,500
Rivers and harbors	49,123	79,115	133,036	152,195	147,470	99,047	76,779	61,573	45,115
Aids and assistance to navigation	2,644	1,990	3,261	992	2,165	1,815	8,633	5,094	9,148

[1] Estimated expenditures for fiscal year 1941 estimated as of Jan. 1941.

Source: Compiled from statement of federal expeditures for public works construction published annually in *The Budget of the U.S. Gov't.* Printed in *Development of Resources and Stabilization of Employment in the United States* (Washington D.C., January, 1941), 82–83, National Resources Planning Board.

TABLE B-1a Water use and control (all figures in thousands)

Agency	1933	1934	1935	1936	1937	1938	1939	1940	1941
Flood control									
Corps of Engineers	$35,118	$41,076	$31,807	$41,303	$49,221	$63,680	$75,454	$103,789	$112,200
International Boundary Commission, U.S. and Mexico		786	2,596	171	1,059	1,299	990	1,960	2,081
Total	35,118	41,862	34,403	41,474	50,280	64,979	76,444	105,749	114,281
Tennessee Valley Authority									
Corps of Engineers									
Tennessee Valley Authority		8,020	31,179	41,565	35,545	36,538	31,543	39,136	60,000
Total		8,020	31,179	41,565	35,545	36,538	31,543	39,136	60,000
Reclamation and irrigation									
Bureau of Reclamation	3,488	3,368	15,731	25,486	36,463	47,640	64,394		
Boulder Dam	19,709	19,534	22,180	18,913	5,588	7,354	9,093	93,642	81,211
All-American Canal		39	1,725	4,864	8,550	7,651	3,550		
Bureau of Indian Affairs	870	2,229	2,912	1,684	1,047	4,337	5,062	5,048	3,140
Small water conservation—Department of Interior									
Total	24,067	25,170	42,548	50,947	51,648	66,982	82,099	98,690	84,351
Transmission and electric plant									
Corps of Engineers	14	2							
TVA (Tennessee Valley Authority)		1,442	1,389	6,640	4,600	7,154	6,745	10,851	13,000
Bonneville Project						15	4,905	2,529	10,000
Total	14	1,444	1,389	6,640	4,600	7,169	11,650	13,380	23,000
Grand total	59,199	76,496	109,519	140,626	142,073	175,668	201,736	256,955	281,632

Source: *Development of Resources and Stabilization of Employment* (Washington, 1941), 82–83.

TABLE B-1b Public land development (all figures in thousands)

Agency	1933	1934	1935	1936	1937	1938	1939	1940	1941
Parks									
National Park Service	$6,537	$8,675	$13,826	$14,538	$23,190	$18,023	$21,158	$16,072	$17,723
Other public parks									
Total	6,537	8,675	13,826	14,538	23,190	18,023	21,158	16,072	17,723
Forest									
Forest Service,	12,799	25,048	22,784	20,900	22,913	18,462	18,703	12,911	10,658
Total	12,799	25,048	22,784	20,900	22,913	18,462	18,703	12,911	10,658
Wildlife									
Bureau of Biological Survey	6	300	667	1,861	1,939	1,248	1,140		
Bureau of Fisheries	152	268	176	134	48	242	1,607		
Total	158	568	843	1,995	1,987	1,490	2,747	1,098	775
Soil erosion control									
Soil Conservation Service			10,334	22,130		215	2,819	1,824	767
Extension Service				1,950	300				
General, Department of Agriculture	2								
Total	2		10,334	24,080	300	215	2,819	1,824	767
Grand total	19,496	34,291	47,787	61,513	48,390	38,190	45,427	31,905	29,903

Source: Development of Resources and Stabilization of Employment (Washington, 1941), 84–85.

Table B-2. Summary of expenditures for federal grants for public construction classified according to function, fiscal years 1934–40, inclusive (all figures in thousands)

Functions	1934	1935	1936	1937	1938	1939	1940
Water use and control							
Flood control	$29,514	$140	$9,152	$494	$530	$45,646	$25,352
Reclamation and irrigation	4,088	24,101	44,319	57,786	37,175		
Transmission and electric plant	62	35	13,728	9,133		1,130	810
Public water supply systems	200	17,494	36,497	44,386	39,623	62,768	43,124
Public sewer systems	419	34,769	101,165	103,883	88,849	136,330	90,511
Miscellaneous	18	349	1,248	1,728	1,942	2,260	1,619
Total	34,301	76,888	206,109	217,410	168,119	248,134	161,416
Public land development							
Forests	351	2,032	2,134	981	1,416	7,839	4,613
Soil erosion control	81,774	2,194	4,050	6,367	1,012	2,644	1,797
Miscellaneous	321	1,860	17,047	21,904	3,382	7,226	8,930
Total	82,446	6,086	23,231	29,252	5,810	17,709	15,340

Source: *Development of Resources and Stabilization of Employment* (Washington, 1941), 88–89.

TABLE B-2a Water use and control (all figures in thousands)

Agency	1934	1935	1936	1937	1938	1939	1940
Flood control							
Public Works Administration	$11	$140	$9,152	$494	$530		
Works Progress Administration	29,503						
Total	29,514	140	9,152	494	530		
Reclamation and electric plant							
Public Works Administration	25	594	416	1,481	353	$377	$270
Works Progress Administration	4,063	23,507	43,903	56,305	36,822	45,269	25,082
Total	4,088	24,101	44,319	57,786	37,175	45,646	25,352
Transmission and electric plant							
Public Works Administration Total	62	35	13,728	9,133		1,130	810

Source: Development of Resources and Stabilization of Employment (Washington, 1941), 90.

TABLE B-2b Public land development (all figures in thousands)

Agency	1934	1935	1936	1937	1938	1939	1940
Forests							
Works Progress Administration,							
Total	$351	$2,032	$2,134	$918	$1,416	$7,839	$4,613
Soil erosion control							
Public Works Administration					176		
Works Progress Administration	81,774	2,194	4,050	6,367	836	2,644	1,797
Total	81,774	2,194	4,050	6,367	1,012	2,644	1,797

Source: Development of Resources and Stabilization of Employment (Washington, 1941), 90.

TABLE B-3. Summary of federal expenditures, corporation outlays, grants, loans, and guarantees for new construction classified according to function, fiscal years 1933–40, inclusive (all figures in thousands)

Function	1933	1934	1935	1936	1937	1938	1939	1940
Water use and control								
Flood control	$35,118	$72,184	$35,827	$65,119	$51,640	$66,177	$76,444	$105,749
Tennessee Valley Authority		8,020	31,179	41,565	35,545	36,538	31,543	39,136
Reclamation and irrigation	25,832	34,575	75,117	96,524	112,935	105,345	129,154	124,828
Transmission and electric plant	14	9,933	10,267	58,561	22,907	7,169	24,290	17,771
Public water supply systems	10,502	28,522	59,451	82,034	89,321	71,172	85,584	57,536
Public sewerage system	136	21,034	46,070	111,632	106,075	91,021	138,705	93,134
Miscellaneous		952	3,060	2,322	2,238	3,513	3,192	2,676
Total	71,602	175,220	260,971	457,757	420,661	380,935	488,912	440,830
Public land development								
Parks	6,537	8,675	13,826	14,538	23,190	18,023	21,158	16,072
Forests	12,799	25,399	24,816	23,034	23,894	19,878	26,542	17,524
Wildlife	158	568	843	1,995	1,987	1,490	2,747	1,098
Soil erosion control	2	81,774	12,528	28,130	6,667	1,227	5,567	3,738
Miscellaneous		321	1,862	35,146	69,553	3,581	7,810	9,969
Total	19,496	116,737	53,875	102,843	125,291	44,199	63,824	48,401
Transportation								
Roads	171,352	500,773	462,853	630,094	880,702	672,803	1,023,212	730,628
Rivers and harbors	49,123	79,115	133,036	152,195	147,470	99,047	76,779	61,573
Aids and assistance to navigation	2,644	1,990	3,261	992	2,165	1,815	8,633	5,094
Railroads	199	74,864	101,665	25,886	3,400	5,791	11,307	2,033
Miscellaneous	16,716	40,950	24,047	69,872	28,589	29,458	45,643	33,801
Total	245,938	715,793	742,049	905,213	1,106,993	840,263	1,212,657	881,235

Defense								
Navy Department	12,626	14,110	13,686	14,463	19,053	14,979	48,094	81,652
War Department	13,796	35,542	34,280	17,374	23,676	34,375	61,499	72,248
War Department Nonmilitary		424	411					
Miscellaneous			5,518	6,544	16,354	11,556	34,870	22,042
Total	26,422	50,076	53,895	38,381	59,083	60,910	144,463	175,942
Government plant and general facilities								
Public buildings	118,177	204,399	85,163	108,678	137,217	121,055	108,220	97,278
Research facilities	108	2,655	2,524	1,312	908	838	3,034	6,757
Surveys and investigations	4	778	801	253	488	2,041	1,342	230
Welfare and health	19,856	49,582	51,458	79,937	100,433	60,837	95,297	79,803
Law enforcement		1,219	117	272	99	148	105	
Education	633	12,391	80,727	133,495	132,271	111,199	195,611	141,236
District of Columbia	7,736	4,205	8,000	12,345	6,871	7,183	20,495	19,661
Facilities outside continental U.S.	707	1,731	2,642	3,976	13,738	1,940	6,087	3,745
Recreation		35,576	87,232	173,518	186,403	130,781	167,242	93,079
Utilities		29,659	16,394	11,250	58,896	61,699	101,433	141,705
Miscellaneous	217	721	31,876	17,144	20,648	33,613	39,419	41,063
Total	147,438	342,916	366,934	542,180	657,972	531,334	738,285	624,557
Housing, total		7,689	32,066	233,801	505,149	510,622	744,111	910,015
Miscellaneous, total	840	36,856	6,221	8,899	6,627	1,859	16,190	46,179
Grand total	511,736	1,445,287	1,516,011	2,289,074	2,881,776	2,370,122	3,408,442	3,127,159

[1] Estimated expenditures for fiscal year 1941 estimated as of Jan. 1941.

Source: Compiled from statement of federal expenditures for public works construction published annually in *The Budget of the U.S. Gov't.* Printed in *Development of Resources and Stabilization of Employment in the United States* (Washington D.C., January, 1941), 82–83, 100–1, National Resources Planning Board.

Appendix C
Documentation of Harold Ickes's Faith in President Roosevelt's Leadership

"I had not intended to volunteer any advice, or suggestions, in connection with this convention. I have sought out no political leader here, nor any of your friends, but they have been coming to me in increasing numbers, because they are convinced, as I am, that this convention is bleeding to death and that your reputation and prestige may bleed to death with it. Prompt and heart stirring action is necessary. A world revolution is beating against the final ramparts of democracy in Europe. In such a situation no man can fail to respond to the call to serve his country with everything that he has. In such a situation *you are the only man able to give the country that quality of moral leadership without which we cannot hope to save our institutions.*

"In order to be in a position to serve the people and the cause of democracy in such a crisis as the country has never before been confronted with, you not only must be willing to accept a nomination for president, you must see to it that the nomination is forthcoming in circumstances that will assure a successful campaign against the appeasers. *Here in Chicago are more than nine hundred leaderless delegates* milling about like worried sheep *waiting for the inspiration of leadership that only you can give them. These delegates have voluntarily pledged themselves to your cause, because of their faith in your essential democracy,* and yet control of this convention is in the hands of men who are determined to destroy you at any cost. It is the strangest sight in American politics to see a convention dominated by men who are bent upon betraying their leader, their party and their country. And yet people will follow some sort of leadership, accepting the worser if the better does not offer. The Farley coalition is actually beginning to believe that someone other than yourself can be nominated. Failing this their objective is to create such a situation that (a) you will not accept the nomination, or (b) the chances of your success will be gravely impaired. Leaderless, but well meaning delegates cannot be held responsible for such a situation and voluntary leadership

---

*Emphasis added.

is impossible because no one is willing to accept responsibility that may be repudiated. I believe that you should insist that the convention take a platform of your own dictation. This platform should be short . . . and admitting of no suspicion of compromise. You should insist that the party pledge itself to support your administration until a peace loving America can once more look with unworried eyes toward Europe. I believe also that you should insist upon a candidate for Vice President who sees eye to eye with you on both domestic and foreign questions, a man who will be generally considered to have sufficient stature to be the head of the nation. I believe that the convention will take you on your own terms. If it will not do so everyone would hold you to be beyond criticism for declining to take the nomination on lesser terms. No one can clear away the sordid atmosphere in which this convention so far has been conducted except yourself. *My own belief is that a personal appearance in which frankly and clearly you would state the situation which in your opinion justified you in running again would raise this political campaign to such a high plane as would be an inspiration to the whole country.* There are many in Chicago today who actually fear that as a result of the tactics of the Farley Wheeler clique a ticket will emerge that will assure the election of Willkie and Willkie means fascism and appeasement.

Index

253

About the Author

A. L. RIESCH OWEN, a faculty member in Economics and Interdisciplinary Studies at the University of Colorado in Boulder, earned master and doctoral degrees in history and economics from the University of Wisconsin-Madison. Prior to her present position, Dr. Owen held teaching posts at Washington State University and the Universities of Wisconsin (Milwaukee and Madison). Dr. Owen's research abroad included comparative studies of Australian and U. S. economic and social institutions. As one of the first scholars admitted to the Franklin Delano Roosevelt Library at Hyde Park, Dr. Owen had access to the F.D.R. papers, at which time initial research was begun on conservation under F.D.R.'s administration. Subsequent research over a period of years has culminated in *Conservation under F.D.R.* This volume also benefited from a unique series of exclusive interviews with Harold Ickes, Eleanor Roosevelt, and William Plog. Among Dr. Owen's earlier publications is *Selig Perlman on Capitalism and Socialism* (University of Wisconsin Press, 1976).